FINAL THIRD!

THE LAST WORD ON OUR FOOTBALL HEROES

JOHN SMITH

First published by Pitch Publishing, 2022

Pitch Publishing
9 Donnington Park,
85 Birdham Road,
Chichester,
West Sussex,
PO20 7AJ
www.pitchpublishing.co.uk
info@pitchpublishing.co.uk

© 2022, John Smith

Every effort has been made to trace the copyright. Any oversight will be rectified in future editions at the earliest opportunity by the publisher.

All rights reserved. No part of this book may be reproduced, sold or utilised in any form or transmitted in any form or by any means, electronic or mechanical, including photocopying, recording or by any information storage and retrieval system, without prior permission in writing from the Publisher.

A CIP catalogue record is available for this book from the British Library.

ISBN 978 1 80150 400 3

Typesetting and origination by Pitch Publishing
Printed and bound in Great Britain by TJ Books, Padstow

Contents

Acknowledgements 7

Introduction 8

1. Setting Our Stall Out 15

2. Legends 24

3. It's Not All Work, Work, Work 39

4. Behind Every Great Manager 66

5. You Wear It Well 115

6. Your Dukes, Your Cheddars and Your Widdleys of This World 142

7. I Want to Believe 154

8. Stranger in a Strange Land 168

9. Coming Over Here 199

10. Board Games 217

11. False 9 to 5 253

12. What Happens on Tour, Doesn't Necessarily Stay on Tour 265

13. Between the Sticks 279

14. Always Finish with a Song – Or a List 299

Bibliography 307

Acknowledgements

HUGE THANKS to Dan Trelfer for his help in editing this book. I missed writing with him, but he was always there with notes for me. And if Dan liked it, I knew I wasn't going too far wrong.

Thanks to Jane Camillin, Duncan Olner, Alex Daley and everyone at Pitch Publishing for giving me the opportunity to go around again and putting this book together.

Thanks to Alex Horne, Paul Hawksbee and Gabe Turner for their kind words.

Thanks to John Greathead, Ben Cooper, Michael Marden, Jim Henderson, Julian Shea and anybody else who sent me a book or suggested a particular autobiography that I might not have read yet. Much appreciated.

Thanks to Jo, Archie, Evie and Martha for all their love, support and patience. This is for them.

Thanks as always to any footballer who has shared their memories in a book. I will always find it fascinating, and I hope you do too. Football's great.

And a big hello to everyone who knows me, Ken.

Introduction

WELCOME ALONG. Come in, there's no time to waste. We've got the best bits from well over 300 football autobiographies to get through. If you've read the previous two volumes, then thanks for your loyalty and continued interest. If you're reading this third volume first, it's a bit weird, but okay.

The principal remains the same. I've been on an odyssey through the written word of our football heroes and present to you the funniest, most interesting, and most baffling things discovered for you in one handy place. Well, three places now, but you get the idea. Michael Owen may claim to have 'the best shit-filter of anyone', but I think I could challenge him. I've panned for the gold and want to share the things I've learned. Learning can be fun.

For example, along the way, I've discovered that:

- Colombia and hairdressing legend Carlos Valderrama rattled as he ran around the pitch, and you could always hear him coming. Graeme Le Saux observes that he was 'festooned with necklaces and bracelets', which makes him sound a bit like a pirate or an art teacher.

- Paul Scholes loves a pun. When he was at home injured and missed out on Manchester United's embarrassing Club World Cup defeat to Vasco de Gama in 2000, he sent Gary Neville a text message that read, simply, 'Fiasco de Gama'. Very enjoyable.

INTRODUCTION

- Jens Lehmann has been stuck in two different lifts with team-mates (at time of writing). Once with a load of Arsenal lads and once at Dortmund with Jan Koller, which had him particularly rattled as 'a giant such as Koller needs more air than normal people'. If this sparks off a debate in your house or place of work about the best or worst footballers to be stuck in a lift with, you have my blessing.[1]

- Dundee United switched to their famous tangerine kit because in the late sixties, they played a friendly in the US against Dallas Tornado, who played in a fetching 'burnt orange home kit', according to winger Davie Wilson. Barbara Kerr, the wife of manager Jerry Kerr, liked it so much that she requested the change from their old black-and-white kit and carried enough clout to get it done. Just in time for colour television, but imagine how well a chain of events like this might go down on Twitter now.

- Jason McAteer has 'never been one for wearing undies' and insists that 'commando's been my way'. So now you know.

- On the night Stanley Matthews met his second wife Mila, the pair took a stroll around the gardens after a cocktail party in Prague and walked into the swimming pool by mistake as they were 'looking into each other's eyes'. I believe this is what they call a 'meet cute' in the Rom-Coms, although Sir Stan's first wife might not have seen it that way.

- The Paul Newman film *The Mackintosh Man* was filmed at Stanley and Mila Matthews' house in Malta, and in one scene they even had Newman carrying Stanley's own mackintosh after a wardrobe mix-up. No, I haven't seen it either, but I've watched the trailer and there are loads of good people in it

---

1 For me the best might be Stuart Pearce as he's a qualified electrician and might be able to have a go at fixing it. The worst, I couldn't possibly say. Not this early in the book.

like James Mason, Michael 'Paddington' Hordern and Harry Grout out of *Porridge*.

- Due to the prevailing, more innocent times, Jimmy Hill and his first wife Gloria were both virgins on their wedding night, which he blames for their failure to 'adapt to a satisfactory sexual relationship'. Oh yes. Jimmy goes below the waist don't you worry about that. And don't worry about him either. He made up for it later with some surprisingly saucy behaviour.

- Hope Solo's dad was once accused of murder. But it's alright, he didn't do it.

- Chris Sutton reveals that as a young apprentice he stayed in digs where a Siamese cat gave birth to a litter and immediately ate her new-born kittens. He says, 'There were legs and afterbirth everywhere – it was horrific,' and I'm inclined to think that this experience has informed his jaded worldview. Well, it would, wouldn't it? I can imagine him standing there shouting, 'Stop eating your kittens! You're better than that!' while Robbie Savage takes a contrary position behind him and invites cat fans to call in and let him know what they think.

There's light and there's dark, you see, but it all needs taking in.

On top of all the new information I've been bursting to tell you about, there have also been occasions when further reading has thrown new light on old subjects. A previous volume dealt with Viv Anderson and Mark Proctor being left out in the countryside by a reunited Brian Clough and Peter Taylor, who nipped off and left them when they were discussing a possible loan move for both from Clough's Nottingham Forest to Taylor's Derby. However, East Midlands insider and confidante of Brian and Peter, Maurice Edwards, tells us that the pair were still at loggerheads when this happened, that Clough wasn't even there and that he simply sent Anderson and Proctor to knock on Taylor's door to annoy him. Who to believe then? Viv was there at least, while Maurice is

INTRODUCTION

peddling second-hand news, so perhaps we should stick with Viv. Either way, the image of Anderson and Proctor being abandoned in the countryside, telling anyone who would listen 'we've tried to come on loan by mistake' remains powerful.[2]

I also read Howard Gayle recounting a story from Sunderland training under Lawrie McMenemy, in which the team was asked to practise kick-offs with nobody in opposition. The team dutifully worked the ball back to keeper Iain Hesford who wasn't looking, and the ball rolled straight in for a one-nil lead for nobody. The same story was also told by David Armstrong, and dealt with in *Second Yellow*, but involved Southampton, with Chris Nicholl in charge and Tim Flowers in goal. Now, I guess there's an outside chance that McMenemy passed this practice on to Chris Nicholl and exactly the same thing happened. But did it really? It makes me think that one of them must be borrowing the story and re-purposing it. Maybe it's one of those generic anecdotes that gets trotted out as evidence against an unpopular gaffer. Now I'm still a wide-eyed optimist when it comes to our footballers and I want to believe every word they say, even the ghost stories and impossibly witty comebacks in stressful situations which they lay claim to, but this sort of thing has got me rattled. Perhaps sometimes it's better to remain in the dark. For example, I still don't know why Arsène Wenger didn't go to Pat Rice's leaving do and I'm not sure I want to.

Step forward then Jamie Vardy, who can provide reassurance about retaining a bit of mystery, as he struggles to shed some light on his now famous 'chat shit, get banged' tweet. He seems genuinely amazed that people have the catchphrase on T-shirts or 'incredibly, tattoos of it', but by way of explanation, the best the Leicester man can come up with as an origin story is, 'The chances

---

2　On the subject of Peter Taylor, I was also disappointed to find out from his book that Forest's eighties Norwegian player Jan Einar Aas was actually pronounced 'Oss'. That's a sticker-collecting childhood giggle ruined.

are that someone has chatted shit and got banged over the years, but the honest truth is I don't know'.

Another man who does his best to keep us guessing is the archetypal unreliable narrator Neil Ruddock – a man who strings a series of very entertaining stories together whether they happened or not. Take, for example, his version of that lovely story of Harry Redknapp pulling a heckling fan out of the crowd and putting him on the pitch for West Ham in a pre-season friendly at Oxford City. Harry isn't shy about embellishing a story and tells it very well himself, with some customary add-ons, but the bare facts of the tale are that the game took place in 1994, the fan was barracking Lee Chapman, and that when he went on, he scored a goal which was unfortunately disallowed.

In Ruddock's version, Chapman remains, but Razor was playing himself (FACT CHECK: he joined West Ham in 1998); the fan borrowed Rio Ferdinand's boots (FACT CHECK: Rio was 15 years old and not playing), he was 'about forty, by the way, and about twenty stone' (FACT CHECK: he was nothing of the sort) and he played up front with John Hartson and Paolo Di Canio (FACT CHECK: Hartson joined West Ham in 1997, Di Canio joined in 1999 to replace Hartson, and neither played with Chapman, who left the club in 1995). Still, nice story. We all love Razor, if not for his playing career then for his part in the greatest of all *Come Dine with Me* episodes[3], but he does love a yarn. It makes all of this something of a minefield, so let's tiptoe through together.

These inconsistencies are for me to worry about though, not you. In my experience, any risk of a story being borrowed or exaggerated is well worth it for the sheer weight of insight gained by reading these books. How else would we know what the inside of a professional football dressing room is like with its 'heady aromas'

---

3   That is a big call in a crowded field, but I stand by it. Yes, it's even better than THAT one. You lost, Jane. Came second to Fash and Razor. Dear Lord, what a sad little life.

INTRODUCTION

of 'leather, Vicks, Deep Heat, shampoo',[4] or the perils of 'taking your clothes off for the first time in front of 25 strange blokes' when you first arrive at a club. This last observation comes from the almost too entertaining book of Roy McDonough, who claims that in some circumstances getting naked can be intimidating (not for him, naturally), as he claims that new team-mates size up your business 'to see if you're a threat', a bit like stags and their antlers.

That dressing room and the make-up of a squad can be a delicate ecosystem if you want to build a successful team, which is something that Kevin Keegan knows only too well. In the grandly titled *Kevin Keegan Against the World*, Keggy says that a football team 'is a mechanism as intricate as a watch' with many moving parts. Evidently, he also feels that balance is important: 'You need a gambler and someone who is the soul of caution. A girl-puller must be balanced by one of nature's monks. You need a clown, and he needs team-mates prepared to be the audience. You need card schools, and a few fellows who prefer paperbacks.' Whether these are natural characteristics that managers should seek out in their recruitment process, or if players are assigned these roles upon arrival isn't quite clear, but there can't have been too many takers for the monk role. That last one might also have just been because the card school would be unmanageably large if everyone wanted to join in. No doubt Super Kev would have been putting everyone straight and sending the surplus away to read a paperback instead, whether they liked it or not.

With his watch analogy here, Keegan is going for deep and meaningful, and he is far from alone in that. You wouldn't expect anything less of Arsène Wenger and his book is full of more profound insights and chin-stroking self-reflection than you could stuff in the pockets of a full-length touchline coat. Wenger muses at one point about 'the first words I will exchange with God when

---

4   This comes from Mick 'Baz' Rathbone, who is so charmed by the smell of football, that he called his excellent book *The Smell of Football*.

I die', which is a lot less depressing than it sounds. He suggests that he will tell God that he spent his life trying to win matches and try to convince him that it was a worthy use of his time on Earth and that 'football is important to millions of people's lives, that it creates moments for sharing, moments of joy and great sadness, too'. It's touching, thought-provoking stuff. Although I prefer to think that the first thing God will ask him is what happened that night Bobby Zamora ripped his Arsenal team apart and made Sol Campbell go home at half-time, but I guess it depends what mood He's in when Arsène gets up there.

Let me take you by the hand then and lead you one more time through the anecdotal avenues and alleyways of the written word of our football favourites. Well, they're all somebody's favourite, right?

Just go out there and enjoy yourselves.

1.

Setting Our Stall Out

'Remote Welsh Station'

ABOVE ALL other things that we know about footballers, we know that they are, on the whole, sociable creatures. There are very few loners out there. They work in packs and have a special camaraderie, earning the love, loyalty and friendship of team-mates and gaffers galore throughout their career. So, when they put pen to paper for their autobiographies and want a foreword to pep things up a bit and get a sort of stamp of approval, none of them should be struggling to find a willing contributor. Which makes you wonder how some of them end up with what they end up with.

The sort of thing you're looking for is Martin O'Neill saying that his early impressions of Emile Heskey were of a youngster with 'the strength of a titan and the pace of an Olympic sprinter to conjure an incredible performance', or Ossie Ardiles describing Lee Clark as 'my precociously talented midfielder'. Perfect – but as you'll see, such faultless testimonies are few and far between.

One way to guarantee a job well done is to go with a consummate professional, a frequent flyer, a prolific foreword writer from the very top of the tree. If you have the connections and can get either Sir Kenny Dalglish or Sir Alex Ferguson to jot something down for you, you are in safe hands. The pair have such standing in the game that a foreword from them is like a royal seal of approval or a 'Taste the Difference' label in the supermarket. A guarantee of quality. A mere mention of their names adds gravitas to an autobiography and, the good news is, they are both often happy to oblige.

Dalglish does the honours for the likes of Jamie Carragher, Chris Sutton, John Wark[5] and Nick Tanner, which is good of him considering Tanner admits once trying to chat up Kenny's wife without realising who she was at a Wet, Wet, Wet concert.

For his part, Sir Alex gives a reference for, among others, Paul Parker, Paul Scholes and Graham Poll, of whom he says, 'He has taken some of our big games, and he has been hopeless in some of them!' He is joking here by the way and is very nice elsewhere,[6] but it does open the door to the kind of problems I've hinted at.

Many of those asked to pen a foreword seem to forget what they're there for, either making inappropriate jokes, going off on a tangent or falling into my favourite trap of all – damning with faint praise. For example, the much-missed Jack Charlton, when asked to say something complimentary about Terry Curran, comes up with, 'Whatever else I could write about Terry, I could never take away from him the fact he was a very good footballer for Sheffield Wednesday.' A 'very good' is the least you would hope for on a work appraisal, and why even hint at other, darker things you would like to bring up that might be in the debit column? Just say the nice things.

Arsène Wenger describes Ray Parlour as 'a train who could go at a certain pace – not electric but he could maintain high energy the whole game', which sounds like he's saying he tried hard, when in fact he was brilliant for him for many years. Terry Venables

---

5   Among some lovely words about Wark, he plays up his social side and says he 'never went thirsty', which would have no doubt fitted right in with that Liverpool side.

6   Nicer than I'm sure most of us would be, anyway.

was practically a father to Terry Fenwick, dragging him along to almost every club with him, even after he'd retired,[7] but all he can muster is, 'It is fantastic to have stars like Paul Gascoigne and Gary Lineker in your team but you have to have the Fenwicks too. Terry will not attract the public through the turnstiles or lift a game with a touch of genius but he is just as important.' These are both nice in their own way, I suppose, but neither of them are getting carried away are they? Still, it could be worse, Kevin Keegan says of prematurely bald midfielder David Armstrong, 'He just looked old.' We were all thinking it, but just keep it to yourself, Kev. Indoors voice.

Asked to say something positive about Ted MacDougall, Lawrie McMenemy can't quite manage it. Instead, he offers up an anecdote about an intolerant Ted throwing a boot across a room at a young Southampton player who hadn't passed to him at a vital moment. Maybe he means it shows something about the high standards he demanded from those around him, but if there's something positive in there, it's buried pretty deep under the unpleasantness from MacDougall.

Mick McCarthy is, as you might expect, a lot more straightforward, writing for Rodger Wylde that 'I didn't like him', 'actually, I couldn't stand him' and 'I took an instant dislike' to him. He qualifies it by saying he's tongue in cheek, that he didn't like strikers generally and Wylde played for Wednesday while Mick was at Barnsley, but still, this is laying it on a bit thick.

Henrik Larsson makes a better fist of things for Chris Sutton[8] as he starts to talk about 'a very special time for both of us in our careers' at Celtic and says he missed him when he moved to Barcelona. He goes on to say that, 'I had a fantastic time at Barcelona and played in a brilliant team, but I think it would have

---

7   Not Barcelona though. That would have been silly.

8   Sutton goes for a kind of Greatest Hits montage with foreword tributes from a number of people.

been even better for me if Chris was beside me. But that just wasn't possible.' The unwritten, unspoken reasoning here is, of course, that Chris might not have been good enough to go to Barcelona and compete for a place with the likes of Samuel Eto'o at that point, but at least Henrik is too polite to say it.

Matt Le Tissier spends a decent chunk of his book being very critical of former Southampton manager Ian Branfoot, so it's only fair, if slightly unusual, that he gives him something of a right to reply in the foreword. Branfoot comes up with, 'You have to ask why didn't the top managers take Matt? Great players play for great clubs. I never had too many enquiries about him when I was manager,' and just about manages to say, 'I liked Matt as a person, there are a lot worse than him around,' while questioning his work rate and commitment. It's odd that Le Tissier goes for this approach rather than find one of many people that would surely have just said what a wonderful player he was and talked about all those incredible goals, but it's hardly the strangest thing he's done, so we'll overlook it.

The best that Lou Macari can find to say about his Manchester United team-mate Gordon Hill is that he 'loved Norman Wisdom and would do the impression up to twenty times a day', and you can almost hear his teeth grinding as he's writing it. Meanwhile, asked to say a few words for his trophy-laden goalkeeper Andy Goram, Walter Smith appears to be reeling that he managed to be friends with Brian Laudrup while at the club: 'One looked like a Hollywood A-list star and the other had teeth like condemned buildings! They were an odd couple.'

Walter also offers a word for former Rangers winger Davie Wilson's autobiography and, instead of praising him personally, he goes with honesty and says, 'My favourite player was Jimmy Millar as I liked the way he played.' Maybe he should have written something for Jimmy Millar instead then. 'Most folk back then probably preferred Baxter, Willie Henderson or Davie Wilson, but

Jimmy was the man for me,' Walter repeats, in case anyone wasn't sure where his childhood loyalties lay.

Howard Kendall does something similar in Kevin Sheedy's book, saying, 'If I hadn't been able to bring Neville Southall to Everton then Kevin Sheedy would rate as my best ever signing.' He claims that he cannot offer higher praise than that, but it definitely feels like he could. Saying someone is your second-best signing, by definition, leaves a bit of room for at least slightly higher praise. The thing is, he used a similar 'second-best signing behind Nev' line about Pat Van Den Hauwe for his foreword. Southall must love it and be constantly blushing when he dips into the memoirs of his team-mates, but it shows that Kendall shouldn't have been trusted with a foreword. For Mark Ward's harrowing tale of his time in prison on drug charges, Howard jokes, 'By pure coincidence, I had just finished watching an episode of the TV police series *The Bill* when Mark's publisher phoned me at home and asked if I would contribute this foreword. How timely!', which might not have been what Wardy was after.

Some players dip into first-hand anecdotes for their foreword, which gives it the personal touch, even if it doesn't necessarily show the subject in the most positive light. Alan Hansen's foreword for Steve Nicol is littered with good-natured pops at him with the centrepiece being a fancy-dress competition on a Scandinavian cruise the pair went on with their wives. Apparently, Nicol got the wrong end of the stick and arrived as a woman in a 'pale green dress carrying a Budweiser', only to realise it was a kids' competition. Hansen never reveals who Nicol was supposed to be in his outfit,[9] but describes the incident as 'absolutely sensational' and claims, 'I've never seen anyone look more dejected in his life.' This is quite something considering that Nicol was the nearest defender to Michael Thomas when he broke Liverpool hearts at Anfield in

---

9   Marge Simpson maybe, but that doesn't explain the Budweiser. Perhaps it was a Duff.

1989. Surely Nicol was more dejected at that point, if only because he'd possibly lined up the same green outfit for the suddenly off-the-cards title celebrations afterwards.

Mark Hughes takes on foreword duties for another Welsh legend Mickey Thomas. Thomas was a star at Manchester United when Sparky was making his way as an apprentice and starts off well by saying, 'Mickey was definitely an inspiration to me at that time in my life.' However, he goes on to say that the indelible impression Mickey left on him was during a lift back to North Wales one day after training. A clearly still traumatised Hughes says, 'I'm thinking I'm going to be dropped at my mum's just outside Wrexham ... But no. Mickey dropped me off at some remote Welsh station that was on his route home to Mochdre. I had to wait on the platform for three hours for a train to get home.' This sounds like what is known in the trade as 'a shit lift' from Mickey, and not the grounds for a gushing foreword.

Bob Wilson was not only a fine goalkeeper, he was also a consummate broadcaster, so you would think he would be just the man for a well-placed word. However, in writing for his good friend Bobby Gould he musters up the following: 'Bobby Moore, Sir Bobby Charlton, Bobby Gould ... ask for the achievements and great feats of these three footballers and you would immediately remember the brilliance of two of them and maybe struggle with the third.'

This seems a bit harsh as there really aren't many who would match up to those two and throwing Gould under the bus just because his name is also Bobby seems a bit harsh. It's like comparing Zinedine Ferhat[10] to Zinedine Zidane, in a book by Zinedine Ferhat. Wilson didn't even give Gould the chance to get his own back by talking about much better goalkeepers in the foreword to his own book – instead he pressed the showbiz chum button and

---

10   Yes, I looked him up. What of it?

got Michael Parkinson to do it. Whether that paid off or not you can judge for yourselves, but he trots out that old chestnut 'you don't have to be barmy to be a goalkeeper, but it sure helps', and I think we can all do better.[11]

Other showbiz buddies to lend a hand include:

Adrian Chiles for Steve Hunt
'He already had an air of mystery, devilment and the downright exotic about him.'

John Bishop for Dietmar Hamann
'One, I am not Didi Hamann's friend; and two, I spent years watching Didi play and if the foreword of a book is like the literary equivalent of a prematch warm-up, I have decided to act as Didi did in every game I saw him warm up for, by putting in no effort whatsoever.'

Ray Winstone for Frank McAvennie
'Frank the fuck who?'

Dennis 'Stay Lucky' Waterman also did the honours for Alan Hudson, possibly even writing and singing him a theme tune for the audiobook version. So, as you can see, it's a mixed bag of jokes, half-truths and genuine praise.

The good thing about asking someone from outside the world of football to step in is that they are less likely to make it all about them, as one or two fellow pros do. Phil Brown for example, writes something for Dean Windass and dwells on whether he did the right thing bringing such a favoured son back to Hull or not. He says that such a signing 'could be a threat' to lesser gaffers but concludes, 'I was fully confident in my own ability as a manager and as I felt he was the right man for our team then it was a no brainer.' A 'no-brainer' tends to mean a decision taken without needing to

---

11 Emu was right, IMHO.

give it much thought, Phil. The time he spends ruminating on it in the foreword to the player he signed suggests it took a bit more thought than that.

Similarly single-minded is Kenny Sansom who is asked to give a few words to Vince Hilaire's excellent if unimaginatively titled, *Vince*. Sansom skips lightly over Vince himself with a dig about his clothes before dwelling on that fabled 'Team of the Eighties' Palace side and how 'people say that when I left it all fell apart', setting the story straight about how he never really wanted to leave Palace for Arsenal and calling Terry Venables 'a fibber' for saying he did. It feels like he's gone a bit off track here, and it's not like he doesn't discuss such things in full in his own book. Somebody should have reminded him that the book was about Vince Hilaire. To be fair to Vince, he called it *Vince* – he could hardly have been clearer.

Among Chris Sutton's many foreword contributors is former Norwich manager Mike Walker and, given that he takes references from a few different people, including the aforementioned Kenny Dalglish and Henrik Larsson, maybe he could have left this one out. Walker seizes the chance for self-justification, saying about his move to Everton, 'I was accused of being greedy by people at Norwich. It wasn't about money.' He goes on to detail how his contract was running down, the chairman didn't sort it and then the same chairman walked all over his successor John Deehan, leading to Norwich's relegation. You see, it's easy to get sucked in. Even I'm doing it now. None of this has anything to do with Chris Sutton. Maybe it is easy to go off-piste with these things. Your mind runs away from you.

By far my favourite foreword flight of fancy, however, comes from Harry Redknapp. The nation's sweetheart was called upon to introduce Kerry Dixon's autobiography, despite never managing him, playing with him, or even playing against him as far as I can tell. Harry opens up with, 'Kerry Dixon was a great goalscorer, a really good centre forward.' So far so good. However, then it takes quite a turn. He bemoans the fact that a 'huge influx of players from overseas' has left Chelsea, and teams in general, with players that aren't familiar with a club's heritage, saying, 'Half of them don't know what happened five years ago, let alone the real history,' before boiling up to, 'If you talked about Arsenal's Double-winning team of 1971, or Kerry Dixon at Chelsea, they wouldn't have a clue. They come in, they play, and they move on in a few years.' This is astonishing 'man to move away from at a bus stop' stuff from Harry. Nobody asked about this, not here anyway. What is supposed to be a few kind words about Kerry Dixon turns into a rant about the modern game and the bloody foreigners. Extraordinary stuff. Still, at least what we can say is that Harry Redknapp never signed a single foreign player in his entire career on principle.

Maybe Kerry should have written his own foreword, like Ian St John did. St John uses his to rant about Gérard Houllier and the row that they had. It was a row that had completely passed me by but clearly had an impact on The Saint, who goes so far as to say that Houllier 'contributed to the mood that provoked me to write this book'. That's nice. Always good to have spite as your motivation when writing.

The final word on forewords here goes to John Sitton, the former Leyton Orient manager and star of a particularly entertaining or distressing (depending on your point of view) documentary in the mid-nineties. It's a subject that Sitton speaks about at length in his book, telling how it left him ostracised by the football community. Perhaps because of that, but hopefully through his own choice, Sitton decides against including a foreword, saying simply, 'Who the fuck's going to write one?' Well take your pick from anyone mentioned in this chapter, John. Or on second thoughts, maybe you're right.

2.

Legends

'Punch Tree'

IF WE think of this book as a swanky nightclub full of our favourite football characters (and why wouldn't we?), then this is the special, slightly elevated, roped-off section right next to the DJ booth, with table service and the best view across the room, reserved for the legends of the game. A place where we can relax and enjoy some stories about brushes with some absolute giants of the anecdote game. A restricted area and not for everyone, despite their best efforts.

There are those that fancy themselves a bit, you see, like Stan Bowles, for example, who once claimed, 'Nowadays people rate me as only slightly behind George as the best British footballer ever to put on a pair of boots.' Now Stan was a great player and a terrific entertainer, but such self-regard just leaves him outside the front door, arguing with the bouncers. I have never heard anybody say that Bowles was in the same bracket as Best. Not even the most ardent Hoops fans. But the actual George Best? Come straight through sir.

GEORGE BEST

The measure of the guys we're letting in here is that they are figures that other football folk can't resist telling you about. Even if, like

Kevin Keegan and Glenn Hoddle, they are using him as an example of how not to live their lives, they still feel the need to mention Best in their own stories.

It's fair to say that Best is problematic and it's notable that there are inevitably as many stories about his notorious drinking as there are about his prowess on the field. Many autobiographies even borrow that famous, probably apocryphal anecdote about a hotel worker walking in on George in bed with a Miss World, knee-deep in cash and champagne and asking, 'Where did it all go wrong?' Everton winger Kevin Sheedy is certainly not the only one to use it, but he is the only one to feel the need to add 'but I prefer a different question – where did it all go right?' Well, yes Sheeds. That's sort of the point of the anecdote.

Northern Ireland team-mate, Derek Dougan, says of Best, 'He had what it takes on the pitch, but not off it and found two lives, as a footballer and as a showbiz personality, incompatible.' It is true that the two sides of Best's life compete for space on the pages of these autobiographies. Viv Anderson has one story of each. In the booze and showbiz corner, he tells of a very glitzy night out at Tramps (it's always Tramps) with Best, Simon Le Bon of Duran Duran plus their wives. Well, Viv's other half and Yasmin Le Bon, but not George's. That only became an issue when George got on the outside of a few cold drinks and the others had to look after him – only finding out at that point that they were technically on his stag do as he was getting married in the morning.[12] True to the old song, he had indeed pulled out the stopper and, furthermore, had a whopper.

'We tried coffee, we tried walking him about. In the end, the task proved impossible. George passed out and that was it. He failed to show up for his own wedding.' Oh, George.

The incident clearly hasn't tainted Viv's opinion of one of his idols though, as the football story he tells is dripping with respect

---

12 I haven't checked the dates but I'm assuming this is what Duran Duran's 'Is There Something I Should Know?' is about.

FINAL THIRD

– up to a point. An up-and-coming Anderson came up against a 'fag-end of his career' Best when they were playing for Forest and Fulham respectively. Viv says 'he was still the man' and that 'he was the closest thing to Maradona this country has ever seen'. We are left in no doubt about what an honour and a privilege it was to be on the same field as such a legend right up till the moment 'as half-time approached, Besty received the ball at his feet and I steamed in. I creamed him. He almost went into orbit. When he landed he gave me a rueful smile.' So much ruddy, bloody respect. But defenders gonna defend. It sounds like George was well used to it though.

Back in Tramps once more (told you), we see the more abrasive side of Best, as Rodney Marsh has him slapping Michael Caine in a row over some chips. Yes, that Michael Caine. Apparently, the actor helped himself to a few of George's first wife Angie's chips and, after a warning, 'George got up, whacked him on the chin and knocked Caine off his chair … Now, not a lot of people know that and how the incident was kept out the newspapers I'll never know.' Extra points for Rodney here for using that apocryphal Michael Caine catchphrase beloved of impressionists everywhere. He's right about the newspapers though, this would be huge news, wouldn't it? Michael Caine nicking chips? The dirty rotten scoundrel.[13]

Self-styled maverick, Terry Curran, is one of many skilful players who clearly modelled himself more than a little on Best – playing with flair on the pitch and with a seemingly insatiable appetite for women off it.[14] And maybe that's where the legendary status truly kicks in. There was nobody like George Best before George Best, but there sure were a lot of aspiring George Bests after him. Curran argues that Best scored the greatest goal of all

---

13 Alex Stepney tells another story about George Best defending the honour of his female companion while a fellow diner helped himself to food from her plate. For the record this was Jackie Glass having her scampi pinched by Pat Crerand in Madrid. This one didn't quite come to blows but what on earth is going on?

14 And on it, once, in the case of Mickey Thomas.

time when he dribbled through the Fort Lauderdale Strikers when playing for San Jose Earthquakes in the USA in 1981.[15] He places it just ahead of Frank Worthington's amazing effort for Bolton vs Ipswich and clearly puts him on a pedestal. Worthington, of course, is another with an echo of George Best about him; the legacy and influence was strong.

Others provide more dissenting voices. Tough, straight-talking Jack Charlton clearly didn't have any time for the nonsense, saying, 'George is still, to this day, a legend – but in my opinion he wasn't a great player. To be a great player, you've got to be a Bobby Charlton, a Billy Bremner or a Dave Mackay – players who stayed around in top level football for 10–15 years.' An interesting point. Best burned incredibly brightly for a short time, and is that enough to secure his status at the very top? I would say yes, but there is an argument for longevity. Interesting that Jack mentions 'our kid' Bobby there as the brothers clearly shared their reservations about Best. According to Alex Stepney, that statue of Best, Law and Charlton outside Old Trafford is an accurate depiction, insofar as the statues don't talk to each other much.

Stepney was there in the good times, but also the dog days, when Charlton was trying to wring the final drops from a long and illustrious career, while Best was arguably drinking every last drop and frittering his own career away. Stepney says, 'There were long days when they simply did not speak to each other,' and that 'I am sure it was George's complete lack of concern for the club that threw Bobby Charlton into the desperately black mood which seemed to envelop him every time he was at the club'. It's sad to think of Charlton, Law and Best that way, whoever you support. On the other hand, maybe George wasn't solely responsible for Bobby's black mood, as he seems to have had the hump pretty much ever since.

---

15 Have a look on YouTube. It's a good goal, but I think we all need to calm down and take the opposition into account. Best has scored many far better goals, against better defenders, surely.

It can and will be an endless debate about where George Best places among the greatest the game has ever seen; that's nothing new – but his legendary status can be felt in the feeling left by all those who played with him, played against him, or just helped him into a cab at the end of a heavy night. Better to leave the final word on him to the man who gave him to the football world – Matt Busby, who says, 'The things he could do with a ball first made you think and then made you wonder. He had a congenital dislike of letting anybody else have a kick at it.' Let's remember him that way.

PAUL GASCOIGNE

There are undeniable parallels between George Best and Gazza. Some of their actions are unforgivable; but what's clear is that the football community, at least as expressed through these autobiographies, was always ready to forgive Gazza at his worst, because they loved him so much at his best. Everybody has a Gazza story – or wants one. Individually, they sometimes come across as a bit of fun (albeit frequently misjudged), but together they paint a fuller picture of an absolute nightmare to be around. You know that kid at school that you were sort of mates with, but mostly out of fear that they might flip out and turn on you if you weren't? Well, we're in that ballpark.[16]

Often the mate that bore the brunt of it all was Jimmy 'Five Bellies' Gardner, who operated for Gascoigne in an undefined role somewhere between minder, live-in chum, gopher, court jester and plaything. The two were clearly great friends and he no doubt enjoyed some benefits from the association, but it feels like he paid the price. His shopping duties included bringing designer clothes on demand from Newcastle to Glasgow after Gazza threw his jumper out of a car window and needed the right gear to get into a club, and the time he had to buy a £1,000 parrot and bring it to a

---

16 A big hello to Darren Madeley from my old school at this point. (Not his real name – he might kill me.)

LEGENDS

pub, where cheeky scamp Gascoigne released it and terrorised the customers.

Sometimes the risk and reward for Gardner was more straightforward. Such as the time Gazza gave him £50 to let him shoot him in the back with an air rifle, which, according to Paul Walsh, left Jimmy 'rolling around in agony almost in tears while Gazza was rolling around crying tears of laughter'. There was another £50 on the table for Jimmy to let Paul hold a lit cigar on the end of his nose for ten seconds: 'Even two months later Jimmy still had a big scab on the end of his nose.' What fun!

That's a lot to take on board and you're probably still wondering why Gazza threw his jumper out of the window. Well, it smelled funny, you see. He'd swapped his expensive shirt with a random woman in the pub earlier that day while out for a drink with some Rangers pals, then decided that he didn't like the jumper she gave him much after all. Oh, and according to Charlie Miller, he threw a headrest out of the car at the same time. This is not to be confused with the time he threw an ice cream out of a car at a cyclist who then justifiably kicked the car door in. That tossed-out jumper left Gazza topless, but not for long. Upon arrival in the centre of Glasgow, he nipped into a charity shop and appeared in 'a full-length ladies' dress for no apparent reason other than to make us fall about the place with laughter', which he kept wearing in the pub until Five Bellies arrived on his designer mercy mission later that evening.

It seems Gascoigne sometimes had an unusual relationship with clothes, as those who have seen him dancing in an open shell suit in the video for his hit single 'Geordie Boys' will attest. Before Chris Kamara began his journey to showbiz presenter, housewives' favourite and Christmas crooner, he was briefly the boss at Bradford City, where he managed Chris Waddle. Waddle invited Gazza along to a home game as his guest and, after he and the inevitable Jimmy Five Bellies emptied Kammy's fridge, Gazza went to the toilet. He came back wearing a tracksuit that he'd found hanging up in the toilets. One of Kammy's. 'He discarded his own tracksuit and appeared on the pitch at half-time to draw the weekly raffle wearing my gear with the CK initials on the breast.' The Geordie Boys soon took off and Kamara claims he later saw Gazza wearing his tracksuit in the tabloids on some misadventure or other. But what of the tracksuit he left behind? Kamara eventually took it home for his son, only to find that 'Gazza had filled the pockets with sandwiches, which had since gone mouldy'. Of course he had. After a few high temperature washes, Kamara started wearing it to muck his horses out.

Here are some other Gazza incidents to help you decide where the line is in terms of acceptable behaviour in the name of fun. There's even a column for your own verdict in case you're one of those carefree / psychotic types that writes in books.

Incident	Acceptable (Y/N)
Climbing in the big tumble dryer and having a ten-minute spin.	
Hiding fish all over Gordon Durie's car.	
Lightening the atmosphere during a tense Rangers team talk by weeing up the leg of an understandably startled Erik Bo Andersen.	
Making Mel Sterland's wife feel welcome by pointing to her big boobs and saying, 'Oooh, you're lovely. I can see why Mel always has a smile on his face, going home to whoppers like them!'	
Destroying a buffet on a private jet he was being shown around, bashing a plate of sandwiches, squashing all the food together and generally leaving a mess for someone else to find.	
Trying to swim from Doug Ellis's yacht to shore while drunk at the 1990 World Cup, getting into trouble and almost drowning before being rescued in a celebrity dinghy by Gary Lineker and Nigel Kennedy.	

Driving the Middlesbrough team bus around the training ground and doing £15,000 worth of damage to it by hitting some concrete bollards.	
Patting an air steward on the bum because he wanted a drink and getting a punch in the face for his trouble. Stuart Pearce says he was left with a 'crumpled face and quivering lower lip' just like after his second World Cup booking against West Germany. Have a word with him, indeed.	
Throwing chocolate out of a hotel window to some Albanian kids on an England trip, before switching to pieces of soap and watching them pick that up and try to eat it too. 'When they realised what they were eating, they went from idolising Gazza to chanting "bastard, bastard",' according to Ian Snodin.	
Acting disabled on a hospital visit to some disabled children. Paul Walsh seems to think he got away without upsetting anyone. Not so sure.	
Leaping on top of a homeless guy asleep in a pile of boxes. According to Pat Van Den Hauwe, 'The old fella was wheezing and could not get his breath, but Gazza thought it was hilarious and was pissing himself.' Gazza gave him £50 for his trouble.	

Boy, that really got away from us at the end there didn't it? And yet this catalogue of ill behaviour (which barely scratches the surface) is universally brushed off by his team-mates who all loved him to bits. Marco Negri claims he was 'often misunderstood' and praises his kindness and generosity, while the other character references all tell a similar tale of a man forever eager to please, who just didn't seem to know where the line should be drawn:

Pat Van Den Hauwe – 'lovely, but crackers'

Mel Sterland – 'a great guy and I've never known anyone like him'

Paul Walsh – 'great entertainment, daft as a brush and nothing more than a lovable rogue'

Always the same story.

There are a lot of 'what ifs' around Paul Gascoigne's career, and they mostly hinge around that 1991 FA Cup Final, when he wrecked his own knee with that horror tackle on Gary Charles. He was coming off the back of a wonderful season and an unforgettable semi-final performance, but should he have played? Was he too hyped up? The fact that Terry Venables admits that Spurs had to tranquilise their star man the night before suggests that perhaps not everything was quite right. Neil Warnock goes one further and says that if Gascoigne had been sent off in the quarter-final against Warnock's Notts County for 'pole-axing' Phil Harding, then Spurs may have lost, and Gazza would never have made that tackle on Charles. He goes on to say that 'Gazza's whole career might have been different', which certainly makes you think, before spoiling it by adding 'and Notts County might have made it to Wembley again'. Let's not get carried away with the quantum leap stuff, Neil. We've all had a drink.

Paul 'Gazza' Gascoigne then. An enigma, wrapped in a riddle and posted through the letterbox of a conundrum. A man who entertained millions but could be, at the very least, a right pain in the arse. Let's leave it here with a bit of fun that we can all get behind – and no, it's not the Raoul Moat incident.

Andy Goram must have been dreading reporting back to Rangers after Euro 96, with Gazza holding all the bragging rights after England's win over Scotland and his own part in it. The Englishman didn't disappoint. Goram walked into the dressing room where Gazza had cones out for goals. 'In the middle of the room, there was another cone with a white mophead stuck in it. That was big "Braveheart", Colin Hendry! Gazza was running up and down, flicking the ball over the mophead and volleying it in, screaming, "Gascoigne scores for England!" Fucking lunatic. That was his moment of glory.'

There you go, something we can all get behind. Right, Scottish friends? Right?

BILL SHANKLY

Next up is Bill Shankly. The man who built the foundations of what Liverpool Football Club is today. Now while that might not be everybody's cup of tea, and we can all agree that all that 'This Means More' nonsense makes us itch, it is fair to say that Liverpool are kind of a big deal in the modern game. It's a huge and undeniable legacy for Shankly, a man whose significant achievements in the game have blinded people to what is otherwise some fairly odd behaviour.

Emlyn Hughes was perhaps Shankly's biggest fan. After all, he gave him his big break and moulded him into a captain of club and country. He alludes to Shankly's 'idiosyncrasies', as if they're all charming, but goes on to casually discuss his rampant xenophobia.

'He hated foreigners. And for all his travel into Europe with Liverpool he never felt at ease. If he stopped someone in the street for directions and they had a foreign accent, his first reaction was to ignore them and ask someone else. Nor could he face foreign food.' Oh, what is he like eh?

Ian St John goes you one further, dropping the bombshell that 'Shankly refused to acknowledge American time'. Upon reading this it instantly became my favourite thing about him. It's wild, isn't it? I mean, he probably should have done, American time is definitely a thing. Although I guess it's only a problem if you're in America – like Liverpool were on a tour once. While the Liverpool players all admirably adapted like normal people, and went to their American beds at American bedtime, it was only really then that Shanks was up and raring to go for the evening. That left him with nobody to talk football (almost certainly football, right?) to except foreigners. Can you imagine? I'm surprised he didn't just throw up there and then.

One thing we can say for sure about Shanks is that he retired too early. He obviously had his reasons for shocking the football world and resigning in 1974, handing over to his erstwhile deputy Bob Paisley, who went on to be even more successful, of course. But Bill couldn't leave it alone. He famously used to turn up at Liverpool for a chat and a mooch about, which I'm sure Bob Paisley was very patient and polite about, but he also used to turn up at Everton's training ground, as his house backed on to it. Furthermore, on at least one occasion, he made his way to Goodison Park and set up camp in the away team dressing room. Alan Mullery takes up the tale from his days in charge of Brighton: 'Bill burst in with a big smile on his face. "Getting ready for the game, son?" he said. "Well, you'll beat this lot, no problem". A minutelater, he'd taken over the team talk and my players were hanging on every word. I let him get on with it. There was no stopping Bill Shankly when he was in full flow!'

In a common theme throughout this chapter the eccentricities of these characters are presented as charming quirks, but mostly they're just annoying, to be honest. Imagine this same story with, let's say Graham Potter playing away at Man City and Sir Alex Ferguson marching into his dressing room uninvited, taking over the team talk and helping himself to a sports drink, and it seems crazy rather than cute, doesn't it? It feels more likely that security might step in rather than everyone laughing the whole thing off.

You might think that laughs were in short supply around Shankly, but don't be misled by that gruff demeanour. He could do slapstick with the best of them, such as the first time he drove his automatic club car, put it in drive and went straight into the car park wall. But he was always ready with a quip too. Emlyn Hughes[17] recalls a training session match with the gaffer joining in, when somebody scored a debatable goal against his team. Shankly turned to the notoriously taciturn Chris 'Silent Knight' Lawler to give the verdict:

'To tell you the truth, boss, I think it just crept in under the bar.'

Shanks exploded. He raged, 'Jesus Christ, son, you've been here 12 years and never said a word. And now, the first time you open your mouth you tell a bloody lie!'

---

17   I told you he was his biggest fan.

I bet he was just waiting all that time to get a word in.

BRIAN CLOUGH

Now then young man. As the final head takes its place on the anecdotal Mount Rushmore, it might as well be a big one. Let's really talk legends. Brian Bloody Clough. If the measure of a legend in the autobiography world is the number of people that have a story about them, then Clough is vying with Gazza for page space. Everyone that came within the Clough orbit has got a story or two, and once again, in common with the other characters in this chapter, he is another titan of the game whose quirks are sometimes overlooked, or dismissed as eccentricities – in his case, due to his undoubted managerial genius. With all due respect to, let's say, Steve McClaren, it's difficult to think of a manager of that stature being forgiven for a quarter of the things Clough got up to, including a nut-grab on Diego Maradona.

Once again, presented by the storyteller as just a bit of fun, Steve Hodge recalls Nottingham Forest playing Barcelona at Camp Nou in 1983: 'As we lined up in the tunnel Clough walked down the line of players before stopping right in front of a bewildered Maradona. "You might be able to play a bit," said the manager, "but I can still grab you by the balls!" He then did just that before striding off towards the pitch.'

Now it's possible that Maradona knew who Clough was at this stage of his career. It's also possible that he didn't. What we can be sure of is that the diminutive Argentine genius would not have understood a word Clough said to him before he engaged in a bit of light sexual assault.[18]

Clough apologists will at this point be rallying round and saying this is just a bit of horseplay, designed to put a superstar off his game

---

18 Worth noting that this tale comes from Steve Hodge's book *The Man With Maradona's Shirt*. It raises questions about what Clough might have called his own autobiography if he went down the Diego route.

and give his own side an advantage. In which case the prosecution would like to bring up the wedding Clough crashed when his Forest squad were staying at the same hotel as the festivities in Scotland. Things began well with the generous boss ordering champagne for the happy couple, but took a turn for the Maradona a few glasses in. A slightly traumatised Steve Hodge remembers Clough intervening as the couple took to the floor for their first dance: 'Just as they were about to embrace, Cloughie appeared from nowhere, grabbed the groom's kilt, and did an impromptu checking of the poor man's wedding tackle.'

Such happy memories of a very special day there. It's fair to say that when the ushers signed up, they didn't expect 'escorting a European Cup-winning manager out of the hall for putting his hand up the groom's kilt' to be part of the job description. The duties are normally a lot more seating, flowers and car parking based on these occasions.

Previous volumes have been full of odd behaviour from Clough such as sending Peter Shilton to train on a roundabout, taking his players round the red-light district on a European trip, and chucking his assistant off the coach on the motorway because he forgot the talcum powder, but the hits just keep on coming. Ron Atkinson says that Cloughie 'didn't exchange a civil word with me' in all the time he was Manchester United manager, but the moment he left it was all smiles and drinks in the office. And Terry Butcher recalls some Ipswich officials going looking for Clough at the City Ground for the obligatory drinks and pleasantries after a 3-3 draw but 'found him stunned, sitting in his office with Peter Taylor and Kenny Burns in complete darkness' – but who among us has never turned the lights off and pretended we weren't in to avoid somebody? And not drinking with Ron Atkinson can't be a crime can it? I'm prepared to forgive all of this.

However, we then get to the punching. Aside from infamously cuffing pitch-invading fans around the head, the Forest boss was also known to have punched both Stuart Pearce and Roy Keane when they were in his charge, which can either be seen as brave or extremely foolish. Somewhere on that same scale, but up towards the silly end, for sure, sits the time Clough took his Forest lads for an idyllic-sounding stroll through the Austrian countryside on a trip away to play Sturm Graz in the UEFA Cup.

Steve Hodge, who spends so much time telling us Clough stories that it's possible he suffered from some sort of Stockholm Syndrome, tells us that as Forest walked through the woods, Clough stopped everyone by one particular tree: '"This," he announced, "is a punch tree." We all looked at the tree, then at the manager, then back at the tree. Everyone has to punch it. Such was the absolute power that he held over his players, no one was going to say "no" to Brian Clough.'

I know that some people decry the level of player power in the modern game, but I'd like to think somebody nowadays might say no, or at least give their agent a quick ring before committing to this. It's great that the man inspired such unswerving loyalty, but this is crackers, isn't it?

Clough's adventures in the transfer market are also a rich breeding ground for stories. Like an unpredictable lover, he's kissing Lee Chapman during negotiations one minute and telling Kevin Bond to get his bloody hair cut before never calling him again the next. Even once players had signed on the dotted line they couldn't be certain where they stood. If Clough thought he'd made a mistake, he didn't waste time trying to correct it, as the likes of Asa Hartford, Gary Megson and John Sheridan found out when he shipped them out again before they had so much as found a regular peg in the dressing room. Former Barnsley striker David Currie was another. There was no disciplinary breach, no bad attitude, but once Clough had a proper look at him on the training ground, he told him, 'I must have been daft to sign you,' asked him if he had bought a house in the area yet, and when told that he hadn't, said, 'Son, I wouldn't fucking bother.' Brutal. There is of course so much to be said for Clough, his success and his methods to get his teams there, but it's fair to say that if he took against you, there wasn't much you could do about it – except move to Oldham within weeks, like the no-doubt relieved Currie did.

On the other hand, occasionally Clough's very singular methods could give a player a boost, so let's finish with one of those. Terry Curran, who got an earlier mention in this chapter for his Best aspirations, played for Clough in his early days at Forest, and spent much of his time driving down the M1 from Doncaster to Nottingham. One day, Clough greeted him before training and took his car keys off him. After the session, Curran couldn't see his Triumph Spitfire anywhere: '"Where have you put my car, I can't see it?" I said. "Oh yes, you can – it's over there!" he said. Unbelievably, in the time I'd been training, he had sold my car and bought me a new Capri. I was flabbergasted.'

Trading a Triumph Spitfire for a Ford Capri in the space of an hour could only be more seventies if they cracked open a Watney Red Barrel to celebrate. Some players might have been upset by it but Curran says, 'The way he handled the situation made me feel ten feet tall,' – so fair enough, although a Capri was no car for somebody ten feet tall. Clough was worried about the miles his player was having to drive, so got him something suitable to do it in. What we do know is that if Clough decided a week later that he didn't like the Capri after all, he'd have sold it just as quickly and bought him a Vauxhall Viva.

3.

It's Not All Work, Work, Work

'The Practicality of the Plastic Straw'

I'M SURE that everyone with this book in their hands has at some point fantasised about being a footballer. Some of us may even have come close to making a career of it before a knee injury, a taste for the nightlife or a crippling lack of talent ruled us out. Just imagine it for a minute though. The goals, the crowds, the adulation, the unfathomable riches – and of course the spare time. Because if there's one thing we know about footballers, it's that between the hard but relatively short work on the training ground and the matchday commitments, there's a fair amount of free time. In this chapter, let's examine exactly what everyone gets up to; because when it comes right down to it, you're as nosey as I am.

Imagine being faced with so much free time that you could indulge yourself in every book, box set, museum visit, language, college course or music lesson you ever wanted to experience. It's the dream. I can hear you scoffing at the idea from here – the suggestion of footballers wandering around the Natural History with a ukulele slung over their shoulder and a bag full of Yeats poetry, but it's true, if you look in the right place. And by the right place, I mean the women's game, because, well, women are better people, aren't they? Hope Powell was England Women's team manager at the 2011 World Cup and describes the following downtime utopia: 'Karen Bardsley was a good artist and was always drawing in her sketchbook ... Anita Asante was doing a PhD in Network Policy and Women's Football, and she'd spend her down time studying. Eni Aluko was studying to become a lawyer.'

You're right to:

a.   be impressed by the diversity of interests and application. and

b.   assume that male camps are very, very different.

Not to generalise too much, but when their male counterparts get together, it tends to be less about studying for PhDs in Network Policy and more about pooing on balconies, pooing in pillowcases or pooing off the top of wardrobes – and a game of pool if you're lucky. Perhaps that's unfair, as those were isolated scatological incidents rather than hobbies; although two of those were Paul Merson, so it's possible it qualifies at least as a pastime in his case. What we can say with certainty is that the menfolk are more likely to indulge their baser instincts during their time off.

Even though certain players attack it with such gusto that it takes up most of their thinking and their spare time, and could in some quarters be regarded as their only genuine hobby, we're reckoning without what eighties tabloids always called 'bonking'. I know, I know, I'm sorry. You're interested in a bit of titillation, but I just won't bow to it. Previous volumes have devoted chapters to the sordid details of the sexual appetites of these boastful men, but not this one. No siree. Oh, alright then, but just a few quick teasers:

'She didn't waste much time before undoing my kecks ...'
Mick Quinn

'Back at her place, she started to strip, and Roy started to strip – so I joined in.'
Perry Groves

'The four of us slipped through the back and performed a whole repertoire of tricks in a room half full of beer kegs.'

Frank McAvennie

'Bozzy got into some spanking and toe-sucking and what have you ...'

Dwight Yorke

'We were high-fiving each other over her back.'

Jermaine Pennant[19]

That's your lot. Speculate all you want about the other people involved in these tawdry tales.[20] You can chalk it up to further reading on your part because we have higher-minded business to discuss. Very much like Gary Neville who tells us that 'between the ages of 16 and 20 I dropped women completely'. By his own admission, the young G Nev may have struggled anyway during his late teens, but the decision to abstain was more about reducing distractions: 'They were going to be expecting phone calls and pestering me to do this or that. My only priority on a Friday night was resting up in bed.' That may sound a bit dull, but trust me, such a cautious approach comes as something of a palette cleanser once you've been knee-deep in the mucky memoirs of the likes of Quinny, Yorkie and Jermaine Pennanty to be honest. Let's also have a quick word at this point for Richard Edghill, another member of the 'Manchester Defenders Stopping Indoors Club', who despite being mostly 'sat at home watching *News at Ten* or *Question Time*', earned himself a bit of a reputation around town because team-mate Jeff Whitley was gadding about and telling all the girls his name was Richard Edghill instead.

Quite why Jeff picked on Edghill when he had his own brother Jim Whitley knocking around Maine Road at the time (who he surely looked more like) I don't know. Poor old Richard though –

---

19 I believe high-fiving above a threesome is called 'An Eiffel Tower'.
20 Although in finest *Through the Keyhole* style, in some cases, the clues are there.

being blamed for affairs when his only interest was current affairs. No, you shush.

Another vice which really swallows a lot of a player's time is, of course, the demon drink. Back in the day there were a number of characters that committed so hard to time at the bar that would have passed that ten thousand hours threshold of becoming an expert in no time at all, but it can't really be considered a hobby now, can it? Not with all those genuine victims it leaves in its wake. All I'm saying is you don't get clinics for stamp collectors to get clean, do you?

Among the many harrowing tales of genuine alcohol addiction encountered in the research for this book, none are as inspiring as Tony Adams and his story of pulling himself back from the drink brink. Having really plumbed the depths in the darkest of his boozing days, he came out the other side, and had to fill all that time in other ways.

In his quest to quit drinking he thankfully had the unfailing support of his close friends and team-mates as he sought fulfilment elsewhere. Paul Merson speaks of Adams 'learning French on top of reading, playing the piano ... and sometimes talking in a way I don't understand', (that might have been the French, Merse), while fondly reminiscing about his drinking days at a particular hotel where Adams 'headbutted a television and also thumped David Hillier'. You can tell which version of Adams he prefers, even if David Hillier didn't. Honestly, between thumping David Hillier and dropping Steve Morrow, it's a wonder any Arsenal midfielders could get insured for working with Adams. David Seaman also grumbles that post-booze Adams 'bores the pants off us with his philosophies, his piano lessons, the plays he has been to see, the books he has read' and says that players would fake phone calls to get away from the Tony 2.0 chat. There's that support network I talked about.

All of the Arsenal lads are obsessed with big Tony's piano lessons, with Ray Parlour failing to be impressed by his progress

IT'S NOT ALL WORK, WORK, WORK

and wildly underestimating the time it takes to get good at it. He recalls an away game with the Gunners when Adams had brought his portable piano on the coach with him to practise at the hotel: 'He has now been learning for twenty weeks and gets on the coach to tell me he is ready to play the song he has been practising for me.' When the big moment arrived a no doubt nervous Tony adjusted his treble and bass settings and launched into 'She'll Be Coming Round the Mountain', but Parlour was unimpressed. 'I was gobsmacked. Twenty weeks for "Coming Round the Mountain"? I was expecting Bach!'

Not only was Ray left non-plussed by the performance, when he told the rest of the lads at breakfast next morning, he says there were the inevitable half-joking suggestions that, 'it's time to get him back on the booze'. Thanks for understanding guys. Expecting Tony Adams to be at Bach levels of piano-playing after 20 weeks is like expecting Bach to play in defence for Arsenal in the same amount of time. Although they have had worse.[21]

Joey Barton is another whose pursuit of self-improvement was met with scorn at every turn. Every *Guardian* appearance or Bob Dylan T-shirt met with eye-rolling you could see from space in some quarters, but you can say what you like, he might be the only person to have ever shared a training ground with Richard Edghill and been watched on *Question Time* by him.[22] Barton is only too aware of the sniping that greeted his attempts to better himself, but shrugs it off, saying that such people 'spectacularly missed the point. My interest was the result of a deeper way of thinking, inquisitiveness rather than pretension. I have become conditioned to looking beyond the obvious.' So there. Dabbling in the works of Plato, Seneca and Aristotle gave him a deeper understanding

---

21 Would he be better at Right-Bach, Left-Bach, or Centre-Bach, do we think? Please yourselves.

22 Did they overlap, City fans? Not you new ones, the proper ones. It would only have been with Barton as a youth player but it's better for the paragraph if they did, isn't it?

of everything, even breathing new life into his appreciation of something as banal as a glass of water: 'I'm now disposed to look at it from different angles. I'll study the sunlight glinting through the glass, and across the liquid. I'll recognise the beauty in the fragmentation of the ice. I'll appreciate the zest of the lemon slice, and the practicality of the plastic straw.'[23] This is all well and good, but I'm now imagining him reciting this to a room full of Arsenal players while Tony Adams bashes out something avant-garde to accompany him on his Bontempi in the background, and between you and me, it is not going down well.

While Barton seemed to focus on improving his mind, Adams also sought the great outdoors in his efforts to experience new things. It's possible this great escape was an attempt to briefly get out of the company of his less than encouraging team-mates, but at one point Tony found himself buying himself a little speedboat. However, just like your average *Bullseye* winner from the 1980s,[24] he had little experience of handling such a vessel and struggled with it on his maiden voyage on the Thames from Putney. Adams remembers, 'I backed the Jag and the trailer on to the slipway and uncoupled it, jumping on as it began to float into the river.'

Unable to get it going, he floated past Craven Cottage and travelled the full length of the course of the University Boat Race until he came to rest in some reeds at Kew, like some kind of full-size (Victor) Moses. Despite famously being a man not afraid to raise his arm and appeal for something, it seems the sometime England skipper was too embarrassed to ask for help. Instead, he simply waited for the tide to turn and floated all the way back. Though how he stopped when he got there, and whether the Jag

---

23 Of course, now we know that plastic straws are killing beautiful sea creatures, their dark side needs to be considered, along with the impracticalities of paper straws, which go soggy too quickly. So maybe there really is a lot to think about after all.

24 If you're not watching the *Bullseye* repeats on Challenge most nights of the week by the way, I'm not sure we can be friends. It remains the greatest game show of all time. I like to think I could write another book on it.

was waterlogged when he did is all disappointingly glossed over. Minor maritime mishaps aside, I say fair play to Tony Adams for emerging from his lager haze and rediscovering a lust for life.

Another football renaissance man is Pat Nevin. You know Pat Nevin, one-time tricky winger, now full-time Chelsea apologist Pat Nevin. Well, I've got something to tell you about Pat Nevin. It's a bit of a bombshell so you might want to sit down.

Are you ready? Strapped in? Here we go:

PAT NEVIN LIKES INDIE MUSIC!

There, I've said it and it feels good to get that out in the open. You probably didn't know that because he so rarely mentions it. Apart from all the time, when he constantly does: 'I had been a music lover all my life,' see. 'My musical tastes were always a bit left field,' told you; 'There was also the burgeoning Postcard Records scene with Orange Juice, Aztec Camera, The Bluebells, Altered Images, Josef K – the list goes on,' is that so? 'So it would be no surprise a few years later to find me at an early Siouxsie and the Banshees gig or even early New Order or The Cure,' – it's exhausting.

Don't get me wrong, we're probably all big fans of at least some of these acts – he has great taste after all. It's just that something sticks in the craw with the constant references to things like the 'incredibly youthful' U2, or the 'scarcely known' Simple Minds, and early this and early that, and dare I say it, early The Others.[25] If you've heard of someone, he heard of them first. It's all designed to hammer home this idea that 'I didn't exactly fit in with the footballer types', which is all fine and dandy and probably true, but you're left with the distinct impression that Pat doesn't just think he's different to every other footballer, he thinks he might be

---

25 Mid-noughties chums of The Libertines who had a song called 'Stan Bowles' – just to keep things football.

a little bit better. Not at football of course,[26] he has a good handle on his talents in that department and may even undersell himself somewhat – but rather better in terms of being a supercool-trendy-hip-swinging-cool-cat, or whatever the kids call it these days.

Nevin recalls a game in his youth football days when he had a bet with a team-mate about who could score the best goal. The prize was an album for the winner bought by the loser, and he was considering *Wilder* by The Teardrop Explodes or *Heaven Up Here* by Echo and the Bunnymen having already just bought *Movement* by New Order and *Faith* by The Cure. This is during what he describes as his 'existentialist, Albert Camus-worshipping phase'. Yeah, we all like music and reading, mate. Elsewhere he describes the transcendent feeling of a good concert, which, again, we've probably all felt, but says, 'A gig by the Durutti Column was so beautiful and emotional that my eyes were still watering the next day at training' (explained away to the players as just a bit of hay fever, obviously). Obviously, because they're all brutes aren't they, Pat. They simply wouldn't understand.

He paints a picture of himself as turning his back on the likes of Terry Wogan's chat show, national newspapers and lads' mags, where he was, naturally, in high demand, but having all the time in the world for a Muriel Gray music show, indie fanzines or the *NME*, all in the name of portraying himself as somehow different from all the other boys. It just feels like it must have been tiring maintaining this level of cool all the time. In football parlance, he is having himself. It feels like sometimes he probably just wanted to pop *No Jacket Required* into the tape machine in the car and have a game of golf but couldn't because it's not what Bernard Sumner would do. Like I say, good music though.

---

26 He could never claim that after that infamously bad penalty he took for Chelsea against Man City in the eighties which commentator Barry Davies described as the worst penalty he had ever seen. And Barry Davies has seen a lot of penalties.

I'll tell you who does play golf, just about every other footballer known to man. Terry Curran advises all young footballers to 'choose golf instead of betting – the other obvious way of killing time', as if it's a binary choice, while Matt Le Tissier gratefully declares, 'I have a job I enjoy which allows me to play as much golf as I like,' which means he probably spent most of his time out on the course as a player, although these days arguing on Twitter must really eat into his tee-off times. By reputation, Le Tissier is one of the better footballing golfers, or golfing footballers, along with the likes of Gareth Bale, Jimmy Bullard and Gary Lineker, who seems to be able to turn his hand to most games like a latter-day Sport Billy, but the one we almost lost forever to the greens and fairways was Alan Hansen.

He has a chapter in the wonderfully titled *Tall, Dark and Hansen* called 'When Soccer Came Second', which details 'a spell when I believed that I might just be able to make the grade as a professional golfer. It would have been a much more enticing prospect, at that time, than playing football.' Say it ain't so Alan! And yet he continues to insist that 'golf was more important to me then' and that 'football came a poor second'. At one point, Hansen played off a two handicap and even qualified for the Scottish Boys' Championship on one occasion where he finished seventh. Thankfully for him, Liverpool and *Match of the Day*, common sense prevailed, Alan calmed down and realised that football is a much better game, and that golf should be kept to his spare time. After all, professional golf is something footballers have a crack at when they retire from football, but we didn't see Colin Montgomerie strapping his boots on and turning out for Leeds once he got out of the stick and ball game now, did we?

If Hansen lacked the dedication to turn golf from a bit of a knockabout into a genuine alternative career, then where does that leave Bobby Robson, who was once paying so little attention during a round that he fell head-first into a bunker. Kevin Beattie brings us the tale of Bobby's Ipswich lads enjoying a game of golf in Scotland ahead of a game against St Johnstone when Bobby was reading a paper mid-round, missed his step and plunged forwards into the trap. 'The sand was flying everywhere and when he stood up he had sand in his ears, his mouth, his hair, and probably anywhere else sand can get.' Robson moulded that group of players into an over-achieving success, winning the FA Cup and UEFA Cup along the way, before bagging the top job as England manager and eventually becoming a national treasure and earning a knighthood. But for those that saw it, I'd be surprised if he ever lived down the time he emerged from a bunker with half of a crumpled *Daily Mirror* in his hand, blinking and spitting sand everywhere.

The Rangers striker Marco Negri is another we can put in the column of 'tried and failed' when it comes to golf. In his entertaining autobiography *Moody Blue* he talks of a less than successful round at a course in Scotland, when he boomed a shot off the tee and hit the lawnmower of a greenkeeper some way off target: 'He responded with a right hand, using his index and middle fingers to form a "V". But not a sign of victory.' Thanks for clarifying, Marco. He says the irate victim of his wayward shot was 'screaming, "Fuck off! Hopeless c***!" I picked up my clubs hurriedly, and wisely decided to quit the game while still a novice.' Probably for the best.

Maybe Negri should have tried his hand at that other great passion of our football heroes – fishing. Although having said that, it immediately conjures an image of Marco haphazardly casting off only to find his hook embedded in the lip of that same greenkeeper from the golfing incident, who would no doubt curse him again if he could only get the words out.

One thing is for sure, the striker wouldn't have been short of someone to go with. Rangers team-mate Paul 'Gazza' Gascoigne is, of course, one of the great footballing anglers, or angling footballers,[27] along with the likes of Jack Charlton and Vinnie Jones. Lee Bowyer even ran a carp lake in France between his playing and managing careers. Most passionate ex-pro of all perhaps, though, is Jimmy Bullard. The man who is all energy and noise when entertaining us on *Soccer AM*, likes nothing more, it seems, than getting down to a quiet riverbank and being at one with nature once more. He says, 'It's pure instinct because, once upon a time, we all had to catch fish to eat so we could live. So it's all about hunting and there's a proper craft to it which I love. That skill element shouldn't be dismissed.'

Put like that you can see the appeal and these footballers love it. Jeremy Goss says that at one point half of his Norwich team considered themselves 'committed anglers' while David Seaman barely stops talking about it.[28] The England goalkeeper who has won every domestic trophy and played for England at World Cups and Euros claims that 'one of my biggest thrills, though, was a fishing video I presented with a long-time friend of mine, Andy Little. It was called "Gravelpit Carping with Andy Little featuring David Seaman."' We've all seen it, surely? No? I've got my fingers crossed that in a moment of *Homes Under the Hammer* style, on the nose musical choices, the whole thing was soundtracked by Wu Tang Clan's *Gravel Pit*, but I'm afraid if it's a fishing show without Bob Mortimer and Paul Whitehouse on it, I'm probably not going to watch it. Sorry Seamo.

Cricket is another game that many footballers are into during their time off, and quite right too. It is the next best sport after all. Geoff Hurst turned out for Essex in a first-class match once while West Ham team-mate Jim Standen won both the FA Cup with the Hammers and the County Championship with Worcestershire

---

27 Please admire the restraint shown in not saying anything about Raoul Moat here either.

28 Maybe, just maybe David, there were times when Tony Adams sat patiently and nodded while you droned on about fishing. Did you ever think about that?

in 1964, which must have been quite the summer for him. Dennis Compton famously combined the two to possibly the highest level of anyone, while Chris Balderstone had parallel careers and even played cricket for Leicestershire and football for Doncaster Rovers on the same day once. Let's also not forget Ian Botham fitting in a few games for Scunthorpe around swashbuckling cricket, disciplinary hearings and charity walks with elephants (or did I dream that last one?). Andy Goram also managed to play both football and cricket for Scotland, scoring four against Australia once. In cricket, not football, which admittedly makes it slightly less impressive.

Other enthusiastic amateurs included commentator Brian Moore, who played to a decent standard as a youngster and even shared a field with Colin Cowdrey once, and Ian St John who lists bowling TV bigwig (that's right, bigwig) Michael Grade in some sort of celebrity knockabout as one of his proudest moments in the whites. There's also Roy McDonough who is described as 'a very good cricketer' by his sexual sidekick Perry Groves, and Didi Hamann, who took lessons from his sporting pal Andrew 'Freddie' Flintoff of Ashes heroics, pedalo and *Top Gear* fame; but their stories in this area are merely preludes to tales of sex and gambling, respectively, so let's pull the covers on over those and go indoors instead.

There we will mostly find Matt Le Tissier, who claims that at one point he was spending around 10 or 11 hours at the snooker club after training, presumably in addition to the golf. That seems excessive, unless he was playing Peter Ebdon, in which case it's only a couple of frames once you factor in the slow play and endless conspiracy chat. Elsewhere, Bobby Gould recalls just how competitive the snooker got at Coventry, particularly the time that Gould and coach driver Hughie Spencer were giving out 'a rare pasting' to George Curtis and John Sillett, who did not take it well. 'They chased us down the corridor afterwards, caught Hughie and jammed a metal waste paper bin over his head. It stuck fast and a taxi had to be called to take him to hospital to have it removed.' Did this really happen? I'm putting it in the same category with those other injuries that may be real or might have just been read about in *The Beano*. The thing I don't understand is why anyone involved in a row over a snooker match would ever use anything other than their cue as a weapon. I mean, it's right there, it's got a heavy end for bashing with or a pointy end for poking with. And then there are the balls if you can get your sock off in time. We've all seen *Scum*. I'm not condoning it, I'm just saying.

Which brings us nicely to the darts where people are given sharp pointy things to throw across the room. Devotees of the sport / pub game (delete according to your own delicate sensibilities) include Colin Todd, who Peter Taylor claimed 'would rather play darts in a pub than win an England cap'. He uses it as an example of a perceived lack of ambition in his life, even going so far as to claim it as a flaw he carried on to the pitch, where he 'would play short stuff instead of delivering the killer ball'. Nah, leave Toddy alone, I reckon he just liked a game of arrows.

Peter Crouch brings us the surprising news that not only did Spurs team-mate Sandro become 'obsessed with darts' but that he also 'had boards shipped back to his mum's in Brazil and began an unlikely friendship with oche legend Bobby George'. Now that is an enduring image. Gorgeous Bobby George, one hand dripping with gold, the other holding a pint, watching proudly on as Sandro tries to hit the lipstick. If he hadn't needed to stay local to London for handy Bobby George access, it's possible that Sandro might have found his spiritual home at Newcastle a few years earlier under Sam Allardyce, where darts seems to have been taken almost (who are we kidding?) as seriously as the football. Shay Given says that his brother-in-gloves Steve Harper was the logistics man and organised darts leagues among the players, comprising the Premier League for the top darters, with the rest competing in 'The Moroccan Open' (no disrespect to Morocco!). It does feel like there's some disrespect to Morocco here, but as they don't have a rich tradition at the elite level of darts, I'll let it slide. It seems that James 'Machine Gun' Milner was the titan of the tungsten around St James' Park way, with Given saying, 'He would throw fast and straight all day long.' You would expect nothing less from Milner, would you? Mr Consistency in football, darts and a number of other things I shouldn't wonder. Probably got a well-stocked tool shed. I bet he knows about cars as well. He's got that look about him. He'd make a good brother-in-law, I reckon. He would help you move house and stuff like that. Sorry, I got lost there for a moment, where was I?

Tennis was big at Spurs in the early 1980s when the shorts must have been so very short. Glenn Hoddle says that Garth Crooks 'shared my passion for the game' and the two would slug it out over five sets 'playing for a big prize in our eyes – our pride'. Is it just me, or does that game not sound like that much fun? You imagine that the rules were very strictly adhered to in that one, including end changes, ball changes and barley water consumption, unlike Stan Ternent's memory of playing doubles against Peter Reid: 'Reidy lobbed the ball high and, as I ran back to take a shot at it, I tripped and fell over a low bench. It was match point but I was writhing in agony.' Now at this point over on centre court at Spurs, Glenn or Garth would have consulted the regulations about how to resolve the issue, but would certainly have postponed proceedings. Reidy thought different: 'Fuck him,' he said, and took the points. He took great pleasure in playing out the final rally over my prone body. Peter Reid there – what he lacks in Corinthian spirit, he makes up for in straight talking and killer instinct on the tennis court.

Other participation sports enjoyed by the football fraternity in their time off include ten pin bowling (Terry Dyson), water polo (Pat Partridge) and cage fighting – wait, what? Paul Sturrock had a player with him at Southend called Bilel Mohsni (who some Rangers fans may remember from a brief spell at Ibrox), who had what Sturrock describes as 'a wee altercation with an Orient player'

IT'S NOT ALL WORK, WORK, WORK

in which he grabbed some scissors from the physio's office post-match and tried to bust into the away dressing room to attack the guy.

In the short term, four players wrestled him to the ground, presumably while his target made his escape, but the slightly longer-term plan was to channel his aggression by getting him into cage fighting. Sturrock says, 'Many a day he came back with a black eye and a bloody nose, which seemed to work for a while, but his discipline on the pitch was always an issue.' Now who would have thought it? Sending somebody with too much aggression into an environment where he would require even more aggression, just to avoid a beating each week doesn't feel like a solid gold plan. Maybe Sturrock felt that aggression was like some sort of allowance that you start the week with. If you can use it all up by Tuesday, you won't have any more till the following week. This is unfortunately not correct. It's a case of the more you spend, the more you build up – like some sort of aggro Nectar Points.

Jimmy Hill lived such a full, rich and varied life that I am quite surprised he didn't have a go at cage fighting himself at some point, but if he did, he doesn't mention it in his book, and you would think he might. However, he does boast that his TV work allowed him to indulge some of his sporting fantasies outside of football. His programme *Sportswide* saw him join in a 'kids mini stox' race, which is evidently some kind of go karting. But instead of treating it as a bit of fun, Jimmy got his toe down and finished a creditable third, claiming a small trophy. As he presumably towered over the first and second place holders on the podium, he chose to ignore the protests from his opponents, children remember, one of whom claimed foul play due to Jimmy's size, age and experience and wanted the prize instead. Jimmy, showing all the belligerence that once saw him get the maximum wage for footballers abolished, told the sore loser, 'Well, you're not getting it!' … 'You'll get a chance to win another, I won't!' And that young lad went on to grow up and become Jenson Button. Not really – I don't know what happened to him, but he probably just went home and cried. Cheers Jimmy.

Hill was also able to wangle himself on to the Grand National coverage one year and managed to indulge his horsey fantasies by getting to jump the first fence. On a horse, you understand, not with a standing jump (he's not Duncan Mackenzie). Jimmy was a big horse fan after moving to the countryside and even joined in with the local hunt to terrorise foxes. If you've always thought that Hill had a haughty, pompous air, just imagine how much that would be magnified by having him on a horse in a pair of jodhpurs.

Of course, the way that Jimmy got into horses, via the hunt, wasn't the way that most footballers get into horses. There's a rich tradition of football and horse racing crossover with many figures like Mick Channon, Mick Quinn, Michael Owen (wait, why are they always called Mick, and Sir Alex Ferguson (oh, right, as you were) all owning or training horses. Not Glenn Hoddle though. Although he says he loves the races, he admits that he's 'actually petrified of animals themselves'. Fair enough. Best to stick to tennis where there's even a net between you and your opponent to keep you safe. Such was Mick Quinn's commitment to the cause that at Portsmouth he had a portable TV and during Alan Ball's pre-match pep talk 'would duck into the shitter and watch the races on my little telly with the sound down'. I'm guessing that furtively watching the racing on a tiny TV isn't the worst thing Quinn has done in a toilet cubicle, but it's certainly no substitute for being there. The roar of the crowd, the thunder of the hooves, the audible ripping of the losing tickets, all of these sounds are proven to improve the mood of a squad of footballers. They can practically get a day at the races on prescription in the name of team building.

In Peter Swan's compelling book, he recalls a Hull City day out organised by Billy Whitehurst, who despite his fearsome reputation, was clearly quite a good organiser. It was Whitehurst that collected the money from manager Stan Ternent, arranged the coach and issued instructions to arrive at the ground at 8:30 sharp, and to wear suits 'because I've ordered tickets for the posh enclosure'. Unfortunately, at the appointed time there was no sign of Whitehurst or the coach, and not for several hours afterwards either. Eventually the Hull lads gave up and took their suits and binoculars to the bookies to watch proceedings there. Perhaps due to being scared of Whitehurst, everybody was very forgiving of him and accepted that his 'intentions had been honourable'. Nobody took him to task once they were told that he had unfortunately 'succumbed' the day before the trip and put all the trip money on a dead cert that 'went belly up, and so did our trip to Cheltenham'. Ah, there it is you see – the gambling. Somebody should have told Billy that there's no such thing as a dead cert, but it seems that people were too frightened of him to tell him pretty much anything really. To err is human. To err when you're big and people are terrified of you is pretty much a free pass.

Ledley King and Ashley Cole crossed the North London divide to own a horse together called King of Defence,[29] while Robbie Fowler and Steve McManaman famously laughed up their sleeve at how funny they were with their stable including Some Horse and Another Horse, so called for the commentary LOLs – but if you can't afford a horse then there are always little horses, or 'greyhounds' as some folk would have you call them. Paul Weller (not that one) part-owned a greyhound with Glen Little and describes it, accurately, as 'one of those things that footballers do with time on their hands', while Malcolm Allison got involved too and found it a murky world.

One of Allison's acquaintances was a villain called Joe Lowery, who Malcolm tells us was doping dogs, including one that belonged to Alf Ramsey in his playing days. Allison recalls watching a hurdle race as 'Alf's dog hurtled towards the first obstacle – then collapsed

---

29 Presumably Ledley put more money in to get his name above the door. If it was a 50–50 split then they could have done worse than Old King Cole.

a couple of yards short. I was standing next to Joe as the track exploded with angry yells. It looked very bad, and Joe murmured to himself: "Sod me, I gave it too much. It should have gone with the hurdle."' Evidently, it's a tricky business to get the doses right. Now whether honest Alf was in on the scam we don't know (surely not) but Allison soon took a step back himself.

Another greyhound man was Rangers winger Davie Wilson, who also lists shooting, photography and fishing in his interests and 'ran a speedboat for a period of time. I can't recall why I did the latter, though, as I suffer from seasickness and even today I won't go on a boat.' How do you end up with a speedboat you don't want? Did he win it on *Bullseye*?[30] Pigeons were his great love though. From a young age, he says, 'I would always be trying to trap pigeons when I was out playing with my pals,' which must have made for some interesting games of football over the park. It was an interest that Wilson maintained to a ripe old age and nicely tees up a look at some of the other miscellaneous interests enjoyed outside the game.

DAVID BATTY – MOTORBIKE RACING

I imagine that actually taking part in racing bikes, and possibly even owning a motorbike, was strictly off the menu during his playing days, due to those stick-in-the-mud, risk-averse insurance folk, but that didn't stop David Batty being a proper fan boy. He says, 'You never fall out of love with bikes,' and recalls going weak at the knees when he met Carl Fogarty and especially Ron Haslam. He describes peeing next to Rocket Ron at Silverstone as 'my happiest memory' and even got an autograph once they had both washed the drips off. I'd have liked to have been there for this, not least to find out how riders manage a wee in those leather suits they wear.

---

30   There it is again.

MARC OVERMARS – MODEL CARS

David Seaman brings us the news that Marc Overmars was a bit of a loner and spent much of his time and a small fraction of his earnings collecting matchbox cars and even some 'that are big enough to sit in. That is one weird hobby.' Who died and made David Seaman the Hobby Sheriff? Let Overmars crack on. The thought of him doing doughnuts around the marble halls at Highbury in some sort of tiny ride-on Jeep is very pleasing.

ANDREA PIRLO – PLAYSTATION

Pirlo has always struck me as someone who thinks very deeply about things, so for him to say that 'after the wheel, the PlayStation is the best invention of all time', is both very big talk and one in the eye for the printing press, the combustion engine, and the Xbox. A further bombshell comes when he says he always plays the football games as Barcelona 'apart from a brief spell way back at the start when I'd go Milan'. That one's a smack in the face for Juventus. This guy doesn't care who he upsets.

ZLATAN IBRAHIMOVIĆ – GEARS OF WAR

Zlatan is another gamer and admits to marathon sessions on Gears of War going on deep into the night when he should have been resting up for training, but it obviously hasn't done him any harm. At the time of writing and no doubt at the time of reading and at the time of finding this book in a box in a loft several years from now, Zlatan is still going strong. He admits to being addicted to the game (Gears of War, not football) and says, 'I'd often play online with other people – Brits, Italians, Swedes, anybody, six or seven hours a day, and I had a gamertag. I couldn't be known as Zlatan online. So, of course, nobody knew who was concealed behind my online tag.' So, if you were similarly enthusiastic about the same game around the same time, there's a chance you've played against Zlatan Ibrahimović. Which is not nothing, is it?

Inevitably, the man with the highest opinion of himself in world football claims 'I crushed everybody', but unless he goes online as IAmZlatanIbrahomvic_01 how are we to know?

BRYAN ROBSON – PAC-MAN

Before we had your Gears of Wars and your Calls of Duties and your Assassins Creeds of this world, but after we had your Pongs of this world, we had Pac-Man, which took the world and seemingly the World Cup by storm. Terry Butcher reports that the England camp at the 1982 World Cup was gripped by it – perhaps a little too tightly. 'Bryan Robson was the Pac-Man champion. He spent so much time on the machine that the controls gave him blisters on his hands and he needed plasters from the team doctor.' This is, of course, the least of the problems that Robson has given team doctors at World Cups as later years would see, toes and arms dropping off him like a badly rattled Mr Potato Head.

STEVE CLARIDGE – DANCING

Robbie Savage is a man who got to week 10 on *Strictly* so speaks with a bit of authority when he says that Leicester team-mate Steve Claridge can cut a rug. 'You should see him on the dance floor. He never drank, but he is one of the best dancers I've ever seen.' Maybe they got the wrong one on *Strictly* and we can only pray it's not too late to see Claridge, socks down around his ankles, shirt untucked, doing a passable paso doble in front of Dave Arch and his wonderful, wonderful orchestra.

ALAN SHEARER – SINGING

Shay Given reports that Alan Shearer had a place in Portugal where he and his friends would go during the holidays and spend the night tearing it up in a karaoke bar, with Shearer gamely belting out 'All Night Long' by Lionel Richie. Given reports that his buddy 'knows it word for word and likes to think he's good but he's horrendous'.

I haven't done much karaoke myself, but I can say from experience that 'All Night Long' is a tough one to sing, what with all those jambo jambos and all that, so let's give him a pass on it. By his own admission, Given was 'no crowd pleaser either' as he had a stab at Ronan Keating from Boyzone's 'Life is a Rollercoaster'. Ronan was right, it really is.

MARCO NEGRI – DRACULAS

When he's not terrorising greenkeepers with shanked tee shots Marco Negri likes to indulge his fascination with Draculas: 'I have always been fascinated by the macabre story of the cruel Vlad Tepes (Vlad the Impaler), better known as Count Dracula'. Told you. He even visited the Carpathians in the middle of winter and saw the castle. I wonder if he's ever been to Whitby for the Goth Weekender?

LUIS SUÁREZ – BOARD GAMES

Suárez says that during his time at Liverpool he and Lucas Leiva and their partners would often double date and play Monopoly together. 'Did I cheat? When I could,' is his confession, but if you're letting Luis Suárez be the banker in a game of Monopoly then, frankly, you deserve everything you get.

GARY NEVILLE – PAINTBALL

Whatever created the team spirit among the Class of '92, it wasn't the paintball. Gary Neville claims it was good for them but that might be because 'I shot Butty right in the head from point-blank range' rather than the other way round. 'I was jumping about screaming and Nick rubbed his head, going barmy. It was a great laugh,' chuckles the evil Neville brother.

MIKE HOOPER – BIRDWATCHING

Apparently, the Liverpool and Newcastle sometime stopper loved nothing more than watching the birds and told Paul Lake while they were both receiving treatment at Lilleshall that they 'were in a twitcher's paradise'. Lovely, wholesome stuff this. Chris Packham would be proud, although I'm sure you also now have Coolio's biggest hit running through your head.

GRAEME LE SAUX – ANTIQUES

While most of us limit our antique hunting to dipping into the very many hours of *Antique Hunters* on TV these days, Graeme Le Saux used to get out there amongst it, channelling his inner 'Bedknobs and Broomsticks' as he went up the Portobello Road. Le Saux collected 'antique tins and old football boots' among other things and even took an evening class in antiques, 'funded by the Professional Footballers' Association'. There's a lot to, very delicately in case we break something, unpack here. First thing to say is that it's a lovely hobby to have. Secondly, you've got to wonder if he ever found some magical boots and played in them like in 'Billy's Boots' and, finally, exactly how did he convince the PFA to pay for his night school?

IAN HOLLOWAY – MAKING CHICKEN HOUSES

Ian Holloway began making 'chicken houses for the hens we'd bought and did a bloody good job, even if I do say so myself'. He tells us that *Soccer AM* visited his home to do a fake advert for his wares, but he was disappointed that it didn't result in 'one or two orders from football supporters around the country' – not even one. To be fair, that would rely on a *Soccer AM* viewer having chickens of their own but no houses for them, or at least one who was thinking of getting chickens, and could convince their partner that what they really needed was a coop made by the former QPR and Blackpool boss.

It's a bit of a stretch but let me say here and now that if I fell into any of those categories, I would have gladly bought a Holloway Hen House.

BRIAN McCLAIR – SHOPPING

Brian McClair is funnier than you might think from his gruff, on-the-pitch demeanour, so when he claims that 'many of my most enjoyable hours are spent in Sainsbury's, with the occasional foray into Marks and Spencer' it's just possible that he's having us on. And yet, I sort of agree with him. He says that 'getting behind a trolley is great therapy', and it's true that there is a certain mindfulness to be found in the cold aisles,[31] before it all gets shattered by the frantic attempts to keep up at the checkouts as your chosen goods come flying down the ramp at you. Of course, it's all online deliveries these days, isn't it? I wonder if Choccy's made the switch. Let's hope not, for his sake.

GLENN HODDLE – FOREIGN PROPERTY

Glenn brings us the news that he and Gary Lineker had use of a Spanish villa through a timeshare deal 'with a number of personalities in snooker and horse racing, for a 32-year period'. Glenn's a bit of a tease and doesn't tell us who the others involved are, but I'm guessing he knew, as it would affect your decision to get involved wouldn't it? Willie Thorne (it was definitely him, right?) would be okay but if you had three weeks after Alex Higgins in the eighties, you would have spent it clearing up and repairing the smashed windows. Also, tantalisingly, the lease must be up some time around now and I'm wondering if Glenn and Gary still use it, or if they've sold it on to younger players like Glen Johnson and Ross Barkley. You know, Glenn-Gary-Glen-Ross. Please yourself.

PETER SWAN – VIEWING PROPERTY

You would think that finding somewhere to live when you change clubs might be a chore, but Peter Swan and Keith Houchen seem to have enjoyed the hunt when they came together at Port Vale and

---

31 Unless you get a wonky wheel. Nothing worse, is there?

used to drive each other around for a nose about. On one occasion, Houchie was taking in a fancy place in the countryside built on a hillside on three levels, with a garden at the bottom. While Keith was getting the inside scoop from the estate agent out back, Swan waited, bored in the lounge on the top floor, until he 'noticed a leather pouffe alongside a chair in the lounge'. At this point there were clearly only three options:

a. Admire the pouffe and wonder where it was from.

b. Ignore the pouffe, because when you've seen one pouffe, you've seen them all.

c. Launch the pouffe out of the back door and down the steps towards Houchen and the estate agent.

Despite it weighting a ton, Swan went for option c: 'With about ten steps to go it was barrelling along at a fair old lick and still they hadn't noticed … but, at the very last moment, they seemed to hear a noise behind them, turned round and leaped for safety.' Well thank goodness they did, and I like to think that Houchen struck the exact same pose as his famous cup final diving header for Coventry as he soared through the air, but there's no word on who pulled the item of furniture out of the hedge and dragged it back up three flights of stairs. Luckily, claims Swanny, 'I was able to convince the bemused estate agent that it had all been an accident.' I have my doubts about whether he truly convinced anybody that it was an accident but naturally Houchen thought the whole thing was hilarious, because, well, footballers.

Of course, as far as some pros are concerned, you can keep such adrenaline-fuelled hobbies as pouffe launching – all they really want is to be curled up with a good book. So, who reads what among our bookworms? Alex Ferguson goes for 'biographies of the dictators' (do your own jokes), while the young Alan Shearer was keen to get his hands on 'Princess in Love, which has attracted a massive amount of coverage in the newspapers'. Hope Powell says that within her squad 'Casey Stoney loved her Martina Cole and Mo Hayder crime novels', while Kenny Dalglish doesn't seem to mind what it is as long as 'it's big writing with small chapters and there's something happening!' and namechecks James Patterson as fitting the brief. Ian St John says he tended to go for mysteries and espionage as well as 'the odd racy one that for plot relied heavily on the joys of sexual intercourse'. Stuart Pearce admits to being a late bloomer who 'never read a book until my thirties' but made up for it with a voracious appetite for novels from then on: 'I enjoy thrillers with a twist, *The Silence of the Lambs* is one, and Sherlock Holmes stories. From there, I went to Oscar Wilde's *The Picture of Dorian Gray*. I really enjoyed it and it encouraged me to experiment. I've tried such diverse authors as Patricia Cornwell and Tolstoy.' Well, it's good to mix things up. Imagine sticking to one genre and reading, say, 300 football autobiographies over a few years. That would just be silly.

Some players aren't satisfied with simply reading fiction, instead they set about writing it. Yes, yes, there's Steve Bruce with his Steve Barnes thrillers, but years before that Terry Venables co-wrote a lot of Hazel books which were successfully adapted for television,[32] while Jimmy Greaves spent about as much time as Steve Bruce did in coming up with a name for his alter ego as he wrote about a 'young playboy footballer called Jackie Groves who scores goals and also scores heavily with the girls'. The first novel he co-wrote is called *The Final* and I urge you to look it up if only for the vintage saucy cover. Meanwhile, John Toshack wrote poetry and even had a collection, called *Gosh It's Tosh* published in the seventies, despite team-mate Phil Thompson declaring that they were 'crap in fairness'. Everyone's a critic.

Other talented players with a pen in their hand include David James and John Gorman. David Seaman says that Jamo 'does good

---

32 These were written with Gordon Williams who wrote the source novel for *Straw Dogs*, trivia fans.

caricatures of other footballers', which isn't easy with goalkeeping gloves on, while Gorman had a regular slot in the Spurs programme with a cartoon while he was injured there as a player. He says, 'The cartoons became so popular that I decided to do a calendar with a player on the page of each month, including me with a screw sticking out of my knee!' This didn't stop at a bit of fun though, as Glenn Hoddle used to drive him round to various pubs and shops where Gorman would flog them. The start of a beautiful friendship.

Was your mum always saying to you 'only boring people get bored' too? I kind of get it now. Strip away the golf clubs, the antiques, the fishing gear and the speedboats and if you can still entertain yourself, then truly you will never be bored. It's why I think I might have been okay on *Big Brother*. I feel like I could take myself away from the ego clashes and rows about shopping lists and you would just find me in the corner conducting an entire World Cup with a rolled-up sock. Channelling a similar 'make your own entertainment' energy was Jeremy Goss at Norwich in the nineties, where 'Mike Walker, Gunny and me used to have punching competitions, usually on away trips, each of us taking turns to give the other a punch in the six pack area'. Two things to note here are, firstly, that Mike Walker was the manager and, secondly, that this only happened on away trips, presumably when boredom reared its ugly head. Punching each other in the stomach when playing at home would be daft, after all.

Lee Sharpe recalls a game that also might well have hurt, which he and his pals played in digs as apprentices. 'Darkness' involved turning off all the lights and closing the curtains so that everyone was sitting around in the pitch black. 'Then people would throw things around the room, anything and everything – ornaments, shoes, pictures – but you weren't to make a sound; if you did, you had to let everybody give you a dig.' What passes the time better than trying to stifle a scream as a vase bounces off your temple in complete darkness? And please just believe me when I say that this wasn't even the worst game that Sharpe and his buddies played in those digs. You don't want to know.

Similar DIY entertainment was made up by David Batty, who when he wasn't asleep and dreaming about being Ron Haslam, would stay awake and terrorise his roommates. At Leeds, Peter Swan would wake in the night to find Batty staring at the TV 'where he'd drawn a target on the screen with toothpaste'. Batty would then fire rolled up tissue through the straw at his target. Swan didn't share Batty's enthusiasm for the game or even Joey Barton's enthusiasm for the straw, so when young David asked him to join in, he told him 'I'd got better things to do'. Quite right Swanny, that furniture isn't going out of the window by itself now, is it?

4.

Behind Every Great Manager

'Tennis Elbow in His Foot'

SIR STANLEY Matthews gained justifiably legendary status with his wing wizardry and his incredible longevity as a player, entertaining paying crowds with his trickery well beyond his 75th birthday, probably. What he failed to do, however, was make much of a mark as a manager. He is, of course, not alone in that club, but in his defence, it is a really hard job. Reflecting on his inauspicious time in the dugout at Port Vale he lamented that 'it's not easy being a football manager; you're a Dutch Uncle one day, physiotherapist the next, and psychologist the day after'. And he was right, of course. These days modern football clubs have legions of physiotherapists, squadrons of psychologists and any number of Dutch Uncles[33] on hand to provide a manager with all the support he or she needs. These backroom boys and girls are vital to a team's success, and stand directly behind a winning manager's beaming smile, along with those boards with all the betting and holiday logos on. A manager is only as good as their staff.

There was a time though, when that staff, instead of running to hundreds of expert professionals, was a small and hardy bunch,

---

33 Me neither. Unless he literally means an uncle from Delft, we can all only speculate

splitting all the jobs between them, without a care for having the correct equipment or indeed the qualifications to take them on. Have-a-go heroes, every one of them.

Legendary manager Bill Shankly didn't need to be all things to all men in his Liverpool pomp, because he had Bob Paisley for that. The man who went on to win four European Cups, countless domestic trophies, and more Bells Manager of the Month bottles of scotch than he could have drunk in a lifetime, wasn't always so grand. Before he was number one, he was Shankly's erstwhile number two – and he got all the good jobs. Known as 'Rats' because of his time as a Desert Rat in the Second World War, Paisley was well used to conflict, so Shankly used him in difficult situations. 'Bob was the hatchet man. Shanks didn't come and tell you if you weren't in the team ... it was Bob who would sidle up and inform you that you were out.' This is from Kevin Keegan, who surely can't have been dropped too many times, but who was clearly stung by it when he was. He's a sensitive soul.

Ian St John brings us two stories that show the full breadth of what Paisley had to put up with for the greater Liverpool good. The first came during an away trip to play Inter, which involved a stay on the banks of Lake Como. Sounds idyllic, and it would have been, were it not for the church bells ringing in the village. They obviously didn't know Shanks was coming. Poor old Paisley got the shout: 'Bob, you'd better get those bells stopped, they're going to interfere with the boys' sleep.'

'Bill,' Paisley replied, shaking his head slowly, 'those bells have been ringing for centuries. Do you think they're going to stop them for a bunch of footballers from the other side of Europe?'

Undeterred, Shankly insisted: 'Well, you'd better do something about it,' he demanded. 'You'd better climb up that tower and muffle the bells.'

Now Bob was a resourceful man but there was clearly a line to be drawn and he drew it at scaling Italian church towers and muffling their bells. He did go and ask politely, but the Italian church isn't known for being open to new ideas and the bells kept ringing.

Anyone already feeling that Shankly was unreasonable here should brace themselves for the second tale, and wonder exactly how Paisley decided what he would and wouldn't do. St John was sent off for Liverpool in a Boxing Day game at Coventry in 1967. He had reacted and punched Brian Lewis at a free kick after Lewis had grabbed his balls and squeezed hard, years before Vinnie Jones got a Hollywood career out of it. The Saint had clearly let his halo slip and was castigated by those who didn't have the full picture. But the management had a plan.

The following day, St John says that Shankly summoned him to the treatment room with Bob and told him to get on the table. 'As I lay there, Bob was dabbing a piece of cloth into iodine and boot polish. He then proceeded to daub the mixture on to my groin and genitals.' Well, of course. Once both future managerial legends were satisfied that their star man's plums were of a sufficiently plummy hue, Shankly threw open the door and called some press men into the room, where Saint sat stripped to the waist, the unconventional way round and invited them to 'take a look at this outrage'. Well, I've heard it called a few things now. The right reports were subsequently written, by the aghast newsmen, but St John still got an FA ban for the punch. So, what have we learned here? Firstly, that the FA aren't as easily fooled as the press. Secondly, that if you want to make it look like your knackers have been knackered (for whatever sick perverted reasons you people get up to), then iodine and boot polish is just the ticket. And finally, that those backroom boys sometimes are asked to go above and beyond the call of duty.

Shankly and Paisley were, of course, ably supported in their time at Anfield by the famous Boot Room. An inner sanctum of knowledge, wisdom and presumably boots, that is given a special sense of reverence by many who experienced it. Despite the inauspicious surroundings, 'right next to the drying room', Kenny Dalglish talks with wonder about the brains trust formed in there by the likes of Tom Saunders, Joe Fagan, Ronnie Moran and later Roy Evans and says, 'It was a real privilege for anyone who was asked to step into the Boot Room.' Sounds magical. Opposing managers would be invited in to say hello, and seemingly all of them lapped it up, either out of respect, or curiosity about the fabled grotto. However, this friendly pretext masked a hidden motive. All the while these starstruck visiting coaching staff 'were being quizzed for information about their own young players, their strengths and weaknesses and what they were like as individuals. The staff never spoke to anyone in there without trying to extract information from them. It was brilliant.' Still, they no doubt gave them a cup of tea and a digestive while they harvested everything useful that they had to offer.

Of course, the sneaky old Anfield Boot Room boys had to do more than use their Good Kop Bad Kop interrogation technique to earn their money. One of Roy Evans' jobs was to make sure everyone was asleep at night on away trips, either with a quick check or a sleeping tablet, while Ronnie Moran was given the prestige job of handing out the numerous medals at the end of, let's face it, most seasons. It was a job he did with all the pomp and ceremony of someone handing round some Quality Street that need finishing in the first week of January. There was no pyrotechnic display, no plinth, no 'Sweet Caroline' out on the pitch. More than one account has Ronnie walking into a celebrating dressing room and simply plonking the box of winners' medals on the table. Alan Hansen says that Moran would ask, 'Who's played thirteen games?', which was at that time the qualification for a medal, while Kenny Dalglish says that Moran would simply say, 'If you think you deserve it, take one.' Dalglish adds, 'That was their way of saying "you got your reward for last year, now let's start again", but it all feels a bit functional, doesn't it? Let's let people enjoy winning for the summer at least, otherwise what are we doing it all for? Where's the romance? I thought "This Means More".'

This no nonsense, business as usual attitude seems to have permeated the club in the days of the Anfield Boot Room, and who can knock it given the success they had, I suppose. Several sources tell us that training was often little more than five-a-sides or full-scale practice matches – and we can't deny it made them very good at football. It's an attitude best summed up, according to Ian Rush, by Ronnie Moran, when he was asked to say a few inspirational words pre-match one time:

'You know that Rudyard Kipling poem, "If", where he says, it isn't whether you win but how you play the game that matters? Great poem, except for that part, which is bollocks. As far as this club is concerned, winning is all that matters.' Oh. It was a gruff demeanour that extended to his physical care of the players. Before Jan Mølby's debut for the Reds, some of his team-mates suggested he should try asking Moran for a massage; something he was no doubt used to at Ajax, being a Continental type: 'Fuck off!' shouted Ronnie. 'You earn the fucking right to have a massage! Go out there and play some games and then I might consider it!'

This perhaps shouldn't come as a surprise given the medical set-up at Liverpool, and indeed most clubs, at the time. It was an era when the 'physio' seemed to be whichever coach had a bucket and sponge in his car boot that day. Paul Walsh describes the treatment room at Liverpool as 'like a museum, with a wax bath and a load of rickety, archaic equipment' and the treatment itself not much better. Once, when Walsh was receiving ultrasound on an ankle injury, Moran was reading the back page of the newspaper, got distracted by it and ended up halfway up his leg. When Walshy pointed out the error he was abruptly told, 'It's your fault, you little cunt for bringing the paper in here in the first place!' You don't get that with Bupa. It seems like you couldn't win with Ronnie, anywhere except out on the pitch. And he was a right Sweary Mary.[34]

The medical care at Liverpool in days gone by could generously be described as shoddy. Kevin Keegan recalls a time when the backroom staff were so perplexed by a niggling foot injury he had that a specialist was called in, who was less than helpful, declaring, 'I've never seen anything like it. The only thing it can be is tennis elbow in his foot.' Poor old Paisley dutifully relayed this message to a no doubt accepting and understanding Shanks.

Roy Evans was no better. Steve Nicol recalls a horrific injury he sustained at Norwich when he broke his jaw and smashed some teeth: 'Roy Evans – our so-called physio – came running on with a bucket of water and absolutely whacked me across the side of the head with a soaking wet, freezing cold sponge.'[35] It's not what you need is it? It turned out that nobody on the staff knew what Nicol needed, as he was allowed to play on with his broken jaw, then go out for a few beers afterwards, before eventually going to hospital the next day, where he was told he couldn't eat for six weeks.

However, in a move that feels like it should be accompanied by a wink and a thumbs up, like something from *Whizzer and Chips*, Nicol boasts that he 'managed to separate the wiring just enough at the top of my mouth so I could squeeze some Golden Wonder beef and onion crisps through the gap'. Let's not forget it was a different time. I'm not sure you can even still get Golden Wonder beef and onion.

This make-do-and-mend approach to medical matters was rife in the British game at one time. Naturally, they were way ahead on the Continent. John Charles left Leeds for Juventus in 1957 but

---

34 Walsh didn't have much luck with treatment at Liverpool. He recalls visiting the club doctor at his dimly lit home with a piles problem. He was told to bend over near the window and, when the doctor opened the curtains for more light, Walshy found a bus stop full of people looking at his bum.

35 It was only in a Screensport Super Cup game too. I'm not sure I'd want to lose teeth for anything less than an FA Cup quarter-final.

FINAL THIRD

says that they already had 'three doctors on permanent call, three specialists in different areas. The physiotherapy was of the highest quality' in stark contrast to the British approach of treating 'the best players in the land with a bucket of ice-cold water and a sponge'. At home, that bucket and sponge was considered a cure for everything at one time on football fields up and down the land. It was the great leveller – whether it was little Jamie copping a ball in the face for his Under 9s team or a seasoned international in the First Division with a minor meniscus tear, both are getting cold water sloshed on it with a sponge bought from Halfords.

Lee Chapman says that Leeds physio Alan Sutton once tried to use it on a broken arm in a game against Manchester United. You won't be surprised to learn that it did not fix it.[36] Perhaps even worse, was Neil Warnock (in his hard to accept days as a tricky winger) being told to run pretty much everything off, including on one occasion, a ruptured spleen. Warnock was clattered by a knee in the back playing for Hartlepool. At half-time in the game, he was about to ask to come off when his manager ripped into him for his guts and his performance, so he stubbornly carried on, despite the searing pain: 'I put my hand on my side and I had got a lump the size of a football on the side of my back. I asked the physio, Tommy Johnson, to have a look at it. He was horror struck. "I've never seen owt like that," he said.' Although to be fair, unless it was a grazed knee or a hangover, any British physio of the time would probably have claimed to have never seen anything like it.

Now, I don't have much of a medical background myself but even if you could convince me that you can carry on playing football without a functioning jaw, arm or spleen, I would have to draw the line at the legs. And yet Alistair Robertson once broke his leg in the first half of a game for West Bromwich Albion before

---

36 Mel Sterland says that on trips to the hospital for treatment, Alan Sutton showed him the dead bodies in the morgue on request, so maybe his judgement on any number of things might be questioned.

being told that he was 'as soft as shit' by touchy-feely manager Alan Ashman and sent back out. Robertson says that physio Tom Jones (not that one), Doctor Rimmer and trainer Jimmy Dunn all looked and found nothing wrong. 'The following day it transpired I'd broken my leg.' Robertson was out for 14 weeks. It's almost as if it might be worth having people who know what they're doing around to have a look at injuries.

It's fair to say that professionalism may not have been at current levels back in the day. Tony Cottee recalls Rob Jenkins at West Ham keeping 'a few cans in the fridge in the treatment room at Chadwell Heath. Indeed, it was a pre-condition of Rob's that before he'd treat a player on a Sunday morning, you had to bring him in four cans of Heineken!', while at Fulham Jimmy Hill says he walked into Frank Penn's treatment room to find a greyhound under the heat lamp receiving a massage while players waited outside. And yet these people have the big decisions in their hands. We always hear about players undergoing fitness tests before a game as they return from injury and assume that these are rigorous, taxing affairs designed to put any question of a recurrence of the injury beyond doubt. Not so. Paul Weller (not that one) says that, at Burnley, physio Jimmy Holland's fitness test consisted of sending a player to run up and down the stairs, while Nick Tanner recalls Roy Dolling at Bristol Rovers being even less painstaking, seeing him 'get a ball, launch it as far as he could and give you 20 seconds to go and get it and bring it back to him. If you managed that, it was a case of, "Yep, he's all right."'

When you know, you know. Even on matchdays it seems that many weren't prepared to give their all in the name of running repairs on these elite-level sportsmen. Jimmy Greaves recalls the enthusiasm of Tottenham physio Cyril Pointon being tested somewhat by the weather: '"Listen you lot, it's pissing down out there," Cyril told us,' presumably as a warning to be extra careful and try to keep a sure foot, right? Not quite: '"If any of you gets injured on the far side of the pitch, I ain't running through all that rain and mud to get to ya. So if ya get injured on the far side, you gotta come over to us in the dugout. If it's a bad 'un, then you'll just 'ave to drag ya' self over." Nice one Cyril.

Perhaps Cyril was right to be cautious,[37] the art of sprinting on to a pitch to tend to a stricken player is fraught with danger. Firstly, there's the possibility of misjudging your run, like Andy Jones at Hull. Peter Swan recalls Jones as a 'real favourite with the fans', presumably because of the sort of knockabout comedy described here. Apart from revealing that if two players from opposing teams were down, Jones would sprint as hard as he possibly could to beat the other physio there, which I always suspected physios do (it's the small victories after all). He also recalls a time he made team-mate Gerry Harrison's injury worse when he slid the last few yards in to treat him, 'overcooked the slide and his right knee went straight into Gerry's bollocks'. It sounds awful. Funny and awful, but he does say that Harrison recovered immediately so maybe there's something in it as a treatment – along the lines of 'I'll give you something else to worry about', although that isn't approved by the British Medical Association.

Secondly, there's the fake-out as players pretend to be injured just to pass the time in otherwise drab and dreary games of football. You might think I mean players feigning injury in order to receive treatment in an attempt to run the clock down in a winning position, but no, like I say, often they just do it to wind the physio up. Ian Snodin says this used to go on, with manager Billy Bremner's blessing at Doncaster, while physio Mick Rathbone says it happened to him too.

Rathbone brings us news of that other, lesser-spotted danger – the ungrateful player. 'Baz', as he was known, was physio at Everton under David Moyes, with Moyes openly describing him as his best

---

37 By cautious I mean lazy and work-shy, obviously.

signing ever. That might be one in the eye for the likes of Tim Cahill, but it all counts for nought if players are going to eff and jeff at him when he's trying to help. Rathbone reports that Thomas Gravesen was a bit, well, unusual, at times[38] but 'mad in the nicest possible way' so that's alright then. Rathbone once darted on to tend to the Danish midfielder and asked what was wrong, only to be met with, 'You fucking tell me, you fucking idiot, you are the medical man!' Mick stayed calm and offered him a drink. 'The game is only five minutes old, you fucking moron!' Rathbone must have had the patience of a saint to put up with all this, but it got worse when he tried to help Gravesen off, only to be told, 'Take your fucking hand off me or I will fucking knock you out!' Charming. Gravesen was making a scene by this point but once they were over the touchline 'he politely thanked me for my help and trotted calmly back on to the pitch'. Understandably, the startled physio was a bit reluctant to help Gravesen again. Luckily, there was always the smaller, more mild-mannered Lee Carsley on hand, in case he really felt the need to tend to a bald Everton midfielder.[39]

What is clear is, that Thomas Gravesen tantrum aside, everyone at Everton respected Rathbone and knew the value of having him. A good physio on the staff can be worth their weight in gold. Pat Jennings cannot speak highly enough of Northern Ireland trainer Bobby McGregor who worked wonders on injured players, getting them fit for their country when they were not fit for their clubs. Nice bloke too, evidently. Jennings describes him as 'constantly cheerful' and 'always ready to put a comforting arm round your shoulders'. Furthermore, 'he insisted upon giving each player a rub

---

38 Rathbone says that one time he was driving Gravesen to a scan and had to fill his car up. Apparently, Gravesen got out and stood next to him at the pump, 'then followed me into the shop and stood next to me while I paid', all without so much as asking for a Twix.

39 It's a fair indication of my football obsession that when I first saw those pictures of Jeff Bezos and his brother wearing the blue suits they returned from space in, my first thought was that they looked like Thomas Gravesen and Lee Carsley. They did though.

down after every training session because he believed it was part of his job'. Bobby sounds dreamy.

Bristol Rovers clearly had another good one during Bobby Gould's time. He recalls ringing up Brian Clough and asking if he would bring his Nottingham Forest side down for a friendly, only to be told, 'I'll bring a full first team down to play your lot as long as your physio will massage my feet.' Now unless Clough was intending to walk down to Bristol with his Forest lads, I think that must mean that he was aware that the unnamed Rovers physio had a particularly good reputation for foot rubs. This speaks volumes for Clough's scouting network (more of which later), that not only did he have his finger on the pulse of where the best players could be found, he also had extensive knowledge of where best to get his toes tickled.

It is universally acknowledged that the physical wellbeing of footballers in England improved tenfold once Arsène Wenger arrived in England. He brought with him what he refers to as 'invisible training' – helping players to look after themselves away from the training pitch – and we can definitely trace a higher degree of professionalism all round back to that point. Tony Adams and his back pain can testify to that, even if the new regime came as a shock at first. Adams tells of his first meeting with new osteopath Philippe Boixel: 'On telling him that my tailbone hurt he put on some rubber gloves, inserted a finger up my anus and promptly massaged my prostate. I was in agony.' But crucially, 'when I left that room I was pain free'. Previously this might have involved a physio giving out two paracetamol and his very best wishes, but no longer. Really putting the Arse into Arsenal there.

* * *

Benches and dugouts these days are barely worthy of the name, they've grown to the size of an airport departure lounge and could seat an orchestra, but it wasn't always the case. In the past when space was at a premium there was only room for the sub,[40] the physio / sponge wetter, the manager themselves and an assistant. This meant that the choice of second in command was paramount; you had to choose who was whispering in your ear very carefully. The assistant manager is a vital cog in the machine of a successful football club. Matt Piper says that 'a good No.2 will strike a balance between being your mate and acting as a reliable go-between with the manager'. Unfortunately, he frames this by saying that Steve Cotterill at Sunderland was none of these things, calling him 'smarmy, cocky and arrogant' and declaring, 'I didn't trust him one bit,' which is a bit of a shame, but at least he knows what he does and doesn't like. Perennial assistant manager Alan Curtis also knows the score, outlining his job as follows: 'Apart from training the players, I also had to act as a buffer between the players and manager at times. My aim was to deal with any issues the players had before they escalated and reached the manager, and I'd like to think I was quite successful in this.' He surely must have been. Alan Curtis has been assistant at Swansea under many different managers so he must be doing something right. He's always been there, like Jack Torrance in *The Shining*, but with less paperwork.

Whether the assistant manager is a social chameleon like Curtis, Tony Parkes at Blackburn or Duncan Ferguson at Everton, that can adapt and work with several different gaffers, or the more traditional type that loyally sticks with one boss, following them from club to club and acting as a trusted lieutenant wherever they go, they are called upon to perform a wide variety of duties. Sammy Lee used to be wired up to Sam Allardyce and do his touchline bidding while Bigger Sam sat in the stand with a brew. Kevin Bond has clocked up any number of miles driving Harry Redknapp from Sandbanks and back and Peter Swan even says that there was a rumour at Plymouth that Kevin Blackwell used to

---

40 That's right, one sub. Deal with it Millennials and Gen Z-ers.

cut Neil Warnock's lawn for him (which we can only hope is true). Harold Shepherdson, World Cup-winning assistant manager to Alf Ramsey, even found that his duties included finding Gordon Banks some Beechnut gum to chew and smear all over his gloves on semi-final night against Portugal in 1966. Conditions were wet and Banks needed more than his usual stickiness to keep Eusébio and the lads at bay, but there was no gum in the dressing room.

Luckily, Jack Charlton had handily spotted a newsagent up Wembley Way on the drive in; Alf barked at Harold and Shepherdson was 'out of our dressing room like a track-suited rat out of a drainpipe'. Luckily, he clearly kept some small change in his tracky-bottoms and the shop was still open because Harold came scurrying back across the Wembley car park just in time to reach Banksy at the back of the England line-up, just as the band came off the pitch and the teams went out. Banks chewed, spat and rubbed while H got his breath back and the rest is history. Banks and his sticky, saliva-spattered gloves kept Eusébio at bay (apart from that penalty – for that he would have needed Juicy Fruit) and England went through to their date with destiny. It could all have been so different but for Shepherdson's mercy dash.

Another England number two, Les Cocker, found himself even more of a players' plaything at England get-togethers. As part of what was no doubt a strenuous workload, Cocker would apparently go for a little row in a boat in the hotel pond each morning. He obviously felt it was blowing the cobwebs away but, frankly, he was asking for trouble. As was only proper, Gordon Hill and Kevin Beattie rigged the boat one morning so that it would sink, because why on earth would you let a man indulge in a simple pleasure when there's a way to ruin it with misguided banter. The boat duly sank, Merlin and Kev panicked and guiltily dived in to rescue him, only to find that the water 'only came up to our knees!' Cocker knew this all along, of course, because it's the assistant manager's job to know. To stay one step ahead. Beattie says, 'Les was laughing his head off and the rest of the squad were hanging out of their bedroom windows, shouting and applauding.' Bringing the squad together, you see.

Unfortunately, the commitment to peace and harmony, whether wet or dry, isn't always the way assistants work. Some know which side their bread is buttered and maintain a fierce loyalty to the management, which can rub players up the wrong way. We all remember the infamous Graham Taylor documentary, which still might be the greatest piece of television ever, and we all remember breakout star Phil Neal incessantly repeating everything Taylor said back to him, presumably to ingratiate himself with the gaffer and get closer to some free Elton John tickets.

Mick Quinn reveals, however, that Neal did the same thing at Coventry under Bobby Gould, where he earned the nickname 'Phil the Parrot', for agreeing with every single syllable his gaffer uttered. Maybe he just genuinely agreed with everything. Bob Wilson brings us news of Bobby Campbell upsetting the players when Bertie Mee brought him in to help him at Arsenal, tearing into them on his first morning before his first tea had gone cold: 'I was the first to be told success had made me soft and that I wasn't producing what I had shown previously. Seven months out with injury never came into his assessment. Pat Rice came next, Peter Simpson and Peter Storey followed.' This carried on as Campbell worked his way around the stunned group until Bob McNab decided enough was enough, told him to poke it up his whiskers and 'stormed out of the dressing room'. That feels like it could have gone better. There's making an impression, there's laying down the law and then there's this. Bobby seems to have confused Arsenal's training ground with prison. Here, there was no need to follow the unwritten rule of walking in and taking on the biggest inmate on day one. He could maybe have just taken some cakes in or something nice.

Bobby Ferguson at Ipswich seems like he got it right when assisting Bobby Robson. He ran a tight ship and berated players when he needed to and even warned tough nut Terry Butcher: 'You laugh at me. I'll make you cry before you're finished,' – but how can you not laugh at a man who used 'camel' and 'ruptured crab' among his repertoire of insults. Assistants need to be adaptable when hurling insults around. In the modern age with cosmopolitan dressing rooms full of players from all over the world, you can't go blundering in calling people ruptured crabs and expecting to get your message across. Phil Thompson knew how to move with the times. During a Liverpool dressing room row away at Southampton, Thommo had a dig at German defender Markus Babbel for pulling out of a tackle. Babbel searched for the right words to fight his corner and, according to countryman Didi Hamann, came up with 'fuck-off-you-are-ze-shit-house'. At that point Pinocchio might have been too flummoxed to retort but instead he fought fire with fire by coming back with 'you are the schizenhousen', which if it isn't right, it should be.[41]

On that occasion Gérard Houllier managed to step in and stave off the worst Anglo-German conflict I can think of, but others weren't so lucky. Kieron Dyer says that Steve Clarke once memorably stood up to Duncan Ferguson at Newcastle and got a ball kicked at him for his trouble, while fights between players and assistant managers are ten-a-penny at Manchester City where Rodney Marsh reports that Ian MacFarlane once 'flew across the dressing room and threw a punch at Tueart, hitting him hard in the throat. Everyone was completely in shock.' None more so than Dennis Tueart, I shouldn't think. Stan Bowles also tells of a fight he had with Malcolm Allison when he was at Maine Road. The chances of two such combustible figures ending up in a scrap were probably high and things came to a head on the training ground, not coincidentally, just before Bowles left the club. His version

---

41 While we're on a German diversion, Ruud Gullit brings us news that they have a word for the kind of curved ball played across field in front of a defender's outstretched leg, the likes of which David Beckham specialised in. It's called, pleasingly, 'Bananenflanke'. Honestly, they're way ahead over there.

BEHIND EVERY GREAT MANAGER

has Big Mal throwing a punch first 'but I ducked and lashed out, catching him with a right hander to the side of the head'. Bowles instantly worried he'd bitten off more than he could chew against the bigger man but 'luckily, Johnny Hart, the reserve team coach, dived in to pull him off me, just as he was about to tear me apart'.

Instead of causing fights and expecting your Johnny Harts of this world to sort it out, stepping in and making peace when the heads have gone seems more like it should be within the assistant boss's purview. At Arsenal, Tony Woodcock recalls a hotel fight after a couple of cold drinks between Kenny Sansom and Alan Sunderland, which sounds like it could potentially have been the best corridor fight outside of *Oldboy*. Manager Terry Neill opened his door to see what the commotion was, took one look and decided he didn't fancy it after all, leaving trusted lieutenant Don Howe to come storming out in his undies to settle things down: 'He thought the hotel was on fire. But he said, "Come on lads, break it up, break it up!" So they stopped for a second. And the hotel security guards were there too, so everyone cleared off back to their rooms.'[42]

Unfortunately, Sansom knocked on Sunderland's door looking for round two and this time there was only physio Roy Johnson on hand to try to calm the situation. 'Roy said, "If you are going to hit Kenny, you are going to have to hit me first." So Sundy did. But it all died down after that.' It's all about rank and respect you see. Nobody would have dared to hit Don Howe, fully dressed or in his pants, but here was poor old physio Roy Johnson, lacking the required clout to pull rank and bring things to a peaceful conclusion and ending up with a smack in the chops for his trouble. We can only hope that somebody brought out the bucket and sponge for him.

A good assistant manager will do whatever is required to make their gaffer's life easier. Sometimes, that will be kicking Mark Lawrenson repeatedly up the arse in the name of toughening him

---

42 I like to think he twanged his pants as he got to his own room and announced, 'That's Howe it's done!', but I'm afraid there's no evidence for that.

up, like Arthur Cox did at Preston; other times that will involve moving in with Phil Brown, like Brian Horton at Hull. Horton says that the two shared a house in Ferriby, in what sounds like a perfect set-up for a sitcom[43] and lived 'like an old married couple', complete with the odd blazing row and storming out. There were good times too though. On one occasion the two were out for a curry together when the restaurant owner asked Brown to do his infamous on-the-pitch team talk for his staff: 'Phil stood in the middle and pointed at one of the waiters and said: "You need a haircut. It's a disgrace your coming to work like that," and went on from there.' I've always got the impression that Brown would need little persuasion to pull this out and Horton may have had to listen to this sort of thing a thousand times, but there were fringe benefits as the singing for their supper worked a treat and the two of them made off with a 'little banquet' of Indian food they were given to take home with them.

Mark Bright brings us a lovely tale of Peter Eustace going above and beyond the call of duty, attempting to be helpful when he was assisting Howard Wilkinson at Sheffield Wednesday. Before Bright made his big move to Leicester from Port Vale, he went along to Hillsborough for a chat with Wilkinson and was shown to his office where he waited outside for a few moments. As he waited, Eustace walked in and started quizzing him: 'Are you good at heading?' he asked. 'Good with both feet?' A nervous Bright nodded and before he knew it Eustace had disappeared and come back 'clutching a pair of boots and some training kit. He stuck them in my hands, told me to get changed, and within minutes we were in his car and heading off to the club's training ground.' In what might technically be regarded as a bit of light kidnapping, Eustace, known by some of the players as 'The Squire of Stocksbridge' due to a perceived arrogance, had gone rogue here. Arriving at the training ground

---

43   Surely 'Who's the Boss?' if that hadn't already been taken.

he put Bright through a full workout to see what he was made of before delivering him back to Wilkinson's office. Far from being part of some good cop, bad cop routine between Wilkinson and Eustace, the boss had absolutely no idea that it had gone on and wondered why Bright was so knackered and thirsty. Eustace had clearly overstepped the mark here by puffing out a prospective player without permission and it's notable that Bright didn't join Sheffield Wednesday until two moves later; once Sgt Wilko and Eustace were long gone and the coast was clear.

If Peter Eustace falls short of being one of the great deputy leaders of the football world, then who are we dealing with at the very top? We've spoken about Bob 'Bollock Dauber' Paisley at Liverpool, Archie 'School of Hard' Knox clearly gets a lot of respect for his work with Alex Ferguson and Walter Smith, and there's a lot to be said for Jimmy Murphy. Murphy was, of course, Matt Busby's assistant at Manchester United and it's clear how much Busby valued his contribution, saying, 'If he judged a player, I found that his judgements almost always confirmed mine.' It also sounds like they had a laugh finding that out too. 'In our relentless search for the best of the boys there are Busby-and-Murphy adventures in the James Bond class (without the ladies, of course). We have travelled thousands of miles together. He has been my protector against pests, of whom football has its quota, my great aid in triumph and tragedy'. Murphy was, of course, immortalised in that great BBC drama about the tragedy of the Munich air crash and its aftermath, *United* in which he was played by David Tennant from off of *Doctor Who*. Similarly, our number one number two was also the subject of a film, *The Damned United*, in which he was played by Timothy Spall, Barry from off of *Auf Wiedersehen, Pet*. Ladies and Gentlemen, Mr Peter Taylor.

Peter Taylor – The Ultimate Assistant Manager
It might just be the case that Brian Clough has had more books written about him than any other figure in British football, and

it's easy to see why. His achievements are impressive and well documented, his charisma is legendary and his story is well worth telling, repeatedly. However, it's fair to say that a significant chunk of that story, and indeed the success, revolves around his relationship with Peter Taylor. It was a relationship that began during their playing days at Middlesbrough but started in earnest when Clough phoned him up to say 'I've been offered the managership of Hartlepools and I don't fancy it. But if you'll come, I'll consider it.' This 'I will if you will' promising start at Hartlepool was followed by unfathomable achievements at Derby and Nottingham Forest, with well-documented bumps in the road along the way, and a spectacular falling out to end things, with Taylor returning to Derby alone and calling it 'a real football town', in a spectacular kick in the teeth for Nottingham.[44] But what a ride.

When the pair arrived at Derby originally, they really shook things up with Taylor saying, 'I think the casualties at the end of our first season totalled sixteen players, four groundsmen, some caterers, a couple of clerks and a tea-lady who laughed after a bad defeat.' This house cleaning is all well and good among the playing staff, but to look at the Baseball Ground pitch around that time, they might have done well to keep the groundsmen on to throw a bit of grass seed around, and that tea lady went on to join Ajax and win three European Cups, possibly.

While Clough was the front man, PR machine and tactical mastermind rolled into one, Taylor's great talent was for finding players. Not just any players but, more often than not, exactly the right players. Taylor lists missing out on Kevin Keegan as one of his biggest regrets, alongside not missing out on Asa Hartford, which might be a little unfair, but such missteps are few and far between. He talks of the 'thrill' that his first sight of Roy McFarland gave

---

44 This comment is a blow, but Forest fans can soothe themselves with Stuart Pearce's line: 'If I didn't have a club to go to and Derby was my only option, I would rather go on the dole than join them.'

him and can count any number of successful signings that must have given him similar fuzzy feelings.

One or two bits of business are particularly pleasing though. There came a time at Forest when Clough and Taylor decided that goalkeeper John Middleton had lost his way a bit and they were looking to get rid for around £40,000. Almost at that moment Tommy Docherty called from Derby wanting to buy him and there the Clough and Taylor fun began. The pair initially asked for £100,000 and, upon being told that Docherty couldn't go over 60, Taylor whispered to Clough to ask for Archie Gemmill to be thrown into the deal, and so it came to pass. 'Two superb deals had been done completely out of the blue.'

That last tale comes from Maurice Edwards, who aided and abetted Clough and Taylor in their transfer work. He was the power behind the power behind the throne if you will. Edwards sees himself as some kind of ninja figure, operating in the background, lurking in the shadows. He's the rumour of a legend on the wind, or something similar. He says, 'In the many books that have been published about Brian and Peter, my name is mentioned as their chief scout in only a couple. This is probably because I was always able to operate without anyone connecting me with them.' This is all very hush hush. Edwards kept his main job as a newsagent throughout his time with Brian and Pete to throw people off the scent while playing a major role in several of their most famous transfers. For example, it was Edwards that brought Garry Birtles to their attention, a man they paid £1,000 for from Long Eaton, who went on to win the European Cup twice, move for more than a million and play for England. That's some good spotting.[45]

---

45 Edwards describes one extremely hectic-sounding day in his life in which he was up at 4am to prepare his shop for the day before flying to Zürich to watch Grasshoppers on a scouting mission ahead of a European Cup tie and getting back home at half past one in the morning. It's certainly an account of a busy day and goes a long way to showing his worth to the Clough-Taylor partnership. It's also an account that reads like he's providing an alibi for a murder that took place in his village while he was in Switzerland.

FINAL THIRD

Edwards says that one of his other jobs was to follow Kenny Burns and keep tabs on his vices once Taylor had identified him as a target, although in Taylor's book he says he did this himself, so maybe they doubled their efforts just to be certain Burns was worth buying. Following him to Perry Barr dog track, Edwards reported, 'I never saw him have more than two pints any evening, even ordering a shandy at times ... he did not bet on every race and his largest investment was £20.' All very restrained, besides which Burns 'spent much of his time kicking a ball about at the side of the stadium with the young lads, enjoying himself immensely'. It was spying time well spent. Burns signed and was a revelation at Forest, becoming a vital part of their subsequent success and winning player of the year. He might even have had £20 on himself to do so if he had any sense.

Taylor was not afraid of signing players with flaws, saying, 'As well as gamblers, we've signed drinkers and provided them with booze under our supervision. We've signed chain-smokers too. We have a stock transfer question, to which we usually know the answer, "Let's hear your vice before you sign? Is it women, booze, drugs or gambling?"' The thinking was, that if they knew what the issue was, they could manage it. It's admirable to have such honesty and deal with the realities, but I can't imagine too many players told them they had a drug problem, did they? It makes the Forest dressing room sound like being on tour with Led Zeppelin.[46] However, Taylor regards John Robertson as his greatest success, a player that they didn't sign at all, but instead inherited when they arrived at the City Ground.

Robertson, it's fair to say, was a little on the tubby side for a footballer and Taylor gave him the mother of all dressing-downs and urged him to change his ways. Robertson did and he was told and managed to stay just the right side of fat to assist the winner in

---

46 Whole Lotta Clough, anyone?

one European Cup Final and score the winner in another. Taylor claims that 'no deal pleased me more than launching the salvation of a brilliant player who cost nothing' and very pleasingly tells us that Robertson became comfortable enough discussing his weight that Pete was able to joke with him about it, ringing him up and saying, 'Is that your line crackling, or is there bacon sizzling in the background?' Lovely stuff.

As we know, eventually the relationship between Clough and Taylor soured and they eventually went their separate ways, but what a partnership they had. Taylor's hope was that 'football will remember us as pioneers of management – the first to see that two heads are better than one'. It's a touching sentiment and he may have got his wish. These days we can all accept that two heads are better than one, as Gritt & Curbishley, Houllier & Evans and Clemence & Livermore have proved beyond doubt.

Beyond the manager and his assistant there lies the coaching staff, also an integral part of any club. Some, like Eric Harrison, make an indelible mark on young players, expertly nurturing their talent and coming to be recognised as the greatest influence on their careers. Others, like Steve Harrison, do a bit of coaching and loads of dicking about and end up being equally loved. Stuart Pearce says that at Newcastle Tommy Craig would take any out-of-favour first-teamers under Ruud Gullit for a walk in the park and an ice cream, which is a sure-fire vote winner, while Steve Walford was clearly deeply loved at Leicester as his departure shows. Muzzy Izzet recalls, 'We shook his hand, hugged him and wished him well. I remember him turning his back, giving us a final wave and the tears welling up in his eyes. He cried. A few of us cried, too.' This brings a lump to the throat and feels like it should have been accompanied by that minor key closing theme from *The Incredible Hulk*, but it's fair to say not every coach feels the same amount of love.

Wilf McGuinness was a coach under Matt Busby, and while Busby didn't quite hold him in the same esteem as Jimmy Murphy,

FINAL THIRD

he clearly liked him well enough to anoint him his successor in 1969, perhaps as a parting joke. Let's cut to the chase, Wilf was a grass. In his coaching days Alex Stepney caught him listening at the dressing room door as the lads discussed the previous day's match and subsequent night out, finding 'Wilf crouched at the door with his ear to the key-hole. Gotcha!' Stepney doesn't say if the players took any revenge on Wilf the Grass, but if they did, it can't have been worse than the treatment that Jimmy Floyd Hasselbaink and his Chelsea team-mates dished out to fitness coach Roberto Sassi for the crime of, well, doing his job. Hasselbaink says that 'Sassi came to be hated by all the players because he was the one who made us practise hard'. This doesn't seem enough of a reason for the bullying he suffered at the hands of the players. 'Sometimes we would hit or kick him. If there was snow, we would smear it all over him.' On one occasion Sassi tried to escape on the snow and 'in the tackle by Mario Melchiot to stop him escaping, he broke a rib'. Good grief. Hasselbaink and Melchiot are pretty far down a list of the worst people around Chelsea at that time, so we can only imagine what the others were doing to Sassi.

Ernie Walley is another, earlier example of an unpopular coach at Chelsea, although this time I'm on the side of the players. Pat Nevin recalls his diary entry[47] from his first day training under Walley, a coach under John Hollins: 'This man is dangerous for the team. Everything he believes about football, I feel precisely the opposite.' By this Nevin meant that while he was a football purist, believing that the game should be as beautiful and profound as a Cocteau Twins gig, Walley was a knock-it-long-and-chase-it-into-the-corners merchant and a devotee of the POMO (Position of Maximum Opportunity) school of thought favoured by the less romantic types at the time. Nevin goes on to say that Walley had it in for him and was keen to get him out of the team, but that 'he

---

47 Of course he kept a diary.

seemed to despise Micky Hazard even more, but then he was a superb technical player, far too complex for Ernie's unsophisticated methods'. Good player Micky Hazard; if he played for Tottenham and Chelsea and I still like him, he must have been doing something right.

Paul Weller (not that one) is clearly still a little traumatised by Harry Wilson, a coach at Burnley affectionately known as 'the bastard' who he says thankfully wouldn't last so long in the modern game now that bullying is far less acceptable. Weller recalls a moment from his apprentice days just before a match when Wilson sneaked up and booted him up the arse as hard as he could: 'It was agony, horrible, almost sadistic. In real pain I swung round to see who it was and it was him.' Demanding to know why Wilson would do such a thing, his tormentor fired back, 'That's made you mad, hasn't it … Now, stay mad, go out there and do the same to them.' I think we can all agree that this is no way to go about your business, and Weller could have been forgiven if perhaps he had retaliated. He would not be alone in coming to blows with a coach.

Paul Walsh infamously punched Ray Clemence during a reserve game at Spurs which Clemence was in charge of. Clem substituted Walshy and it's fair to say that the striker disagreed with the decision. He challenged it, only to be told, 'Just fucking get off,' by the coach. 'With that, my head went,' admits Walsh, who swore back and threw his shirt at Clemence. He threw it back at the blonde bombshell as he disappeared down the tunnel. 'I span around like the Tasmanian Devil and just smacked him right in the bugle in front of the Main Stand.' For those unfamiliar with the nomenclature here, 'bugle' is cockney slang for the nose, or hooter, while the Main Stand, simply means the Main Stand and you shouldn't get confused by it.

Spurs were playing Charlton here and Walsh says that next thing he knew, opposition coach Keith Peacock jumped on his back and helped Clemence to restrain him, which just goes to show that these coaches will stick together when the shit goes down, whoever they work for.

At Leeds, David Batty says they found a way to undercut the wrath of the coach a bit, long before anything escalated to any kind of bugle splatting. Batty remembers regular rollockings from coach Mick Hennigan in the dressing room, which prompted team-mate Vince Hilaire to take action with a bit of good, clean fun. Hilaire bought six of those dancing sunflower toys that were briefly popular, that swayed to any music or noise around them, and lined them up above where Hennigan's head would be as he laid down the law. As the ranting began, 'Six of them swayed, rocked and rolled along the entire length of the shelf. The more amused we looked the more puzzled, frustrated and angry Mick grew, and the louder he shouted. And the louder he yelled the more frantically those plants gyrated.' See, kids, undermining authority needn't mean resorting to violence. I've just had a look and you can still buy those flowers, you know.

Of course, most coaches are former players whose best days are behind them and those that decide to put the effort in to help bring the next generation through are to be applauded. Arsène Wenger for example, seems like he was always destined for the dugout. Already coaching at Strasbourg at the age of 30 he threw himself into it with a zeal that would see him go on to the dizzy heights of being badly mistreated by ungrateful Arsenal fans in the future. 'Strasbourg was like a laboratory for me … I wanted to look for and to find new methods for giving the players what they needed.'

However, it's fair to say that this commendable enthusiasm isn't shared by all. There are those who feel that coaching badges are a lot of stuff and nonsense and think that their status in the game alone should be enough. Matt Le Tissier describes coaching qualifications as 'a complete waste of time. They were designed for novices, not players who had been at the top of the game for 17 years.' Le Tiss suspects it's all a scam (not for the last time) to 'rake in a fortune for the FA', rather than instil a set of common principles in those that want to mould the players of the future, calling it a 'cash cow'. He has an ally in Jason McAteer, who complains that 'the system gives you no recognition in terms of your standing in the game'. So, if you're wondering why Jason isn't manager of Real Madrid, blame the system. There will always be some debate about whether great players make great managers or not and the truth is, well some do and some don't. Jürgen Klopp and Pep Guardiola being at the top of the English game side by side surely is proof positive that it does not matter if a successful coach has had a modest or an outstanding playing career behind them, so I can't agree with Matt and Jason that you should get handed top jobs on a plate simply because you were a good player.

Following that logic, anyone who's sat in the passenger seat of a car long enough should get a driving licence by some sort of osmosis. Ian Snodin comes right out and baldly says, 'I'm very anti-coaching badges,' in a rant which goes a bit 'freeman of the land' if you ask me. Stopping just short of invoking Magna Carta when explaining why he shouldn't have to take any coaching courses in order to coach, he says, 'People have said to me that I could earn great money in Dubai or America if I get these qualifications but I refuse to do them.' Fair enough, we can't make him. In the case of Dean Windass it wasn't a lack of effort that made him struggle with his UEFA B Licence. It was just a lot of heavy, hard work, slaving away 'sat behind those desks from 7pm to 9pm' listening to coaches. That's right, TWO HOURS in a boiling hot classroom and Windass was ready to snap, or at least get naked. He gleefully tells us that while his teachers were turned away, he stripped off. 'They asked a question and I jumped up from behind my desk to answer it with my hand in the air like a little kid – and my tackle dangling in the fresh air!' Obviously, in a room full of footballers, this went down a storm and, as Deano points out, 'You needed to have a sense of humour like that to get through it.' Two hours.

91

With Le Tissier, McAteer and Snodin on one side, saying their reputations alone should earn them decent coaching jobs and the actual Arsène Wenger on the other side of the argument, diligently learning his trade, you're probably torn about which is the best approach. Well, if it helps, Sir Alex Ferguson also believes that a bit of hard work doesn't hurt, calling the idea of fast-tracking of coaches 'a disgrace. In Holland and Italy it might take four or five years for you to receive your badges. The reason they need to go through that intense, prolonged scrutiny is to protect them from what's to come in management.' Quite right too Sir Fergie, you can't go giving out badges to just anybody willy-nilly. Not even to Dean Windass and his willy-nilly.

If some of our old-school thinkers turn their noses up at the notion of coaching badges, I can only imagine what their reaction to the creep of psychology into the game must be. The psyche of players is an area that clubs quite rightly pay a great deal of attention to in the modern game, whether it's taking care of everyone's mental wellbeing, or trying to secure a vital edge over opponents. Ledley King tells us they had a guy called John Syer at Spurs, affectionately known as 'John the Head'. Not because he had an enormous noggin, you understand but 'because that was his job', which clears things up. King recalls meetings 'where we'd sit together and pass a pen around to each other like it was a microphone, closing our eyes and visualising what we wanted to do on the pitch the next day', but if all this was going on, how come they are still regarded as 'Spursy' all these years, players and managers later?

American goalkeeper Hope Solo recalls another sports psychologist working on team building with her and her team-mates by doing 'relay races balancing an egg on a spoon, passing the egg to a team-mate without dropping it. A lot of people dropped the eggs.' Still, sounds like a bit of fun, doesn't it? If slightly messy unless they were hard-boiled.

Things like this certainly raise questions about whether the players buy into the methods or not. Solo makes it clear she didn't have a lot of time for the egg man, and she isn't the only one to view these dark arts with an air of suspicion, whether it's straightforward psychology or those with more wild and wacky ideas. Player-turned-physio Rodger Wylde recalls Stockport using the services of a so-called psychologist, but the former Sheffield Wednesday man's suspicions were raised by what the guy was wearing: 'He wore a suit, with a T-shirt, and on his feet he wore a pair of white school-like plimsoles.' As far as Wylde was concerned this was the thin end of the wedge and when the psychologist began laying on the centre spot during the warm-up and bringing healing crystals into the treatment room, alarm bells started ringing. To be fair, he was polite enough about it and pledged to at least give the stones a try 'despite thinking it was a load of bollocks'.

Famously, faith healer Eileen Drewery was another divisive backroom staffer with an unusual approach to improving players. Those who mocked are well documented but it's always worth saying that Gazza, Paul Merson and Tony Adams all felt that they benefitted from sessions with her. Now we can all speculate about why those players in particular found some answers from her, but as the always level-headed Gary Neville says, 'If it works for them, I don't see anything wrong with it.' What I didn't know before reading Mark Bright's book is that Drewery had a rival in the faith market, and I don't mean George Michael. Now it's possible that Eileen Drewery worked miracles for the people she treated, but in terms of branding, that name just isn't doing it for me. A bit more pizzazz, you say? A bit more mystique, perhaps? A bit more glamour, anyone? Ladies and Gentlemen, I give you Olga Stringfellow.

Mark Bright was carrying a hamstring injury towards the end of that memorable season they got to the FA Cup Final in 1990, when boss Steve Coppell suggested he had nothing to lose by paying a visit to Ms Stringfellow to see what she could do for him. Steve drove him down to her house where they were 'shown to a room that had some strange stuff decorating the walls. Things like spears, masks and drums seemed to be everywhere.' Undeterred, Brighty gave it a go and sat patiently while Olga did her stuff: 'She put her hand on the sofa with her palm facing upwards, and I had to sit with my hamstring touching her hand as she told me that her energies were moving into me,' then she left the room briefly and returned with a book full of newspaper clippings detailing her previous careers in journalism and romantic novels, as well as various rich and famous people she had treated. Finally, says Bright, 'She put her hand on my hamstring and started moving it up and down, she also began to make some very strange noises that sounded like a horse ... then started talking, but it didn't sound like any language I'd ever heard.' Bright makes it very clear that he's glad he didn't go to his unusual appointment alone and that he and Coppell exchanged furtive, sceptical glances throughout the process, but here's the kicker – it worked. It certainly makes it a better story than if it hadn't, I'm sure you'll agree. Sure enough, Bright played the very next game and starred in the cup semi-final soon after. Get your head round that. A story like this is enough to give you a new-found respect for the mumbo, even if you still draw the line at the jumbo.

Staying at the mystical end of the fixing players spectrum for a moment, we have the unnamed hypnotist brought in by manager Terry Neill at Tottenham as his 'twelfth man'. Pat Jennings ran scared and opted out but says that player after player trooped in for an appointment where each was put under and asked to visualise their greatest game. So far, so good, but then things took a turn away from peer-reviewed science and towards the end of the pier. Jennings says, 'I recall seeing Cyril Knowles so "gone" that he was stretched across the top of two chairs, his head resting on one and his feet on the other, while he responded to instructions to take my weight. I sat on Cyril and he didn't flinch. It was impressive, just like something you might see on television.' Impressive maybe, but necessary? Possibly not. It feels like the hypnotist got a bit carried away and if someone hadn't stepped in it would have only been a matter of time before Steve Perryman was barking like a dog and Ralph Coates was biting into a raw onion believing it was an apple. It sounds like he was working on a solid ten-minute routine for *Opportunity Knocks*. Or *New Faces* if you were an ITV house.

On firmer scientific ground comes Harold Oyen, the man who can claim credit for prolonging Gordon Strachan's excellent career by encouraging him to eat porridge and bananas and stretching a bit. But there was a bit more to him than that. Chris Kamara says that while other Leeds players were 'downing lagers and eating pies before and after matches' Strachan was sticking to the diets and post-match relaxation techniques given to him by the doc. Lee Chapman says Oyen was a proponent of biokinetics, which 'involves the massage of the energy points around the body to enable the energy flow to be at a maximum during the game'. Is this really so different from what Olga Stringfellow was peddling? The lines become blurred, don't they? I'll admit I'm confused and don't know what to think any more. If I had to employ one of them, I would probably go with Harold Oyen as he seems more scientific, but then Chris Kamara hits you with this: 'One of his tricks was to spend a few minutes slagging you off as he loomed over you, holding your arm at a right angle. He'd call you every name under the sun, then he'd ask you to push his arm away.' Kammy says, no matter how fuming you were, it was impossible to shift the looming Oyen. However, he then pulled the switcheroo, stopped the negging and started saying nice things and then, 'When his tone changed, shoving his arm was much easier,' and now I don't know what to think.

If the biokinetics guy, the bananas and porridge guy and the verbal abuse guy are the same guy then I don't know where that leaves us. Perhaps what we need to do to really pin this backroom business down is to look at specific areas and see who really does what.

THE KIT PERSON

You might take it for granted that when your idols run out on a Saturday afternoon (or a Friday night, or a Sunday lunchtime) they are all wearing the right shirt, shorts and socks, but that's not easy you know. That's someone's job to make sure not only that it happens, but that the other team aren't wearing the same kit. Otherwise, that would just get complicated. Of course, I joke – there's far more responsibility to being in charge of the kit than that. Take chilled-out entertainer Allan Saint-Maximin for example. You can lay his kit out for him all you like but that's only half the job. He's going to need wraps on both wrists and both knees and a hairband before he can even consider crossing the white line. The man is like a *Pirates of the Caribbean* extra.

Has the kit person always been responsible for the same things at every club? Or has the role changed? Are they responsible for ensuring there's a bottle of whiskey in the skip like in Sam Allardyce's playing days? Just for a nip 'before running out for the game. It warmed you up nicely and gave you a little glow'. Are they responsible for ensuring that said skips are kept out of the way of enraged managers such as Nigel Worthington? Darren Huckerby says his Norwich gaffer booted one in temper and almost broke his foot.

Are they responsible for all hazards that aren't the skips? In a similar dressing room tantrum to Worthington's, Neil Warnock once tried to emphasise a point to his Burton players by kicking some cardboard, which was actually covering 'one of those old-fashioned metal anvils used for hammering studs into boots'. I'm pretty sure I've seen Tom & Jerry do this. Something about Warnock tells me that he would not have blamed himself for this incident. Somewhere, a kit man has let him down by leaving a large cartoon item in the dressing room.

Are they responsible for drying players off, as Norman Whiteside remembers? You heard. In a reverie about the once-a-season joy of playing at Highbury and making use of their heated marble floors, Whiteside says, 'At Old Trafford we only had people to towel us down after showers; this was real decadence!' If there really were people towelling players off, then it seems a bit ungrateful of Norm to say 'only'. Admit it, some of you are already working out the footballers you would most or least like to towel down, aren't you?

On a similarly damp theme, was the kit person also responsible for running the big bath back when it was a thing? They've all been replaced by much more hygienic showers these days, something that Bob Wilson laments: 'In a huge hot steaming bath after every game we laughed, cried or argued, but we never deserted each other.' Is it steamy in here or have I gone misty-eyed? Bob goes on to claim, 'The hours spent in them definitely played a part in creating a special spirit among a group of ambitious young men.' Maybe Bob's right, maybe there isn't anything quite like a big bath full of ambitious young men.

Even if you are able to take care of your chores as a kit manager, you aren't out of the woods yet, as many perils lie in wait in the dressing room area. Danny Blanchflower recalls a time with Aston Villa when brilliantly named trainer Hubert Bourne ended up in the kit hamper after standing behind a door that Danny and team-mate Tommy Thompson (what is it with these names?) came bursting through: 'Tommy flung it open, hit Hubert on the backside, knocking him into the hamper, the impact closing the lid. Hubert lay there for a while, strait-jacketed by his overcoat before someone discovered his predicament.' The fact that this is from the fifties makes it sound even more like a Norman Wisdom film than it already did. Lovely stuff.

Jock Robertson, kit man at Norwich during their run of glorious European nights in the early nineties, never got bumped into a hamper but he did find trouble of his own in the shape of Chris Sutton. Bryan Gunn describes Jock as 'a lovely old boy, a silver-haired Scot who absolutely lived for the club and went about his job with immense pride and enthusiasm', so it's understandable that away at Bayern Munich was a big game for him too. Sutton upset him by coming out of the toilet, plucking one of his fluffy white towels from the middle of a pile on the treatment table and knocking his carefully laid-out display on to the floor. Jock flipped his lid, called Sutton a 'big lanky git' and squared up to him. 'It was crazy. Jock was only half the size of Sutts, yet here he was trying to wrestle with him. Chris was doing his best to keep Jock at arms' length: "Calm down, Jock. It was an accident for f***'s sake."' Jeremy Goss was also there and remembers this mismatched scrap almost as well as he remembers his goal, recalling Jock's cheeks being 'red raw with rage' and 'Sutty sat there in a ripped shirt and with his hair all over the place', once the two had been separated. Presumably it was Jock's job to find Sutton a new shirt so I'm not sure he can call this a win, but I'll bet those other Norwich players thought twice before reaching for the towels after their famous victory.

Away from the matchday maelstrom, the kit man can get the better of players in less violent ways. Baz Rathbone, who can be considered something of a poacher-turned-gamekeeper, remembers the thrill of his first days as a player at Birmingham when he reported to Ray, the kit man for some boots: 'This room was filled from floor to ceiling with hundreds of blue Adidas football boot boxes.' With eyes alight and possibilities dancing through his head, Baz took his chance to grab what he could from this Aladdin's cave. When told he was allowed three pairs, asked for 'two eights and a nine please' in case his feet grew, but Ray had clearly heard it all before and was having none of it: '"Here," he said. "Here's three eights and tell your brother to fucking well buy his own.'"

Do not cross the kit guy.

THE GROUND STAFF

We all know where we stand with the ground staff, don't we? We know what they do. They look after the pitch. Once more, it's a job that seems to have got more complicated as time has gone by. These days, pitches are perfect surfaces, as flat as snooker tables, as manicured as the greens at Augusta and sometimes with fancy patterns all over them that make them look delicious like Battenburg cake, but look at pitches in the seventies and it seems like the main job was making sure you could see a penalty spot through the mud.

Occasionally, that mud was there not by simple wear and tear, but by design. If you need an impression of what Stanley Matthews' standing was in Stoke by the end of his career, then this will give you an idea. Still playing at 48, Stan had an understandably dodgy knee caused by over 30 years of competitive full-backs clattering him whenever they could catch him. Carrying such a knock, and being, you know, 48, meant that Stan functioned far better on a very soft wet pitch, so Stoke got the fire brigade in, driving in early in the morning without the sirens on 'to the Victoria Ground, where they hosed thousands of gallons of water on to the pitch. Then, just as quietly, they drove away again.' This gave The Potters a greasy, slower pitch when others around the country were dry and cracking apart. This is incredible. We all thought Stoke were cheating a bit when they used to have ball boys on hand with a dry towel for Rory Delap every time he went to launch one of his famous long throws, but here is the actual fire brigade being used to make a pitch wet and muddy, just how Stan liked it. Shouldn't they be out catching real criminals? Oh no, that's the other lot isn't it.

In the early days of Leicester's shiny new stadium, then called The Walkers Stadium and now called whatever it's called, Muzzy Izzet found there was a problem with the pitch surface – it stank. The talented midfielder found he was put off his stroke by a pungent smell of sewage coming off the pitch: 'I don't know what they used as fertiliser that year but it smelled ripe.' Now Leicester fans are free to make their own jokes about shit they've seen on the pitch, but this was a serious matter. Muzzy got a cut on his leg in an early game, and it developed into a more serious problem because 'all the muck and fertiliser from the pitch had infected my leg'. That's made me feel a bit queasy if I'm honest. Of course, the Leicester ground staff might stand by their decision and claim that it's made the current lush surface at the ground, and maybe even their unforgettable Premier League title win possible, because professionals will take great pride in their surface.

Ian Rush came across just such a man on an away day with Liverpool at Roker Park. Rush says the pitch was frozen solid that day and 'it was so cold my hands were numb and blue and the strong wind so relentless it gave me earache'. As the players came off into the tunnel at the break, they passed a hardy groundsman carrying a garden fork, off to do what he could with the pitch: 'He was wearing just jeans and a T-shirt, and tucked into one sleeve was a packet of fags.' Well, where else is he going to keep them? Despite his best solo efforts, conditions were bad enough that the game was abandoned at half-time, a decision he clearly disagreed with. Rush says as the Liverpool players were leaving 'we passed the match referee in the corridor being harangued by T-shirt man. "Frozen? Dangerous?" he gasped incredulously. "Ye soft shite!"'

Once again, as with those in charge of the kit, it's better not to mess with the ground staff. New York Cosmos legend Giorgio Chinaglia wasn't in too lofty a position to cop a right-hander from one member of staff. According to Steve Hunt (in his entertaining *I'm with the Cosmos*), 'Giorgio took exception to a remark made by a man sweeping terraces at Giants Stadium' one day and overreacted with a Cantona-style karate kick. However, not to be intimidated by the attack, 'the man threw his broom down, having dodged the kick, and floored him with one punch'. Presumably before picking his broom up again and sweeping Chinaglia out of the way.

Chinaglia might have had more chance in a dust-up had he been at Fulham in the sixties. Alan Mullery recalls groundsman Albert getting into a row with South African goalkeeper Ken Hewkins because he was trying to mow the pitch while they the team were playing on it. Hewkins 'told him to bugger off. Albert argued back and Hewkins hit him – wallop! – straight on the chin. Albert went down in a heap and his petrol mower swerved off across his beautiful pitch, carving a zigzag pattern across the neat lines he'd cut earlier.' Now we cannot condone violence and it seems like this could have all been sorted out with a quiet word, but I am all for deciding the pattern on a football pitch by having Ken Hewkins whack the groundsman mid-job and seeing where the mower ends up.

APPRENTICE DUTIES

In previous volumes we have leaned quite heavily on the life of the apprentice and the ordeals faced by them in a toxic culture of hazing and bullying passed off as team building, or the dreaded word banter. The tales of hardship are endless, such as Paul Sturrock being made to crawl across the floor of the Dundee United first-team dressing room, a young Terry Yorath getting thrown, fully clothed, into the bath by that horrible lot at Leeds and Steven Gerrard having to work next to the toilets and put up with the 'very smelly fog' apparently generated by coach Joe Corrigan's morning ablutions.

At Sheffield Wednesday in the late sixties, it seems that almost nobody had any clothes on. A traumatised Rodger Wylde remembers only too well walking through the first-team dressing

FINAL THIRD

room and witnessing Brian Joicey 'sat stark naked swinging his considerable length of penis like a whip' and another unnamed player weeing over everybody in the showers, you know, for a laugh.[48] At Hereford, Kevin Sheedy describes finding manager John Sillett, assistant Terry Paine and reserve coach Tony Ford 'standing naked in the bath amidst a collection of broken glass because somebody had gone in and deliberately smashed milk bottles in it'. It feels like all may not have been well at Hereford and presumably the management team learned a valuable lesson to keep vigilant and never to all bath together again. Sheedy got the job of clearing up the mess so that the three nudie-bums could tiptoe out while trying to retain some dignity and authority. Where is your Big Bath God now, Bob Wilson? Where?

It wasn't all broken glass and ball sacks, however; there were some perks. Steve McMahon served his apprenticeship at Everton and had to act as ball boy from time to time. This was in the golden age of hooliganism, but he's prepared to brush off the coins that rained down and occasionally hit him on the back of the head because 'I would spend most of the match collecting the coins – and that definitely meant a fish supper on the way home'. Bryan Gunn was also able to pick up a bit of ready cash at Aberdeen, thankfully without having 20p pieces pinging off his head at all angles. Instead he earned it by babysitting for Alex Ferguson's kids. That's right, in between laying out the training kit, polishing the boots and making sure Willie Miller had his piles cream each morning (true), Gunn would look after the Ferguson children, including future recurring Peterborough manager Darren. Gunn says, 'If they got up to mischief I'd make them do press-ups. We sometimes played snooker on their full-size table, but more often than not, we played football in the garden and then watched *Sportscene*,' which sounds like money for old rope to be honest

---

48 Wylde's full account of this trick is a grim tale beautifully told, but I'm not telling it here. Which proves that Dan was the dirty one all along.

but puts Bryan in the top bracket of footballers I wish I'd had as a babysitter.

DIGS

Gunn sounds like he had the time of his life as an apprentice; as well as fond memories of his adventures in babysitting he had a good time at his digs as well, where he was housed with landlady Mrs Welsh. Gunn says with a lot of growing boys around the place there was a danger of poor Mrs Welsh being eaten out of house and home, so she put up signs saying 'Do Not Enter The Kitchen After 10pm'. Being good boys, her teenage tenants stayed out accordingly but it did mean that every week on pay day Gunny would 'go to the local newsagents and buy a dozen bottles of orangeade and a box of 48 Golden Wonder cheese and onion crisps'.[49] Playing snooker on the gaffer's full-size and gorging on pop and crisps in his room till all hours? This man knows how to live.

Others that enjoyed their time in digs include Mark Kinsella, who, according to the very indiscreet Roy McDonough, 'banged his landlady "Fishy Ann"' at Colchester, and for rather more wholesome reasons, Terry Dyson. Dyson was housed with Peter and Wynn Adcock when he first arrived and Spurs and he had such a nice time he wouldn't leave. He says that when the family 'upped sticks' and moved to Hertfordshire, 'I went with them. They couldn't get rid of me! I spent my whole ten years at Spurs living with them.' Bit weird this isn't it? I mean, it's lovely, but it's a bit weird.

Some couldn't wait to move out. The deeply cynical Derek Dougan claims that 'landladies are in effect "spies" for the clubs and report to the managers whatever apprentices do', while Mark Bright just got the hump at Leicester because one of the family's daughters was a bit bossy with the telly: 'She would come in and think nothing of taking the television remote control and switching

---

49   I wonder if Gunn and Steve Nicol ever bonded over their love of Golden Wonder.

channels, even though you might have been watching something.' To be fair, that is really annoying when that happens. These petty grievances pale into insignificance, however, when we consider the living arrangements of Perry Groves at Colchester. Groves was housed with groundsman Tom Cheney and the two did not get on. Perry felt that Tom could have been a bit more forthcoming with the lifts into work and his resentment grew to such a fever pitch that when poor old Tom went into a diabetic seizure at the ground one day, Perry was slow to help. As the kit man (see, ever dependable) called for someone to get a sugary tea, Groves set off, but only very slowly. Eventually, he came back but 'as I got to him with the lifesaving cuppa, I thought, "I'll make you suffer for not giving me a lift," and deliberately dropped the tea, making it look like an accident, of course'. Perry brushes this off as a light-hearted caper but this is genuinely chilling. His autobiography is called *We All Live in a Perry Groves World* but groundsman Tom nearly didn't, thanks to him.

REHAB

Had they tried to make Amy Winehouse go to rehab at Lilleshall, she might have been a bit less reluctant – it sounds a right laugh. If I'm honest, I've never quite understood where Lilleshall is or what Lilleshall is. I've always thought of it as a fabled place like Atlantis, Brigadoon, or Tebay Services. At one point it was a 'centre of excellence', but it was also a place where injured players from clubs around the country would go to recuperate and receive treatment.[50] Anyway, as I say, it sounds like a good do, apart from the painful injuries of course. Peter Swan says that without the imminent matchdays approaching, a vibrant drinking culture reigned supreme. He fondly recalls a local night club 'called Cascades, about seven miles away. We renamed it CatchAids. There were some right

---

50 I'm still not sure why it was there or who funded it. Probably Bill Gates or something.

slappers in there.'[51] Swan says that while the wily old foxes knew where to draw the line, some of the younger lads would be tempted and as soon as they disappeared off with a girl the rest would drive off and leave them behind to find their own way back – or not.

When Paul Lake was there, he spent time with the likes of Ally McCoist, John Barnes and, most notably, Vinnie Jones. Jones took a dislike to a PT instructor who was a little overfamiliar with the players, and decided to take decisive, massively overreacting, retribution: 'He proceeded to haul this startled bloke out of the campus in true hod-carrying style, before bundling him into his boot and taking him for a bumpy, wheel-spinning, two-mile joyride to the front gates and back.' It's worth noting that this is yet another violent Vinnie Jones story that he doesn't feel warrants a mention in his own book. Perhaps his part in *Lock, Stock and Two Smoking Barrels* is just CCTV footage of him going about his business.

PLAYER LIAISON

Player liaison is one of the newer roles in the game. Dedicated professionals who spend their time settling new arrivals in, helping out with furniture, energy providers, family visits and the like. We've all heard some of the preposterous things which modern footballers have asked of their club's representative but it seems it was ever thus – there just wasn't a name for it. Alan Smith says that before there were such people, physio Gary Lewin was the go-to guy at Arsenal. Lewin is described as a 'bubbly, good-natured character', and let's see where being friendly got him. 'Paul Merson, for instance, once rang in the middle of the night because, while asleep, he'd poked himself in the eye,' and 'Freddie Ljungberg rang at one o'clock in the morning to ask if, at this time of night, he was OK to park on double yellow lines.' These were separate incidents years apart by the way, Ljungberg wasn't driving Merse to the hospital.

---

51   Catch Aids, by the way. Brutal.

DISTRIBUTING TURKEYS

Scoff all you like, it used to be a position of unfathomable power. In olden times clubs would reward players at Christmas with a turkey for the family gathering. You might think this would be a nice thing, but conflict magnet Ian St John even found beef among the turkeys. At Liverpool, assistant secretary Bill Barlow was in charge of the birds and he and St John didn't get along. Barlow seized his chance, as Ian had fallen out of favour and sensed he was on his way out at Anfield.

'He was in the snooker room guarding the turkeys when I walked in. He handed me a scraggy little bird and I asked him if he was joking.' The Saint reached for a bigger, more befitting bird, only to be told, 'No, those are for first-team players.'

St John was fuming, says he 'could see the pleasure in Bill Barlow's face', so he called him a bastard and walked out. He doesn't even say if he took the little turkey with him.

AGENTS

Adebayo Akinfenwa has got it right about agents, and even if he didn't, I would probably tell him that he has. He says, 'Agents are hustlers,' and broadly speaking, that's true. 'The agent you choose should be the one that hustles you the best, because if they're that good at hustling you, imagine how good they'll be hustling managers on your behalf when there's a lot of money at stake!' The man speaks the truth. The agent is the person who helps you with decisions and then you send into bat for you. You can protect your nice-guy image and send someone in to do your dirty work for you while you ride around on a go-kart having fun.

You may think this last part is a metaphor, but it really isn't. Les Ferdinand was due to leave Newcastle for Spurs in the nineties but then an injury to Alan Shearer gave the Magpies second thoughts. They came back with an improved contract offer, sending representatives to meet at Sir Les's agent's house. This was before

Newcastle had all the money in the world so negotiations may have taken a while. Rather than take part in the discussions himself, because of a verbal agreement he had with Spurs, he left the grown-ups chatting while he 'was whizzing about Jon's garden on the go-cart'. Now if this doesn't perfectly distil the relationship between agent and player, I don't know what does. The role of the agent has grown over time and it's arguable that they do now wield too much power. It's all come a long way from Kevin Beattie's first agent scoring a load of free shampoo for him and his Ipswich team-mates or Gazza berating his guy because he was asked to dress in a 'DJ Bear' suit at a London toy fair.[52]

Arsène Wenger is slightly sniffy about agents, proudly stating that he has never had one, although he does have a 'commercial and image consultant',[53] which sort of sounds like the same thing, and fondly remembers his early days in football when there was 'no such thing' as agents. However, it seems like he was glad of them when Sky Andrew was hunkered down with himself, David Dein and Sol Campbell discussing the England defender's potentially explosive move across north London from Spurs to Arsenal, 'gauging the impact it would have', presumably before deciding, 'fuck it' and doing it anyway. You have to know how to play the game you see.

Dinosaur Bobby Gould says he once pulled the plug on signing winger Ricky Otto 'because I threw out a blonde he had working as his agent. I'm sorry but I was just too old-fashioned to be negotiating a transfer with a woman,' the silly sod. Meanwhile, Harry 'Definitely Not a Wheeler Dealer' Redknapp, unsurprisingly, actively embraces the role agents play. H explains in *A Man Walks Onto a Pitch* that a man doesn't necessarily have to walk onto a pitch

---

52 I would love to tell you I have no idea what DJ Bear was, but he was a mascot, a 'Panda for Peace' that went around grounds in the late 1980s as a special envoy, discouraging hooliganism. He was created and often worn by Paul Trevillion of sock tags and 'You Are the Ref' fame. As you will have seen from the Euro 2020 Final at Wembley, the campaign was not 100 per cent successful. Bring him back, I say.

53 You have to wonder where the image consultant was when Wenger started wearing that long coat with the zip he couldn't work.

to assess a potential purchase these days. He says that you simply let it be known that you need a right-back and 'an agent comes on and tells you he has a 20-year-old from Estonia, who is going to be the best full-back in Europe. He sends you a link, you go into the club cinema and a minute later everything you need to know about him is up on the screen – the games he's played, the goals he has scored, match footage, the lot. You can go from never having heard of a player to watching him play a full game in the time it takes to make a cup of tea.' This all sounds very remarkable and an efficient way of going about your business. It must be a blessing for Harry to be able to save all that time, especially when it seems to take him 90 minutes to make a cup of tea.

Jermaine Pennant cheerfully admits he would have been a bit lost without his agent Sky 'same as Sol's' Andrew, although he does stitch his client up a bit over that infamous Porsche story. The story was that Pennant had parked a Porsche at Zaragoza station, left the engine running and forgot all about it as he moved to Stoke in a rush. It was always used as a stick to beat footballers with more money than sense with. Pennant's version is that he did leave Spain in a hurry, but deliberately left the car parked there with the keys in the glovebox for a friend to collect it for him, because of course he wouldn't be daft enough to leave the engine running and forget all about it. However, the agent says of the incident, 'He'd never admit this – but he got out of the car, left the engine running and it took two weeks for the petrol to run out! He denies it. But that's what happened.' Well, this presents quite the quandary. We all think of agents as slippery, untrustworthy hucksters who constantly bend the truth – but for the sake of a better story we want to believe one this time don't we?

TRANSFERS

Often it is an agent who instigates a player transfer, but it's not a hard and fast rule. Tony Cottee concedes that tapping up is a real thing, saying, 'Despite denials to the contrary, in nearly every major transfer, the buying club will have made contact with the player before they make their interest known publicly,' but often that contact can come from surprising quarters.

In Cottee's case he says his return from Everton to West Ham was instigated by scout Ronnie Gale, the man who initially discovered him as a youngster. The two bumped into one another at Upton Park when Cottee was visiting with Everton: 'Whether it was intuition or not, I don't know, but he looked me straight in the eye and said: "You want to come home, don't you?" I said, "Yes, I do, can you have a word at the club and see if it's possible?"' He also says that during a Merseyside derby soon after, he and Julian Dicks chatted about their impending returns to West Ham and thereafter 'hardly made any physical contact' for the rest of the game, which anyone who remembers Dicks will agree must have been quite the effort, regardless.

Maurice Edwards says that he once tapped up Burton keeper Les Green on behalf of Peter Taylor at Hartlepools, while he was refereeing a warm-up match for them. He approached him at a goal kick and made their interest clear, which is a bit cheeky by any measure of cheekiness. Green duly dropped his telephone number off to the referee's room after the match, before being transferred a few days later. Which just goes to show you can't trust a referee.

Peter Swan didn't even need to play a match to get the inside scoop on a potential move from Hull to Port Vale. A barman called Don who worked the players' lounge at Boothferry Park sidled up to Swanny after games and told him that he knew John Rudge, 'insisted that he spoke to the Port Vale boss regularly and said that Rudge was keen on me'. The move went through, after Swan got creative with his medical records,[54] and to repay the compliment the

---

54 Swan was instructed to take his own records along with him for a medical at Vale Park so decided to disguise an existing problem with his right knee by chucking any incriminating X-rays out of his car window on the drive down and telling the doctors that the left knee was the one that needed checking when he got there. Shout out to the diligent medical staff once more.

big man painted the bar for him and even put some Artex on the ceiling for him, 'which was a hell of a job'.[55] I believe that Thiago Alcantara's move from Bayern Munich to Liverpool went down an almost identical manner to this.

MAINTENANCE

One man who wasn't thrilled about Swan's move to Port Vale was maintenance man Bill. After climbing on a roof one day to do some repairs, he made the mistake of making a joke about Swanny, on the ground below. Following all known banter bylaws, Swanny removed his ladder and went off to the gym, saying, 'You're not fucking laughing now, are you?' and leaving him up there for a couple of hours.

Bill would have been better off at Highbury, where there was a bit more respect for the resident handymen. Alan Smith remembers a 'pokey chamber' just off the marble halls where the legendary Paddy Galligan and Pat O'Connor based themselves. Smith says that Paddy even lived in the West Stand for a while and the pair did everything around the ground 'from climbing on top of the stands to hoist the flags on matchday to changing the "next game" signage around the ground'. Smith remembers an almost permanently boiled kettle and 'one or both would be on hand to pass the time of day over a cuppa'. This is more the sort of thing. I like to think that there were two of them so that if any cheeky scamp nicked a ladder, the other one could help them down.

VIBES

Now we come to those people who are just good to have around the place. Once upon a time they may have had a specific job, but it got lost in the mists of time, and nobody has the heart to ask what it was now. Doc Crane was, presumably, the doctor around

---

55 You want to try taking it off, Swanny. Nightmare.

the England camp at some point but by Glenn Hoddle's time his duties seem a bit more fluid. Hoddle found himself berating the doc away in Rome for that famous vital World Cup qualifying draw because he forgot the dressing room key when he took Paul Ince off to stitch his head up, getting puffed out getting there and back and there and back again, but that aside, Glenn bloody loves him.

Hoddle would get Doc Crane to referee five-a-side matches between the coaching staff and the medical team, which seems a bit uneven and, of course, Glenn dominated those. It was also Crane's job to count the players on and off the team bus, though he possibly wasn't very good at that because on one occasion he missed Gazza and they left him behind.[56] You would think you might notice whether Gazza was on your bus or not, but maybe Crane was just taking a bullet, and this was Glenn's first attempt to drop Gascoigne without him kicking off and smashing a hotel room up. To be fair to Crane, it's possible he had sun cream in his eyes. Hoddle remembers, 'The biggest laugh of the Saturday was provided by the Doc on the coach, who was covered in sun cream that wouldn't rub in properly.' In what sounds a bit like bullying, Ray Clemence (presumably basking in the fact that Paul Walsh wasn't around, and his bugle was under no threat) squirted more cream on the doc as he was trying to rub it in. Glenn says it was everywhere, 'in his hair, his eyes, up his nose. It took him hours to get it all out.' Bless poor Doc Crane.

Mick Byrne feels like he might have been the Irish equivalent of Doc Crane. Although it said physio on his passport, Shay Given says that you rarely got more than a cursory back rub out of him, instead referring to him as 'a confidante, a mate and a comedian'. Such was Byrne's popularity within the Republic of Ireland squad that when Steve Staunton brought him back into the dressing room

---

56 If Doc Crane was responsible for counting England players in and out of everywhere then it means it was his fault that Mick Harford made it on to the stage next to him in the wrong shirt when they all sang on *Wogan* that time. Honestly, look it up, I'm obsessed.

after a Brian Kerr-imposed exile 'the place erupted' and within minutes 'he was already banging on doors, leading the lads in sing-song' and generally improving the mood. See what I mean – vibes.

In *Second Yellow* we discussed Sheffield Wednesday's bringer of songs of joy and tears of laughter, Tony Toms. He's another that fits into this minister without portfolio category. The ex-military man and self-confessed 'trained killer' was employed by both Sheffield Wednesday and Kent County Cricket Club 'essentially acting as the entertainment and social manager', despite by his own admission, knowing very little about either sport. According to Rodger Wylde, when he was asked how he managed to hold down two well-paid jobs despite nobody truly knowing what he did, he would reply, 'Bluff and jargon, my good man, are very powerful tools indeed.' There are one or two pundits in the ever-expanding world of televised football who seem to live by these very words.

Let's move on from Tony Toms to Terry Gordon at Oxford United. Gordon wasn't technically employed by the club, he just got in with the players through a friendship with second-poshest-named footballer ever, Peter Rhoades-Brown[57] in the eighties. Gordon would play elaborate pranks on new arrivals such as getting Billy Whitehurst to help him look for a tortoise in the car park and accusing Mark Lawrenson of sleeping with his wife. In the case of Dean Windass, Gordon approached him in the dressing room with 'gun in one hand, an empty whisky bottle in the other' and convincingly threatened to shoot him. A bit of fun, I'm sure you'll agree. With Windass enduring 'the most petrifying moment of my life', eventually Terry smiled and 'stuck out his hand: "My name's Terry and welcome to Oxford United Football Club." Bastard.' This was an initiation ceremony which manager Malcolm Shotton and all the other players were in on. Reassuringly, it was a fake gun, which doesn't feel like it was a given in this situation. Another of

---

57   Forbes Phillipson-Masters, obviously.

Terry's hits was forcing 6ft 7in striker Kevin Francis to run naked around the pitch at gunpoint. Tantalisingly, Windass says that Gordon's pranks 'came to an end the day Paul Tait decided to hit back with a golf club'. I need to know more about this. Believe it or not, more football books need to be written until I get the full story.

* * *

It's easy to see how the backroom staff at football clubs grows exponentially, like that expanding foam stuff in cans that you can get from DIY shops. Arsène Wenger says that at Arsenal, 'When I started, the club had 70-80 staff; then we went to 200, 400, up to 700 staff when I left,' although maybe it went to 699 at that point. Alan Curbishley's *Game Changers* book goes further. The book is a series of conversations with people in the game and includes one with a former head of medical at a variety of clubs, the brilliantly monikered Wayne Diesel. Diesel reels off a list of professionals at a club including doctors, physios, massage therapists, 'pedicurists, chiropodists, osteopaths and chiropractors, and then we had sports science' which includes conditioning coaches and many GPS data analysts. In the same book, Harry Redknapp says that during his time at Spurs 'there were people there on a Saturday and I didn't even know what they were doing there! We had so many masseurs, physios, analysts – so many people.' The cynic in me says he might have signed one or two of them, but it is possible that staffing levels have got out of hand.

The facilities themselves have even got too comfortable. Roy Keane says that at Sunderland they had a briefing room to watch opposition DVDs in which it was impossible to stay awake. He blames the heat and the leather chairs and admits to feelings of guilt about nodding off during a ProZone presentation – but the fault was definitely with the room, rather than with him and his team. 'Years later, after I'd left, I was talking to Seamus McDonagh, who had worked with Martin O'Neill at Sunderland, as Martin's goalkeeping coach.' He compared notes about the room and sure enough, 'he said, "You couldn't keep your fuckin' eyes open, could you?"' This might go a long way to explain Sunderland's freefall down the divisions in recent years. They've had a high turnover of players and staff in that time, but maybe all they need to do to improve things is turn the thermostat down in the briefing room.

If there's one thing that encapsulates the growth in backroom staff more than any other in my opinion, it's another tale from Sunderland. Peter Crouch says he went for a look at Sunderland's Academy of Light before deciding on a move to Tottenham from Liverpool and found that they had their very own in-house 'full barber shop with the right chairs, mirrors and equipment. It's left unstaffed, so that lads can summon their own hairdresser and have them come in and do their hair whenever they want.' That's an actual club barber shop with a rotating cast of hairdressers. Astonishing stuff. We've gone too far. Once upon a time there would have been one person responsible for everything from muffling church bells to clipping your toenails and these days an over-privileged player can stroll into a club's own hair salon, sit down in one of those chairs that goes up and down and say to their chosen stylist, 'Just a little off the top and can I have a Dutch Uncle round the back and sides please.'

5.

You Wear It Well

'Country and Western-Style Rope Tie'

IT ALWAYS strikes me that at the elite level, football is about decision making. The players that make it in the game are those that make the right choices on the pitch and execute them well. Off the pitch, their judgement often seems less cut and dried. I'm talking, of course, about their fashion sense. The world of football is a minefield of peer group pressure, like one enormous school playground, but without the gentler souls who clung to the edges and tried to avoid being noticed. Everyone is piled in the middle, scrapping for supremacy and survival – hoping to avoid ridicule and hang on to their dinner money – and it's brutal. In football, as we'll see, you can be ridiculed for being too scruffy or too smart, for trying too hard or daring to wear something out of the ordinary – but what is the latest ordinary? How do you keep up? Nobody wants to be the guy to wander in for training the day after it's collectively decided that Louis Vuitton washbags are on the way out. Some rise above it all, like Dominic Calvert-Lewin, wearing exactly what he wants and not caring what anybody thinks about it – and all power to him. But some of us, or let's face facts, none of us, are as good looking as Dominic Calvert-Lewin, so the same doesn't apply. For the rest,

115

it's a case of wearing something suitable that won't cause a scene and that won't make you a target.

For managers, things used to be a much simpler affair. It was a binary choice between suit or tracksuit. You may have got the odd famous standout moment like David Pleat's slip-ons skipping across the Maine Road pitch, or Bob Stokoe wearing tracksuit bottoms underneath a mac and trilby combo,[58] like a flasher on the run from a local bobby, but both men were, put simply, attention-seekers. Rarely did we see such deviations from the norm. However, in recent years, since Pep Guardiola arrived on the scene, the lines have become blurred. Pep will think nothing of wearing a hoodie or a chunky-knit jardigan at the drop of an expensive, stylish hat. And just as with playing out from the back, many managers have followed his lead, whether they have the facilities to pull it off or not. Anything goes on the touchline these days, and some really mix it up. Ralph Hassenhüttl for example, refuses to be pigeon-holed – one week he's in baseball cap and training gear, the next he's wearing a waistcoat with his sleeves rolled up like he's just made it through the speeches at a wedding.

Some managers go the whole hog and deck themselves out head to toe in club clothes. Take the Teutonic Tony Pulis – Thomas Tuchel at Chelsea or, indeed, the actual Tony Pulis, well, everywhere really. The pair of them go wild in the aisles of the club shop before the ink is dry on their contract. Emerging from the changing room with everything but their eyes covered in club-branded clothes. It serves two purposes. Firstly, it leaves spectators in no doubt whatsoever whose side you're on. Secondly, it stops you needing to run the fashion gauntlet with your peers.

Mike Walker seems to be a man who fully embraced the change in his status. As a player one or two books reference the fact that he would always wear a suit into training every day, which is

---

58 With what look like brand-new September specials school shoes.

bold and something he paid a price for, as we'll see later. However, once he became a manager, Ian Snodin reports that Walker could be found in 'the Continental nightclub in Liverpool with "MW" on his tracksuit top', which 'just summed him up', apparently, though I can't think what he means. Snodin says it with a sneer as it seems that Walker was not a popular man during his time as Everton boss. So enamoured was he with his 'MW' branding that upon arrival he also 'got the groundsman to paint "MW" on the closest parking space to the entrance' at the Bellefield training ground. That space had always been reserved for the incumbent manager anyway, but Walker decided it needed that extra flourish, which was all well and good until Mark Ward cheekily parked in it and claimed he thought it was for him. Walker didn't see the joke and immediately fined Ward half a week's wages – which he no doubt put straight in his one of his zipped pockets for safekeeping.

Bill McGarry arrived at Wolves in 1968 and was keen to make an impression on his new players in his light-blue tracksuit. It's possible that this ensemble was left over from his playing days at Huddersfield because, according to Derek Dougan, it didn't fit properly anymore, and gave his entrance 'a touch of farce'. Dougan says that the outfit 'did not leave much room for leg movement, so when he tried to raise a leg to put his foot on the seating which ran around the room, he missed and stumbled'. If your opening gambit with an impressionable side involves you falling across the dressing room because your trousers are too tight to lift your leg 12 inches in the air, it's possible that you won't recover your sense of authority from that.

Whether McGarry retained a sense of humour about his wardrobe malfunction is unrecorded, but another manager who did not like jokes at the expense of his clothes was George '1-0' Graham at Arsenal. Around that time, new first-teamers were required to give a speech upon arrival with the big boys and sneaky Tony Adams stitched a young Ray Parlour up, telling him, 'Just mention something about the manager's clothes. He really likes that.' An overconfident Romford Ray launched into his heartfelt words about the honour and privilege to be in such company and representing Arsenal, before finishing off with a cheeky, 'By the way, Boss, all the lads really like your tank top.' George's face was a picture. 'Sit down, son,' he said.

Evidently, Graham was under the impression that he always looked immaculate and didn't take too kindly to the jibe. But as he no doubt withdrew into the shadows, slipped the offending tank top off over his head and used his tears to dampen his hair back into place, Parlour was receiving high-fives and being accepted into the gang and was well on his way to being the life and soul of the Arsenal party, with not a tank top in sight. Maybe the world just wasn't ready for a sleeveless manager at that time. Of course, gilets abound these days and George might have felt more accepted in the current climate.

Neil Warnock has consistently stuck with the formula over what might be 100 years and 50,000 games. Week-in, week-out it's been a tracksuit for him, with the occasional suit for the odd posh day out for a Wembley play-off; and even in retirement (at time of writing, though who knows?) it's difficult to imagine him in anything else. He more than most will have been shocked with what he found at Reading one day when he went to Steve Coppell's office for the obligatory post-match drink, much-favoured by the old school.

I've often found myself wondering if these awkward exchanges take place immediately after the game when still in match gear, or after everyone is showered and more presentable. Either way, it seems that coach Wally Downes preferred to keep things very informal. Warnock and his coaching staff wandered in to find Wally 'sitting in the manager's chair, stark naked other than his T-shirt. For the fifteen minutes they were in there, all he could do was play with his bollocks. That shows you the class of the man.' Well, it certainly shows you something of the man. I assume by this

Warnock means to say that Downes has no class at all – otherwise I've been living life wrong.

At least Wally Downes stopped at half naked with his Donald Duck impression. The potential for even more flesh on show was ever present with Martin Allen. According to FIFA favourite Adebayo Akinfenwa, who played for Allen at Gillingham, 'When he talks, he takes off his clothes. I'm serious. He'll start with a suit and tie, and by the end of it he'll be sitting there with his belly hanging out.' If it was a particularly lengthy and nuanced conversation, he could have been completely in the nip by the end of it. Presumably that's why he doesn't get much work as a pundit between his many spells as Barnet manager; the last thing producers want is for *Match of the Day* to turn into *Naked Attraction*. It's distracting.

Fashion choices on the Saturday night staple are worth a comment at this point. It's liberty hall these days. I blame the move to Salford. The ever-present threat of bumping into the Director General around Television Centre in London clearly kept everyone involved honest enough to keep a jacket and tie on, but now they are off the leash. Back in the days of Lynam, Brooking and Hansen, and even the early days of Lineker, a jacket and tie was very much required. Now I can't recall exactly which maverick pioneer first dared to wear an open-necked shirt on there but pretty soon the regulation kit became trousers and a too-tight crisp white shirt. Paul Ince once shook up the world by wearing jeans on there and we've rarely seen him since. Nowadays, apart from those black shoes with the white soles that they all seem to wear, everything feels a lot more mufti day. Patterned shirts, T-shirts, jumpers, dresses – whatever they like and good luck to them. If someone came on in a tie now, it would look like that bit in *Step Brothers* when they go for a job interview in tuxedos.

It's possible that Sir Alex Ferguson may not approve of the modern trend towards relaxed-fit garments. Certainly, we can find him bemoaning a drop in standards at press conferences where 'we had a lot of young reporters who dressed more casually than the men I had known in my early years. Maybe it was a generational thing, but it just didn't sit well with me.' He should have said something. I'm sure everyone would have been suited and booted before the room had stopped shaking.

Ferguson is a man of impeccable standards in most things, and even in his moment of glory he bemoans the fact that he let those standards slip. In 2008, the night Manchester United beat Chelsea in the Champions League Final in Moscow, it rained heavily. Some of you may remember that it was quite slippery – for some more than others. Well, by far the greatest consequence of the wet that night was that Fergie's shoes got drenched and ruined and he didn't have spares. He apologetically says that he 'attended the victory party in trainers, for which I took plenty of stick from the players'. You see, it really doesn't take much. These United players had just reached the pinnacle of club football, and in the middle of their giddy celebrations, they still found time to poke fun at the gaffer's pumps.

Of course, Ferguson was never afraid to improvise and make a quick change when required. There's the infamous grey shirt fiasco away at The Dell when United were three-down against Southampton and Fergie ordered them to change at half-time. The offending article was from that nineties boom period for shirt sales when kit manufacturers had one eye on whether the shirt might look good with a pair of jeans in a town centre, rather than on a football pitch, and the players struggled to pick each other out when wearing it. That was their excuse for the hammering they took that day anyway. It just proves that nobody is safe from a fashion faux pas even on a matchday itself.

That same Britpop, lads-mags endless mid-nineties summer gave us another notorious shirt in the shape of David Seaman's gaudy red 'Refreshers' kit that he flung in vain at Andy Möller's buzz-killing winning penalty in the Euro 96 semi-final between England and Germany. Seaman says of the kit, 'When you saw little kids with that kit on, it looked good but it looked daft on a grown-up.'[59] Aside from feeling a slight pang of sadness for any adults who wore it down the pub at the time, unfortunately, international football tends to be populated with grown-ups and it left him feeling silly: 'The first time I wore it at Wembley, we were lining up during the National Anthem and I saw a couple of the opposition players laughing at my kit.' Unless I'm mistaken, that heartbreaking semi-final was the debut for that shirt, so I'm slightly annoyed that the Germans were relaxed enough to break their laser focus to mock Seaman and still win. Despite protests to Umbro, Seaman was forced to continue wearing it. Maybe the good folk at Umbro were standing by their design and wondering if it was perhaps the hair or moustache that was causing the sniggers at Spunky's expense.

Seaman can only wish that he'd been as lucky as Gordon Banks once was to run into the world's fussiest referee and been asked to change his shirt. Pat Partridge confesses to not getting on with Banks (which is surprising as both men come across very nicely in their respective books), and this incident is either an illustration of that, or a cause of it. Partridge decided to report Banks to the Football League when he was at Stoke for being 'improperly dressed' during a match. You might wonder what Banks had done to incur the wrath of the Partridge – a sparkly crop top perhaps, or cowboy fringe on his shorts, or even a return to his boyhood clogs – but no. Banks 'turned out in a jersey he had been asked to sponsor with a black collar, piping on the sleeves and buttons at the neck which, of course, could have been extremely dangerous had they come off during play'. That explains it. It's a good job

---

59 As an aside on official England merch, Peter Shilton claims that the 1966 shirt was the first commercial tie-in they had and that inside they carried a label with 'Always wash with Lux soap' on.

Partridge stepped in here. We lost far too many young footballers in the seventies because they choked on buttons that came pinging off Gordon Banks's shirt as he got up to claim a corner.

Another goalkeeper who ran into one or two clothing problems was Bryan Gunn. He fell afoul of that age-old problem of having his pants riding up his bum crack. He said it first, not me. Gunn says that at Carrow Road, the sight of him desperately picking his pants out of his bum when play was at the other end (not easy with goalkeeper gloves on, I imagine), was so common that it became a fans' favourite: 'If ever the Norwich fans got bored, they would urge me to do it: "Gunny, Gunny, pick your bum! Gunny, pick your bum!"'

Now that's entertainment! While other clubs' supporters reminisce long into the night about the showboaters they've loved – that flick by Jay-Jay Okocha at Bolton, that shimmy by Juninho at Middlesbrough, that turn by Dimitri Payet at West Ham – Norwich fans are gathering in the pub and wiping away a sentimental tear for the days when Bryan Gunn would scoop the pants out of the crack of his arse on demand.

Despite becoming something of a calling card, someone at the club suggested that a jockstrap would cure the problem, so he gave it a try. Unfortunately, the first time he slipped it on, 'I bent down to pull it over my trousers and felt something snap in my back.' It's a good job he tried them on over his trousers first, so he didn't end up in such a compromising position as he writhed in agony. Gunn ended up bed-bound for two days and out injured for several weeks. The grass isn't always greener when it comes to underwear. Stick with what you know, even if you've got a hungry bum.

Gunn was no stranger to multiple layers on his bottom half – he says that his school days were littered with ripped and torn trousers from diving on the concrete, so his clever mum sent him along with a pair of shorts underneath. Come playtime, young Gunn was having some fun, removing his trousers, and playing in shorts before putting them back on over his dirty legs at the end. If his school was anything like mine, you would need to think long and hard before you took your trousers off and left them to one side for any length of time, lest you soon became the boy with no trousers because they've been flung up on to a roof.

Peter Reid describes his own adolescent angst at wearing cheap nylon shorts for his boys' team, St Aidans: 'The chafing was unbelievable but I played on, and when I came off at the end I had friction burns on my thighs and around my groin.' Ooh, it doesn't bear thinking about, does it. Reidy tried to treat his sore misgivings with talcum powder and his inner thighs became infected, leaving him in agony. It's not such a big leap to suggest that Peter Reid's sole motivation for making it to the big leagues was to get to wear proper kit that wouldn't leave him with a red raw undercarriage.

When that call to the big time comes it's important to be ready, in case you blow your chance. Reader, Joey Barton was not ready. With Man City 3-1 down to Middlesbrough in the days of Kevin Keegan's reign, the eternally optimistic gaffer turned to a teenage Barton and told him to warm up. Barton recalls, 'I leaned down, found my pads, but scraped my fingertips on cold concrete when I reached for my shirt.' Realising it was gone he surmised that an opportunistic Boro fan had pinched it. He began to do what any of us would have done in the same situation – panic and beg: 'Give us me shirt back. Please. I promise you can have it at the end of the game.' His appeal fell on deaf ears. There was only one shirt because he was a late addition to the squad, so Keggy called on a fully kitted-out Ali Bernabia instead and Barton's debut had to wait. You see, this goes to show that if you leave anything to one side it's likely to get nicked, and this is in a packed football ground with stewards and a police presence. I'm still wondering how Bryan Gunn ever got his school trousers back.

If having your actual football kit ready is top of a list on some mood board somewhere with 'Fail to Prepare – Prepare to Fail' printed across the top in Comic Sans, then 'don't play football in a suit' can't be far away. Alex Stepney remembers an occasion from the brief and disastrous managerial reign of Wilf McGuinness at Manchester United when Bobby Charlton had been excused training but joined the lads on the field for a debrief afterwards, in the rain, wearing his suit.

Stepney recalls Charlton looking uncomfortable in the wet and having his hands in his pockets. McGuinness, ever keen to impose his authority, pounced: '"Right," said Wilf, interrupting his flow, "Bobby Charlton, for having your hands in your pockets you will do twenty press-ups on the spot." It showed appalling lack of judgement on McGuinness's part.' This is far from being an isolated example of McGuiness criticism from Stepney (we've already heard how he caught him snooping), but it must rank up there with the wannabe gaffer's worst moves. Charlton dutifully did the press-ups with Wilf stood over him in a scene very much like Richard Gere in *An Officer and a Gentleman* but he must have lost what little respect he had for hapless Wilf there and then as his tie dangled there among the puddles.

If Bobby was furious with the dry-cleaning bill he incurred, there was another man who actively embraced a mucky suit. Alan Curtis brings us news of Roy Saunders, father of Dean Saunders, and a coach at Swansea. Despite being clean and dressed after training, Roy could never resist joining in a post-session kickabout with his suit on. Curtis says, 'It was hilarious watching him fall arse over tit trying to make tackles in his platform shoes. When we were knocking balls in to the keeper, Roy would be challenging for them with his overcoat on!' This does sound pretty funny to be fair, although it also sounds like he could have done somebody a mischief in those platforms.

Suiting up for the training ground is one thing but Steve Hunt took it to the next level at Anfield during his Coventry days. Displaying a flair for the razzmatazz which would make him so popular with the New York Cosmos, Hunt decided to take advantage of the fact that he had been best man for his mate on the Friday and that the suit didn't need to be returned until the Monday, by going out to inspect the pitch in it for a bet. 'So it was that I found myself in front of the Kop tipping my top hat,' to the home fans before conceding that, 'I may as well have played in my wedding gear; we lost 4-0'.

From top hats to boots and a lovely bit of trivia. When David Beckham announced himself to the world with that glorious goal from halfway against Wimbledon in 1996, he did so wearing Charlie Miller's boots. Miller takes great pride in telling us that at that time both he and Becks were considered the coming men in British football and had snagged their own boot deals with Adidas. On that fateful day in south London, young David had some kind of boot emergency and urgently needed some Predators because he was obviously planning to ping one in from the cheap seats: 'When he contacted Adidas, they had to get him a pair as quickly as possible and just happened to have a pair of mine, which had been custom-made and were waiting to be delivered to Glasgow. They even had my name, Charlie, embroidered on the tongue.' Luckily, they were the same size and the rest is history. A star was born, wearing Charlie Miller's boots. That's an interesting thing, isn't it?

Peter Crouch is a very good authority on things of interest in the modern game, as we know, and he brings us news of a machine that most clubs have 'resembling a giant toaster'. You're already imagining the crumpets, I can tell, but this is for new boots, 'to steam them and make them as soft as old slippers', but it wasn't ever thus. There was a time when players of all levels were encouraged to sit with their feet in water to mould the new boots into the right shape – a policy Wimbledon striker Terry Gibson adhered to. The night before the 1988 FA Cup Final, Bobby Gould says he checked on his players in their rooms and when he got to Gibson's he 'saw these studs sticking out from under the sheet'. Gibbo was apparently wearing brand-new boots, having 'broken them in by standing in the bath for ten minutes, then left them on because his feet were cold. He was stark bollock naked except for his Wembley boots.'[60] I have a lot of questions about this:

a. If Terry was cold why did he keep the wet boots on?
b. If Terry was cold why didn't he put some clothes on?
c. How did Bobby Gould know that Gibson was SBN beneath the sheets, unless his studs weren't the only thing poking out?

Once the suitably rested and questionably attired Gibson was awake the next morning, he would have dressed in his official cup final suit, (which that year were supplied to Wimbledon by Top Man, executive at the time, Peter Ridsdale, high-street retail fans). But Bobby wasn't happy and decided to wear it only as far as the ground before changing into his lucky 'Marks and Spencer blazer, shirt and trousers', which he had worn for every other round. Dave Beasant wouldn't have been so ungrateful; even in his finest hour, snaking along Wembley Way in the coach wearing his XXL Top Man finest regalia, he would have recalled the thrill of receiving his first Wimbledon FC club jumper all those years earlier: 'From being a nobody I suddenly felt I was a somebody, a footballer with a chance to make a name for myself.' Brings a tear to the eye. I may need to blow my nose on my non-Wimbledon-branded jumper sleeve here.

Official team formal wear is a funny area. Glenn Hoddle insists that he brought England's look on in leaps and bounds in the nineties, by delivering grey suits and brown shoes after years of the tyranny of 'blazers, shirts and ties that did nothing for the image of our country'. What do you mean you don't even remember them? Far less precious about his clothes is Paul Merson, who freely admits that 'when I was bang on the cocaine, I sold my Arsenal

---

60   See 'I Want to Believe' for more wet boot shenanigans with Ian Rush.

blazer to a dealer'.[61] That's in the intro to his all too revealing *How Not to Be a Professional Footballer* but I promise if you stick around for the rest of it, some of it gets lighter than that.

Speaking of lighter, the most famous cup final suits of all are the white Armani 'Spice Boys' suits that Liverpool wore at Wembley in 1996. Much has been said about them already, so we won't dwell other than to say that Ian Rush was dead against them. In his rant on the topic, he does reveal, however, that players get to keep all of their cup final suits. He surely didn't get much wear out of the white one but, given the number of cup finals Rush played in, it's possible he never once needed to actually buy a suit of his own. Rush's team-mate that day, Jason McAteer, tells us that as a kid hanging around the car park at Manchester United, he once saw manager Ron Atkinson open his car boot to reveal 'three different suits' hanging up 'for the first team to have a look at'. This is how Man United went about their business in the eighties, before the success, the expensive imports and the number-one singles came along – picking a suit out of Big Ron's car boot.[62]

Under the less 'easy-oasy' Old Trafford regime of Alex Ferguson, Eric Cantona once sent shockwaves through the squad by turning up to one of many Town Hall receptions 'sporting some sort of country and western-style rope tie, the sort of thing you might expect Frank Worthington to wear'. This is Bryan Robson getting the vapours at the sight of it all here. Urgent discussions rippled through the assembled squad as if Mr Darcy had turned up dripping wet before Robbo says he got Eric out of a potential fine by telling a seething Fergie, 'You can't be fining him for that, on a night like this.' Now don't get me wrong, there's an argument to say that anyone who wears a cowboy tie who isn't an actual card-carrying cowboy should be fined for wearing such a thing, but in these circumstances, it feels like it would have been a bit harsh for Fergie to even think about

---

61 I like to think the dealer wore it all the time afterwards.
62 Almost certainly a Jag, right?

it. Or maybe not. Maybe you give them an inch with the cowboy ties and, before you know it, they're leaping into the crowd kung-fu kicking opposition fans. Makes you think.

Ian Wright is of the firm belief that not wearing a tie cost him England caps under Terry Venables. Wrighty was competing for a place with the likes of Shearer, Sheringham, Ferdinand, Fowler, Andy Cole and Ian Marshall[63] in the mid-nineties, so small margins mattered, and the Arsenal legend remains convinced that an incident at Venables' first game in charge, against Denmark, cost him dearly. Wright was a sub that night at Wembley and arrived wearing a Versace 'double-breasted suit that fastened with a kind of wingtip collar, so I wasn't wearing a shirt with a tie. The first thing Terry said to me was, "What? No Peckham Rye?"' Wright explained that with such a suit a tie wasn't needed but 'he looked at me with something between pity and contempt and said, "You need one with England"', and Wright says he knew his days with him were numbered.

I would like to think that Wrighty is reading too much into this. You can question El Tel's judgement in picking one prolific striker over another, but surely this petty tie business can't be the reason. As an argument against Terry Venables, it isn't very tenable.

Paul Lake was once told by Man City manager Mel Machin that his 'Nick Heyward-style Arran jumper and my nearly new cords from Affleck's Palace were unacceptable for first- team travel' and was instructed to get a proper suit instead. Help could have been at hand though. Lake (and every City fan of a certain age) fondly recalls the famous 5-1 win in the Manchester derby in 1989, but he also recalls a United-supporting former schoolmate in the crowd spitting at him. As Lake says, 'Like many of his comrades, he didn't appear to be coping terribly well.' The following week Lake was browsing clothes in a shop when he bumped into the

---

63 Criminally, one of these men didn't get a single cap.

very apologetic spitter who wanted to make it up to him, saying, 'I tell you what, Lakey, pick anything out of this shop – anything at all – and I'll nick it for you.' You can't say fairer than that. Petty theft – it's what brings us all together. For the record, Lake didn't take him up on it, m'lud.

THE DRESSING ROOM

The dressing room is the real fashion battleground where players live or die by their behaviour and clothing decisions. It's even called a dressing room for goodness' sake – it's right there. Before we get knee deep in the poor choices and bad behaviour, let's have a tip of the hat for 'Sir' Les Ferdinand who Peter Crouch names as a rare tidy bear who would 'neatly fold his dirty training kit each day and leave it in a squared-off pile under his peg', instead of creating more work for the 'weary kit man'. An absolute gentleman. Too pure for this world. I bet he tips well at hotels too. It makes me wonder how he got on at Newcastle, which at times seems particularly brutal. Shay Given recounts Alan Smith getting 'battered for dressing like a student' as soon as he arrived, and Charles N'Zogbia getting stick for 'some rascal outfits' such as a Gucci suit covered in flowers which Given claimed gave him a migraine. As I said at the top of the chapter, you'll get grief for not trying to dress smart, and you'll get grief for trying to dress smart. It's a very fine line to be walked.

Naturally, I'm sympathetic to the victim of ridicule in almost every case, but frankly David Seaman is on his own. Peter Reid tells us that at QPR[64] Seaman would 'turn up to training wearing waders after going fishing', while his trying hard outfit in his early days at Leeds consisted of jeans with cowboy boots and a blue velvet jacket. Somewhat inevitably, 'all the lads burst out laughing'. Seaman could have learned from Terry 'Teddy' Curran that you've simply got to own it. Curran is a man who was offered a suit as an

---

64   Yep, Peter Reid and David Seaman played together at QPR. That's not something you've thought about for a while, is it?

incentive bonus when he joined Nottingham Forest, so he knows his clothes; but when he turned up at Southampton, he ran into Alan Ball. Curran says of his first day, 'I walked into the dressing room wearing a short leather Christian Dior jacket I'd paid a cool £400 for and light blue jeans. Bally shouted out: "Where's your motorbike?" "It's outside," I replied. The banter had started straight away.' That is some red-hot banter lads.

Less well-equipped to cope with the cut and thrust of the dressing room was the fledgeling Ian Rush at Liverpool. Before he scored so many goals for the club that he could just tell everyone to shut up and leave him alone, Rush was a bit of a target for the bigger boys. Sympathetic team-mate Howard Gayle says of Rush, 'He spoke with an unusual accent and wore the wrong clothes. He looked out of his depth. It took him a full 12 months to get used to the remorseless criticism, which passed for banter.' Bless him. By his own admission the Welsh striker was shy and 'a bit of a scruff' and became a target of the Scottish Mafia at Anfield. Messrs Dalglish, Souness and Hansen would hit him with jibes like, 'Been repairing the car have you?', 'How many polyesters died to make that shirt?' and 'What's it with you Ian? Quieter you are, the louder your socks?'[65] Rushy tried wearing a neutral plain white T-shirt and jeans to no avail until he relented and started dressing the same as the others to get them off his back and fit in. In one last defiant roar though, he says, 'Although I also now dressed like them, I never bought a Commodores or Barry Manilow album. I felt I had to draw a line somewhere.' Solidarity, brother.

Other players named and shamed for being badly dressed include Neil Pointon at Everton, Danny Sonner at Ipswich and Vince Hilaire at Crystal Palace (the latter two both being accused of dressing in the dark) and would you believe it – Gareth Southgate. He may be considered the thinking woman's crumpet these days,

---

65   These are what I believe the kids call some 'sick burns'.

with schools holding waistcoat days in his honour to salute his sartorial style but there was a time as a lad at Selhurst Park when he was the butt of the jokes from Dave Stephens. "'Hark at Leo Gemelli!" he said, referring to the brand name of the jumper I was wearing. It was one of Mum's specials, bought with the best intentions in the world but, sadly for me, another naff brand.' Now I've never heard of Leo Gemelli, but I've never heard of Dave Stephens either, so I'll stick with the England manager and his lovely mum who went shopping for him if you don't mind.

It's clear to see that there's a pecking order in every dressing room, and just as Dave Stephens was once top dog at Palace, inevitably at Rangers that role was filled by Gazza. That came with the perks that certain behaviours would be tolerated and covered up by team-mates. Charlie Miller reports that Gazza would sometimes go on a three-day bender in something like a Versace suit, which 'would be stinking' at the end of it. Gascoigne's solution was simply to 'take Alex Cleland's nice pristine suit, put it on and hang his Versace one on wee Alex's peg at Ibrox. Alex would just shrug his shoulders, take Gazza's suit, go home in his training gear, get the suit dry-cleaned and bring it in for Gazza the next day.' Either Alex Cleland was too nice for his own good or had self-esteem issues, but as far as Gazza's concerned – it's good to be the king.

One of my favourite dressing room stories involves an overprotective Kevin Keegan sticking up for Andy Cole as only he could. Rob Lee remembers Cole arriving one day in a new jacket, 'one of those fancy designs, probably cost him a fortune – it had a load of weird colours all over the back'. Keegan walked in and fearing the worst said, 'I'm not standing for this. Andy's come in with a nice new jacket today and already one of you has taken a spray can to the back of it.' KK meant well, and to be fair, he's right to be wary. Clothes are often the focus of the pranks / vandalism that take place in dressing rooms. Shoes nailed to the floor, crash helmets filled with talcum powder, suits set on fire – you know the drill.

Jimmy Bullard, a man who would later graduate to some uptown top pranking, insists he was way too much of a wallflower in his early days at West Ham, and wouldn't have dreamt of messing with Paolo Di Canio. Bullard recalls Di Canio being usually 'dressed in tight jeans or trousers, pointed shoes and a funky shirt', and it didn't take much to set him off. On one occasion somebody hung his shirt from an air conditioning duct in the middle of the dressing room ceiling and he was gone, ranting and raving up to Harry Redknapp's office. 'He didn't calm down until the culprit was found, an apology was made and he had made sure no-one ever touched his clothes again. "If anyone ever does that to me again," he seethed, "I'm not playing."' I would pay good money to have seen what might happen had Di Canio ever been at the same club as Roy McDonough. Now there's a man with views about what you should and shouldn't wear. Some keener readers might remember his performance art piece with Perry Groves's pyjamas – well this time the victim at Colchester is old MW himself, Mike Walker. Walker favoured a suit in his everyday wear and once had the temerity to come in wearing a herringbone number, which Roy considered beyond the pale.

Fresh out of the shower one day, McDonough 'grabbed the shirt, tie and jacket off the peg and pulled it over my soaking wet body. I stood there in the mirror admiring myself, top-half suited, but nothing on underneath apart from a pair of football boots, with water still dripping down my legs.' Walker emerged from the shower to find quite the scene, realised what was happening and went after McDonough who remembers Walker chasing him up the tunnel on to the pitch 'screaming blue murder, while my bare cock and bollocks flapped around the bottom of his tie'. That's right, he put the tie on but not the trousers. Well, it stands to reason. Nobody likes pulling on trousers over wet legs, do they?

A nice and, noticeably, and less cock and ballsy wrinkle on this wet suit business, comes from Davie Wilson who played at

Rangers with the legendary Jim Baxter. After one game Wilson was due to meet a journalist for an interview, so he got changed quickly and went in to say his goodbyes to the lads that were still in one of those big baths so beloved of Davie's namesake, Bob. The winger says that 'next thing I knew Jimmy was splashing me with water until I was soaked through. I wasn't best pleased,' but revenge is a dish best served damp. At the next opportunity, Davie did exactly the same thing, but this time he had put on Jim Baxter's suit. Baxter splashed Wilson again: 'However, this time I decided to dive full length into the bath. I resurfaced and reached into the inside pocket of the jacket and pulled out Jimmy's wallet.' I'm guessing that Wilson had to move pretty rapidly to protect his own clothes from Baxter and stop things escalating but, all told, this is a pretty good wheeze, I'm saying.

A quick roll call of other victims include:

Club	Player	Garment	Fate
Everton	Jim Arnold	A tie 'so large you could have made a couple of pairs of trousers or even curtains out of the material'.	Terry Curran says he did him a favour by cutting it 'into a thousand different pieces' with a knife.
Leicester City	Robbie Savage	Gifts from his wife – 'a lovely jumper and jeans'.	The arm was cut off the jumper and the legs of the jeans were in ribbons. Savage 'didn't find that funny' and although no proof was found, he suspects the hand of Dennis Wise in this, and you could be forgiven for joining him in those suspicions.

West Bromwich Albion	Mick Martin	White shoes	Willie Johnston nailed them to the floor, inspiring Bryan Robson to do the same thing to Ray Wilkins when he moved to Old Trafford.
Leicester City	Kasper Schmeichel	All his gear	Launched from a top floor window by Jamie Vardy and Ritchie De Laet because Schmeichel is 'Mr Serious, very professional and likes everything to be done just right'. That'll teach him.

Sometimes, unfortunately, things go too far. Pat Van Den Hauwe is a man prone to occasional bursts of violence both on and off the pitch. He once took a dislike to the tie that his 'top advisor' Nick Trainer was wearing in a wine bar. He suggested that Trainer removed the tie and, when he disagreed, Pat took things up a notch: 'I went into the kitchen area and picked up this huge chopping knife the size of a machete and slipped it down my sock.' Then as the pair left and 'walked down the road, I grabbed his precious neck accessory, pulled the knife out, raised it above my head and chopped the tie off in one slice, missing his nose by half an inch!' Now it seems that many is the tie that's been chopped up in the name of the beautiful game, but there can't be too many that have been chopped up while still being worn. If the socks Pat was wearing were long enough to slip a large chopping knife down, then I would suggest that he's in no position to sit in judgement on anybody's fashion sense, but of course he sees very little wrong with his conduct in the entire episode. It was just a bit of everyday knockabout knife-attack fun on a close friend's 'precious neck accessory'.

As a further example of how these things can escalate beyond all acceptable behaviour, Peter Crouch refers to a 'dark period at Stoke in 2013' that has an air of a Prohibition-era gang war about it. Apparently, things 'began innocently enough with Matty Etherington getting his new leather jacket flushed down the training-ground toilets', which doesn't seem that innocent, but is remarkable at least for the admirable plumbing on display here – that's quite a flush!

An understandably miffed Matty suspected Jon Walters so put dead fish heads in his shoes and car, which certainly didn't calm things down at all. Walters responded by 'getting a severed pig's head from a local butcher's – still covered in blood, dried and otherwise – wrapping it in Matty's jeans and putting it in his locker'. Instead of hitting back directly at this point, Etherington decided to mix things up by trying to put the head in Glenn Whelan's locker, but putting into it the locker of Kenwyne Jones by mistake. Crouchy says, 'Before you know it, Kenwyne has lost the plot and is putting a brick through Glenn Whelan's car window, and Glenn is threatening to go round Kenwyne's house,' presumably while Etherington and Walters clinked glasses and shared a smile over make-up drinks. This will have taken a lot of unpicking, although it does seem that a nice little side-line revenue stream for butchers and fishmongers is offloading your manky leftovers to footballers for business such as this.

You might think that Roy Keane would get involved in these dressing room vendettas, but he really doesn't seem to. Instead, in his excellent second book we find him casting an admiring, supportive glance at a young Cristiano Ronaldo, who he describes as 'good-looking and he knew it', as he gazed deep into the dressing room mirror: 'I'd think, "Good on yeh." Looking at some of the other lads in front of the mirror, I'd think, "Yeh fuckin' nugget."' Quite where Roy draws the line between the good on yehs and the nuggets is never fully explained but it's clear that Ronaldo falls on the right side of that line and has his blessing.

Whether Cristiano was manscaping or not at that point in his career is unclear, and what Roy's views would have been remains a mystery, but the fledgling second-best player in the world would not have been the only one. As far back as 1990 Alan Smith says that Swedish winger Anders Limpar was 'shaving off all his pubic hair' because he told them his wife liked it that way. Smith shared a room with him so he must have taken steps to make sure their razors didn't get mixed up. Robbie Savage at Blackburn recalls a 'buzz, buzz, buzz' coming from the toilet area for about 15 minutes before Lorenzo Amoruso emerged, having 'shaved off every single body hair – and I mean every single body hair. He came out of the toilet looking like a goddess that day!' This may seem like too much information, but it clearly made enough of an impression on the lads to warrant inclusion in their books.

David 'Impervious to Nonsense' Batty surprises nobody in saying, 'I have never been one for spending hours in front of a mirror, unlike some of the guys I have played with.' He namechecks David Ginola and Lee Chapman among those who might 'preen themselves' or 'file their nails in the dressing-room', while he expresses admiration for Stuart Pearce with his 'longish, lank hair but absolutely no vanity'. By this he means he would arrive at team breakfasts 'looking like he'd been dragged through a hedge, with hair all over the place. I appreciated that. He hadn't been poncing about in the bathroom for ages.' Come on David, live and let live, eh? Stuart Pearce might be unlike his *Psycho* namesake in not wanting to hang around the shower too long, but if some of the lads like spending a bit more time looking their best, then equally, good luck to them, I say.

It's an opinion that would be in a minority though – particularly when it comes to hair. Robbie Savage remembers Dean Saunders pinning him down and coming at him with scissors and clippers on his first Wales trip. Luckily, the blonde bombshell managed to fight him off, saying, 'No one touches my hair without permission', and quite right too. Poor old Tim Carter was a goalie with a blonde fringe (or bangs as our American cousins call it), which everyone left well alone until it kept getting in his eyes and caused him to spill a cross and concede a goal for Bristol Rovers. Team-mate Nick Tanner recalls that at half-time 'Bobby Gould took the physio's scissors and cut Tim's hair diagonally to stop it from flapping in his face. It looked awful.' It seems brutal but at least this one is done for a practical reason. Had it been successful and led to an immediate upturn in results, the blue-and-white half of Bristol could have been awash with similar cuts within the week, and Bobby would have had a new trade.

When we talk about footballers' hair we need to talk about perms. It's a shameful period in the game's history and lessons must be learned. There are a lot of apologies and self-justification to be read around the subject. Baz Rathbone says he went for one to fit in with his peers, going to Rackham's barber shop in Birmingham where, given the choice between an £8 perm and a £10 deluxe perm he went cheap. He admits to regrets: 'When I look in the mirror and lament the loss of my barnet, I always wonder if all that is the result of me trying to save two fucking quid.' Meanwhile, Bryan Robson claims, 'The reason I had my hair permed was for convenience, not for the fashion. It used to be a nightmare when I had a shower after training. It was all over the place,' but surely this is an argument for keeping it cut short, not going for a haircut that makes you look like Ronald McDonald.[66]

Phil Thompson, on the other hand, is proud of his own perm and sees himself as a trailblazer. Although he admits taking his lead from Kevin Keegan, who by then had moved to Hamburg, as far as England was concerned Thommo says, 'I must have been an icon for the perm in those days.' He says he had his done in a secret attic above a barber shop, before unveiling it at a League Cup game away at Wrexham. He says that initially 'the catcalls were relentless' but it soon caught on. 'Terry Mac and Phil Neal had it done. Mick

---

66 We don't see so much of Ronald McDonald anymore, do we? They've scaled him back. What happened to the big Milkshake monster? Whither Hamburglar?

Lyons and Bob Latchford followed suit at Everton,' and as this curly style spread like wildfire across the footballing community of Liverpool, Thompson says it began to dominate conversation, with players asking each other, 'How's the perm? Where did you get it done?' It feels like in recent years the rivalry between Liverpool and Everton has got even more intense and bitter and that perhaps the players don't chat across the divide like this anymore. Maybe what we need to bring everyone together once more is compulsory, across-the-board perms for the players. Who's first?

Of course, not everyone was on board with players taking a bit more care with their hairdos. Old-school boss Bobby Saxton once came back into his Blackburn dressing room having visited the opposition Brighton one, trying to motivate his side by saying, 'I have just seen one of their players turn up with a fucking hairdryer,' and insisting that if they couldn't beat them 'I will show my fucking arse in Burton's window'. They won, sure enough, but I'm not sure what Burton's window, Saxton's arse or hairdryers have to do with each other. Or indeed if Burton's would have been on board with the whole idea had they lost. It's difficult to see what they get out of it, promotionally speaking.

Speaking of Burton's, let's take a look at those real fashionistas, who lived out loud and free from the constraints that their fellow footballers tried to impose on them. Obviously, this is all subject to advancing years and changing fashions, but I for one salute the likes of Mick Quinn who says he strived for the 'sophisticated urban soul boy' look in his day with 'a baby mullet', white or cream shell suit 'with a nice Lacoste T-shirt and some big flash white trainers'. You can scoff all you like, but let me tell you, Quinn's mission was to impress women and somehow it worked. Frank Worthington is another lothario with some fashion boasts to share, saying, 'I'd been one of the first men in Britain to get a tank-top, but I didn't like platforms so I had Cuban heels instead.' He was way ahead of George Graham.

YOU WEAR IT WELL

Worthington might have been right about the platforms. Gerry Francis wore them at QPR and was the subject of much ridicule. According to Stan Bowles, 'I remember Terry Venables telling me about coming off the pitch after a game, and he and Gerry were the same height. Next thing, in the bar, Gerry's towering over him, and Terry's talking to his belly-button!' What I would say is that, given what we know about Gerry Francis and his singular commitment to that hairstyle that he's had since the early seventies, he's unlikely to have allowed a bit of ridicule to alter what he wore. I'm guessing he wasn't talked down from those platforms, but rather came down of his own free will in due course.

Much more surprisingly than Worthington and Francis, Ben Thatcher considered himself a snappy dresser and aimed to be known as 'the best dressed player in the Premier League. That's where I'm investing my money. The gear. Good clobber,' according to Muzzy Izzet. I don't know how far he got with this as I've never knowingly seen a picture of him in civvies, but he was aware that David Beckham was playing at the same time, right? As far as I can see, Thatcher could have spent as much as he liked on Prada suits, he was always more likely to be a contender for the most violent player in the Premier League rather than the best dressed one. Perhaps we should compromise on 'the best dressed violent player in the Premier League'.

Rodger Wylde was more concerned with cultivating a 'rock star' image on the field with his 'long hair, shirt outside my shorts and socks round my ankles' which he says that Sheffield Wednesday fans lapped up, 'hungry for a new hero to worship'; while Howard Gayle is more interested in fashions off the pitch. He says, 'My uniform was standard: beige or white pants with flared bottoms known as Oxford bags, or Wrangler jeans, a Budgie jacket with a tank top underneath, then Hush Puppies on my feet. I was proud of my roots and had Afro hair.' It's a strong look, I'll give him that. Gayle is also very interested about the fashion among the hooligan

139

set during his time, claiming that supporters of London clubs all 'dressed really badly, arriving at Lime Street in leather coats and sheepskins' which he says weighed them down in any chases which ensued through the back alleys of Liverpool.[67]

What with the perms and the Oxford bags, it seems that Liverpool was the place to be for fashion statements, which is possibly why John Barnes went there. Ian Rush stood in awe as Barnes would 'arrive for training wearing a vivid yellow or orange jacket and black or lime green shirt'. Bold, as it's easy to get it wrong. Didi Hamann says that on the day he signed for Liverpool he was pretty pleased with how he looked as 'the whole outfit worked well together', but instead *The Liverpool Echo* later described me as "wearing the kind of brown outfit that parents forced their six-year-olds to wear in the mid-1970s"' and his new team-mates told him he looked like a geography teacher.

Wearing enough tweed for seven geography teachers, here comes Garry Birtles who Forest and England team-mate Tony Woodcock recalls was 'into the baggy look: baggy woolly trousers and jackets. I used to call him Charlie Chaplin.' Woodcock says that Birtles once surpassed himself on an England trip when players were instructed to dress in 'smart casual' to travel, only for Birtles to come down from his room 'in this heavy tweed and wool suit with a shirt and dicky bow on'. Obviously, the rest of the squad enjoyed the moment at his expense but 'it seemed that the more comments he got, the more outrageous he seemed to get', and good on him for that, although the bow tie must have been like a red rag to a bull for the jokers in that squad.

For the final word on football fashion, we're sticking with Nottingham Forest and with John Robertson. He talks with admiration about his team-mate Jimmy McCann's sartorial elegance, saying, 'Jimmy was a bit of a snappy dresser and used to

---

67   Maybe a need to be light on your feet is why the trend for Sergio Tacchini tracksuits came into that culture, but that might be for another book.

YOU WEAR IT WELL

wear these skin-tight V-neck jumpers. I used to look at him and think, "God you look good in them".' This is lovely and it's nice to have someone in the macho world of men's football besides Roy Keane have an honest, platonic admiration for how another man can look – but it's tinged with sadness. Roberston goes on to say, 'I used to borrow them from him and for a time thought I looked the same but in all honesty I just didn't have the figure to pull it off.' A heart-breaking realisation, that. There's Jimmy McCann swanning around looking the business, then John Robertson borrows the same jumper and ends up looking like a saveloy because he doesn't have the figure. You and me both, John Robertson. You and me both.

6.

Your Dukes, Your Cheddars and Your Widdleys of This World

'Smacks of the Factory Floor'

SIR PAUL McCartney, the nation's second-greatest knight of the realm,[68] once mused on the potential for a collective public fatigue regarding 'Silly Love Songs', before quite correctly pronouncing, after a moment's reflection, that this seemed not to be the case. One might wonder the same thing about football nicknames – but three volumes and several chapters into this odyssey, let's go ahead and assume that you can't have too much of a good thing. So here we go again.

The art of the nickname is endlessly fascinating. Some of us have them, others don't, footballers, by and large, do. If they're lucky it will be a term of affection rather than ridicule but there doesn't seem to be any way they can control it. The occasional player might wander into a club and try to launch his own nickname like Gordon 'Call me Flash' Watson, but most players are just going about their business when suddenly the hammer falls and the nickname arrives – and it sticks forever.

---

68   Sir Tricky Trevor Brooking since you ask.

John Charles is one of the lucky ones – the Leeds and Juventus legend was variously known as 'The Gentle Giant', 'Prince of Wales', 'Il Re,' 'The King of Soccer' and 'King John'. He is the Lord of the Nickname, you see. He can't help attracting them. Charles was a great player and a fine figure of a man, who earned his gentle tag with his strict sense of fair play on the field, but if anything, it's all a bit too grand. What he needs is a 'Ginger Pubes' or 'Toolbox Head' to balance things out. You know, to keep his feet on the ground. The likes of Robbie 'God' Fowler, or Gordon 'Merlin' Hill, might have got a glimpse of the reverence afforded to John Charles, but oh, how Genaro 'The Gimp' Gattuso, Archie 'The Poison Dwarf' Gemmill, or even Peter 'Modo' Beardsley would have longed for just one of his noble monikers.

Sir Alf Ramsey, famously not a fun man, had a nickname in his playing days that is unpalatable to our modern sensibilities, and probably shouldn't be repeated here, so obviously felt that, deep into his management career, and with a World Cup on the sideboard, he commanded more respect. When he arrived at Birmingham City, where Mick Rathbone was playing, he laid down the ground rules early on, telling his squad: 'I don't like the words boss or gaffer – it smacks of the factory floor – and Alf is far too familiar. If you call me Sir Alf, then I think we should get on famously.' Nipping any dodgy nickname business in the bud early doors there. No fun to be had. At all. Having a go at the factory floor, though. Honestly, Alf, we all know you're from Dagenham and put the posh Chris Eubank voice on. We see you.

Still, if you are going to have a nickname it may as well be one that's taken more than a moment's thought. Often, team-mates will go for the lazy option. I'm saying that Cheddar (John Chiedozie), Widdley (Chris Waddle) and The Duke (Mark Viduka) are just the right side of acceptable.[69]

---

69   If only because The Duke might be a reference to James Grodin's character in top ten film of all-time, *Midnight Run*.

FINAL THIRD

Laying forlornly on the other side of the fence, however, are the likes of:

John Pemberton – Pembo (yawn)
Glenn Hysen – Hiso (unnecessary)
Owen Coyle – Oweny (perverse)
and
Mike Newell – Newelly (Come on everybody. Do better.)

We even have the curious case of the admirably monikered Ambrose Foggerty who was at Hartlepools with John McGovern. Even when he neatly side-stepped the tried and tested Foggy, he ended up as 'Amby'. Honestly. McGovern says that he even used to arrive for training every day in a suit, and they still went with Amby. The man was seemingly bulletproof. He could have turned up with a parrot on his shoulder and only spoken in rhyme and still have ended up as plain old Amby. This shows a surprising lack of imagination in a town that once elected a man in a mascot monkey suit as mayor.

Affable Bryan Gunn concedes that he and his Norwich pals 'just weren't particularly good at nicknames' as he laments failing manager Dave Stringer with 'String Bean'. Gunn says his gaffer 'wasn't particularly skinny', which is a real shame as it might have worked a lot better. Mind you, String Bean is better than Bobby 'Burton's Window' Saxton, who went by 'Sacko'. Which feels pretty route one and safe, until you consider his profession. Then it feels unfortunate.

The trouble with these slight tweaks on actual names is you can get yourself in a right mess. For example, Darren Bent and David Bentley were at Tottenham together. Ledley King refers to Bentley as 'Bents' and Bent as 'Benty', when surely Bent could just as easily have been 'Bents' and Bentley 'Benty'. It's not sustainable. It's mind-bending stuff. It's a good job they never signed Michael Bentine.

YOUR DUKES, YOUR CHEDDARS AND YOUR WIDDLEYS OF THIS WORLD

Despite being both underwhelming and lacking imagination, there is a comfort and familiarity about this form. There must have been a time at Charlton when Lawrie Madden was simply known as 'Mads' or 'Maddy'. Then he left some poo in his jockstrap one day and suddenly he's 'Skidders' until he changes clubs, burns down the training ground (possibly) and leaves the area.

Skidders is not alone in deriving his nickname from his slapdash toilet habits, of course. Skidders is not even alone among his Charlton team-mates of the time to do so. Paul Walsh also tells us that Wayne Turner once stopped in the middle of a dual carriageway to defecate, and that 'his work of art looked like a Walnut Whip with a little signature peak at the top'.[70] Henceforth he became known as 'Whip'. What on earth was going on at Charlton at that time? There was shit everywhere. Whip at least sounds like something you could bluff your way out of. It's a bit more cryptic than Skidders. In fact, David Fairclough at Liverpool was also known as 'The Whip' according to Phil Thompson, due to 'the shot he had with his left foot', and with such different origins it doesn't seem right that they ended up being called the same thing.

Where signature moves and scat fail to throw up a nickname, physical quirks will often do the job. Luggy (Paul Sturrock), King Conk (Phil Thompson), Boxing Glove Head (Iain Dowie) all had to live with what their maker gave them, while Brian Marwood got off lightly with 'Buns' as a nod to 'the ample shape of his posterior' according to Lee Chapman. Des Walker got called Arkle after the famous racehorse, not because of his incredible pace or engine, but because of his prominent teeth. Ben Thornley had to put up with 'Squeaky' because of his high-pitched voice, Alan Shearer called Kieron Dyer 'Pinhead' for having a tiny head ('whenever I headed the ball, Shearer would make a noise imitating the sound of air leaking from a ball to pretend I'd popped it' – which is

---

70 You can insert your own joke here about whichever band you think are middle-of-the-road shit.

145

admittedly, pretty funny) and even lovely old Bobby Robson was rather insensitively called 'Cloth Ears' in his Fulham playing days due to a hearing defect. Kids, and footballers, can be so cruel.

Poor old Paul Hart was christened both 'Fossil' and 'Horlicks' by the hip young gunslingers at Hillsborough when he was there. Lee Chapman says he was called Fossil 'because of his lived-in looks' and Horlicks 'because most of his conversation had the same effect on people as a bedtime drink'. Poor old Harty. Meanwhile, to take it back to the bowels, both Sam Allardyce and Brian Laws let us know that Mark Lillis was known as 'Bhuna', not only because he loved a curry, but because 'when Bhuna farted, you stood well back'. I can't imagine that Lillis was the only player of his era enjoying a curry, and certainly not the only one that farted (even Dennis Bergkamp farts), so imagine just how bad both his curry craving and his gas must have been to mark him out for the name.

Similarly, in a very crowded field, imagine being so good at consuming booze that you end up with a nickname that reflects that, like 'Fish' (Paul Hinshelwood), 'Sponge' (Tommy Baldwin), 'Old Lager Legs' (Mark Hughes) or 'The Ledge' (Terry McDermott – short for Legend). Just how much would you need to drink to earn such a name, within a peer group that can, famously, really put it away? Somewhat surprisingly perhaps, the king of the drinkers is former Spurs star David Howells. Neil Ruddock (no stranger to a pint glass himself) tells us that Howells was known as Oliver Reed: 'The joke doing the rounds was that Olly Reed died because he'd been out on a session with David.' Presumably this wasn't 'doing the rounds' when the pair played together at Spurs, because Oliver Reed was still alive and high-kicking on *Aspel* back then. But as previously discussed, anyone who has read 'Razor' Ruddock's books will get used to his concept of time being more skew-whiff than one of those Marvel Multiverse capers. Let's just assume it came up after their retirement, and poor old Ollie's demise.

YOUR DUKES, YOUR CHEDDARS AND YOUR WIDDLEYS OF THIS WORLD

All drink aside, Howells provides the perfect link into our next batch of nicknames – those derived from popular culture, which will always have a special place in my heart. We're betting without Triggers here, as almost every club seems to have one player who might be found wanting on a quiz night, but here are some of the better ones in handy table form.

Player	Nickname	Reason
Michael Carrick	Spuggy	As a teenage Geordie in London in the nineties, this feels inevitable. *Byker Grove* was all the rage.
Tugay	Worzel Gummidge	Due to the wonderful, updated version of *Worzel Gummidge*, this one doesn't hit home so hard. Tugay doesn't look anything like Mackenzie Crook's version of Worzel – but he sure does look a lot like the old John Pertwee version. Not his Handsome Head though. That has more of a Robert Pires vibe to it.
John Blackley	Sloop	Paul Sturrock reveals that his assistant was called Sloop after the Beach Boys song, 'Sloop John B' – which is a pretty good nickname to be fair.
Ledley King	Ledley Scissorhands	I like this one. Ledley struggled with a handful of cards when trying to play Kalooki on the team bus in his early days, dropped them everywhere and Chris Armstrong christened him Ledley Scissorhands.
John Gorman	Spartacus	Once turned up at Tampa Bay Rowdies in 'cut-off jeans and some sandals', and Rodney Marsh thought that was enough.
Jim Beglin	Dex	'Come on Eileen' era Dexys Midnight Runners went big on denim dungarees. Jim once dared to rock the same look at Liverpool training, and that was enough.
Andy Townsend	Shaky	After Shakin' Stevens. He once wore double denim into training and that was enough. (As I said in 'You Wear It Well', this kind of thing is a minefield.)

147

Mark Atkins	Arrows	Bit complicated, this one. David Batty explains that it was 'because he looked like Nigel Mansell who drove for the Arrows team back then'. Wouldn't Nige, or Mansell have been better then? Besides which, I'm not convinced he looks much like Nigel Mansell.
Andy O'Brien	Postman Pat	I'd love to tell you this was because of his exceptional delivery, but of course Shay Given asks 'have you seen the size of the nose on him?'
Phil Thompson	Buzby	As another centre-half who got himself a bargain down the nose shop, this one must have come as a blessed relief. Thompson had a special World Cup nickname in honour of the British Telecom mascot bird of the time because 'he spent so much time on the phone to his wife', according to Terry Butcher, which is a lovely thing. Call me cynical, but I can't help thinking it had a little to do with the beak too.
Lee Clark	Roy	Good one this, if a little niche. David Batty named him after the killer character from thriller *Primal Fear* played by Edward Norton. Seemingly because he lost his rag in training once or twice. Niche. And sorry if that spoils *Primal Fear* for you.
Richard Edghill	Said Aouita	'I used to beat Ian Brightwell in training – that's Ian Brightwell the son of Olympic athletes Anne Packer and Robbie Brightwell I might add … and of course from then I got the nickname Said Aouita.' Edghill is justifiably proud of his running exploits here but I'm not sure his Said Aouita tag merits an 'of course'. Coe, Ovett and Cram were still fresh in the mind at that point, so Aouita wasn't the obvious nickname and it's all the better for it.

YOUR DUKES, YOUR CHEDDARS AND YOUR WIDDLEYS OF THIS WORLD

Gareth Southgate	Nord	Wally Downes named Gareth 'Nord', because the way he spoke reminded him of *It'll Be Alright on the Night* host Dennis Norden. It's all I can hear now.
Jimmy Carter	Peanut	Perhaps inevitable because of namesake President Jimmy Carter's peanut farming background. Considering Carter (the winger, not the president), weed down the legs of both Perry Groves and Paul Merson on his first night out at Arsenal he did well to hang on to Peanut.
David Armstrong	Uncle Festa	An old staple for a bald player. According to Mel Sterland, it was Carl Bradshaw who named him after the uncle from *The Addams Family*. Armstrong only trained with Wednesday for three days. Perhaps that's why. For his part, Armstrong says that in his younger days at Middlesbrough he was called 'Spike' by Basil Stonehouse. He or we have no idea why, but I think we can all agree that a man with a name like Basil Stonehouse has got no business dishing nicknames out.
Gary Stevens	Grease	Gary Stevens of Brighton, and later of Spurs, was nicknamed Grease 'because he had black hair done in a quiff like John Travolta', according to Brian Horton. I'd have preferred Zucko in the circumstances, but Grease will do.
Mick 'Baz' Rathbone	Baz	Baz is a nickname that has grown to almost become Mick Rathbone's actual name like Razor Ruddock or Freddie Flintoff. He tells us he got it on day one at Blackburn when Alan Birchenall decided he should be called Basil, after Sherlock Holmes actor, Basil Rathbone. Fair play Alan Birchenall. Over time it got shortened to Baz but the origin story is a strong one.

Alex Ferguson	Taggart	Gruff Glaswegian football manager Sir Alex was inevitably nicknamed after the gruff Glaswegian TV detective. This was mostly unspoken, until the self-confessed 'profoundly stupid' Paul Parker made the mistake of calling him it to his face one day. Imagine the swearing. He's lucky there wasn't a murder.
Glen Little	Blakey	While at Burnley, Glen Little was known as Blakey because he looked like the *On the Buses* character – and side by side, there's certainly something in that. All well and good until you factor in team-mate Robbie Blake, who boss Stan Ternent also called Blakey, in a situation of Benty proportions. According to Paul Weller (not that one), 'If ever they were in the side together and Stan was shouting and balling instructions, "Blakey, get stuck in ... Blakey shift yourself ... Blakey you're fucking hopeless ..." it was a fair bet neither of them knew who he was shouting at.'
Billy McNeill	Cesar	Brushing over the fact that he was sometimes known as Billy McBingo by his unimpressed players during his short stay in charge at Aston Villa, I had always assumed that Billy McNeill's nickname was Cesar because of his imperious, unflappable leadership skills in his playing days at Celtic. Not so. According to Steve Hunt, he received intel that 'in fact, Billy's nickname at Celtic was after Cesar Romero; the actor who played a getaway driver in *Ocean's Eleven*. The reason apparently was that Billy was the only Celtic player to own a car.' Sometimes that's all it takes.

There is, of course, that rare sub-section of players whose nicknames derive from other players who went before them.

YOUR DUKES, YOUR CHEDDARS AND YOUR WIDDLEYS OF THIS WORLD

Combining samba and sarcasm, both Mel Sterland and Mark Bright ended up being named after Brazilian internationals. Sterland was Zico, partly due to his tremendous shot but mostly, according to Lee Chapman, because 'Mel has always enjoyed his food and his stockily built frame provided a vivid contrast to the lithe form of the original Zico'; while the man universally known as Brighty, was christened Serginho during a dry spell at Leicester, after the famously inept striker that held back that wonderful 1982 World Cup side.

Serginho (the name, not the player) is genuinely creative and it's a bit of a shame that it lost out over time to the more prosaic Brighty – though not for Brighty, of course. Sterland meanwhile would surely have preferred Zico to what Jack Charlton used to call him – 'The Flying Pig'. Pig derived from his habit of hoovering up leftovers at mealtimes, while flying came from a time he missed the team bus down to London and had to chase it in a friend's car to catch it.

Now we're getting somewhere. At last, some genuine flair and panache. Some nicknames are ten-a-penny, like 'Son of …' for the manager's favourite, 'Village' as in village idiot for the dimmer bulbs in the squad and BBC (Balls, Bibs and Cones) for a less than inventive coach, but in amongst it all there are some absolute gems.

Fitz Hall's nickname, 'One Size', quite rightly gets a lot of attention for how good it is, but I've recently discovered that John Dreyer was known as 'Tumble' and I think it's right up there with it. Mickey Adams was known as 'Fusey' at Southampton because of his infamously short temper, Steve Stone was apparently 'the Magpie' according to Stan Collymore because 'if you left your toiletries bag open in the dressing room, Stoney would be straight in there. He wouldn't bring any of his own gear with him, no shampoo, no deodorant, no nothing,'[71] while Mark Hateley was known as

---

71 I'm not sure we can start having a go at Steve Stone for not bringing any shampoo now, can we?

151

'Topper' during his short time at Leeds because 'everything you'd done, he'd done twice as well and twice as fast the week before'. Lee Sharpe says that Hateley didn't care for the moniker and hit him on the head with a pool cue when he once accidentally said it out loud in a bar, sending Ian Rush into hysterics.

While you recover from the realisation that Mark Hateley and Ian Rush were both at top-flight Leeds as late as 1996, let me hit you with another cracker. Northern Ireland's Gerry Armstrong became the nation's hero when he scored the winning goal against hosts Spain at the 1982 World Cup. It was a good finish and a momentous game, either of which could have cemented him a top nickname. Instead, it was his prowess in the never-ending round of press attention that followed that earned him the frankly excellent 'Don Quick Quote' from team-mate Sammy Nelson. How good is that?

Shay Given brings us a couple of big hitters in his enjoyable and enjoyably titled *Any Given Saturday*. First up it's Ireland team-mate Keith O'Neill who was known as 'BSE' because he was 'like a mad cow', but better than that is former boss Brian Kerr. Kerr was known among the squad as 'The Flamer' because 'he used to send everybody a text after a game, thanking them for their efforts and sign it, Thanks B.K and that's how he became named after Burger King's finest', which is just lovely.

Another boss who was asking for trouble was Jimmy Mullen who ended up being known by his players as 'Jimmy Burnley' while at Turf Moor. This didn't come, as you might hope, from him being so loyal to the club that he became synonymous with it, but rather because one night he got drunk and locked himself out of the hotel fire door. While the man described by Paul Weller (not that one) as an 'enthusiastic drinker' was beating on the door like Fred Flintstone after the cat has put him out: 'He was trying to say "I'm Jimmy Mullen from Burnley, let me in."'But he was so confused it became, "I'm Jimmy Burnley, let me in."'

YOUR DUKES, YOUR CHEDDARS AND YOUR WIDDLEYS OF THIS WORLD

The name stuck. Footballers are cruel. One sign of weakness, one mistake and they're on to you.

Never a truer word said. The world of football looks like the dream from the outside, but once you're in there scrapping, it can be as brutal as school and a question of survival once you've been saddled with a nickname that undermines you.

Across a career, the origins of a nickname might even get misted up and forgotten about, but the name and the sentiment remain. It may have come about for a myriad of intricate and complex reasons, but players are busy and can't be expected to keep up with all of it.

One such case is Charlton legend, Derek Hales. Paul Walsh says that Hales was known as 'Killer' around The Valley – of that, he is sure. It would be fair to speculate that this was earned by his legendary status at the club as a clinical finisher. A man whose ruthless efficiency in front of goal, along with a droopy moustache that certainly didn't hurt, gave him the air of a ruthless gunslinger and cold-blooded killer. Well, sort of. Walsh says that it was partly because of that and 'partly because his family owned a butchers with a slaughterhouse attached to the back, where he used to work occasionally'. Ah yes. That might be it. Cheers, Walshy.

7.

I Want to Believe

'Croissant of Luck'

VERY MUCH like Matt Goss from eighties favourites Bros, I too made a conscious decision, because of Stevie Wonder, not to be superstitious. Others are not so lucky. They find themselves in the grip of unseen forces, their destiny being decided by the cosmos while they dance like marionettes on strings down below. The only way people who feel this way can exert an influence of their own on their fate is by sticking to a strictly maintained regime of touching good luck totems or wearing some lucky pants. Perhaps in a perpetual search for some sort of edge over their rivals in the highly competitive world of football, our heroes seem to be in thrall to superstition more than most.

Just to be clear I'm not touching the religious beliefs of players. Except to say that Andrea Pirlo felt close to a higher power as he strode up to take his penalty in the 2006 World Cup Final: 'I then lifted my eyes to the heavens and asked for help because if God exists, there's no way he's French.' It's possible that this raises deeper questions about the whole nature of players praying and assuming that their God will be on their side rather than anyone else's, but I think the otherwise dreamy Pirlo might just be being rude here and it's best not to dwell. As I say, I'm skirting around religion because

I WANT TO BELIEVE

a person's faith is not something to be mocked. Unlike a belief in that horoscope cobblers.

Terry Yorath surprised me by being involved in that sort of thing, but a casual remark such as 'I'm an Aries and once I decide on something, I do it' was enough to set the alarm bells ringing. Glenn Hoddle is, of course, fully on board with the zodiac game and has probably been knee-deep in Justin Toper press cuttings for years. He's a Scorpio don't you know, and slightly underplays things by admitting to 'some faith in astrologers' before detailing how he clearly has rather a lot of faith in astrologers, actually. Exactly how that ties in with, or competes against, everything else he places great faith in, I don't know, but as long as he and every other Scorpio the world over, who surely experience exactly the same things at all times ever according to their horoscope, are happy, I'm happy.

Most players don't give their horoscope a thought. How could they? What possible influence could the stars have over their lives and careers and the events of today's game? No, no, no – far better to rely on pre-match lucky omens to give you a boost. Neil Warnock likes to see a wedding before a game 'because it's lucky to see a bride'. Okay, I can see this. Teams stay in hotels for away games, and there's every chance that same hotel might host a wedding over the weekend. Bumping into a bride anticipating a very happy day in her life might at least put a spring in your step, if not directly affect your result. I'm sure Phil Thompson has something similar: 'It's strange how you grab hold of things as omens. When we had played Bucharest we had witnessed a crash while we were in the team coach. In Liberec we witnessed another crash. The same thing happened in Greece. It all seemed to be fitting into place,' he says. Oh, Phil. This is a bit of a downer after Warnock's wedding enthusiasm. With that many accidents in the vicinity of the Liverpool coach, can we be certain that their driver wasn't just running people off the road all over Europe? Still – a win's a win.

Of course, you can't rely on weddings and car crashes and other chance encounters to provide the good luck that extremely fit, extremely skilful, well-trained, professional footballers seem to think they need. They must force these things with their own rituals and regimes. Here then, is a full guide to the superstitious pre-match routines of our football heroes.

THE DAY BEFORE THE GAME

Kenny Dalglish is leaving nothing to chance and starts early ahead of Saturday's game. He says he would always have to get the tea for John Wark and Graeme Souness at Liverpool's training ground and 'then we had chocolate biscuits and had to take them in the same rotation'. King Kenny says he tried not to be superstitious at the start of each new season 'but I couldn't help it', and to be fair if there's a chocolate biscuit in it for you it's easy to see why you might be tempted to fall into superstitious ways.

Apart from Lee McCulloch performing his special boot preparation of cleaning them in the sauna, rubbing special Italian oil into them and giving them a squirt of 'Febreze because they stink', the eve of the game seems to revolve mostly around nutrition. Pepe Reina says that the night before Spain matches, his hotel room would become the social hub, with players coming along 'eating croissants and drinking milk' in what sounds like a lovely kind of slumber party with exclusive entry for those with elite passing ability. This business became known as 'The Croissant of Luck', which I believe has been considered as the title of the next Indiana Jones film.

No such thing would have happened at Liverpool in Phil Neal's day. He is adamant that 'you may think it's daft but we never eat bread on Friday or Saturday, only toast'. I mean I do think it's daft that Phil doesn't know that toast is essentially warm bread but if nobody had told him before now, I don't want it to come from me. Honestly, bread changing into toast is the most obvious transformation since Clark Kent took his glasses off and became Superman – in fact I don't think bread is even trying to hide the fact that it is the real identity of toast – but it all seems to have fooled Phil.

Chris Sutton would have had bread, toast and anything else on a Friday by the sound of it, saying, 'I always used to eat tons of food the night before the game, stuff like roast dinners, spaghetti bolognese and lasagne,' I assume not all at once, but you never know. He said he followed his Billy Bunter-style feast up the next day with loads of coffee and trips to the toilet to shift it all. But let's not get ahead of ourselves thinking about Sutton having a pre-match poo just yet. Not until Jamie Vardy has finished his lucky eve-of-the-match tawny port anyway.

THE MORNING OF THE GAME

It's Saturday morning now and Lee McCulloch is up and about, safe in the knowledge that his boots don't stink and are all prepped for the game. He's having coffee, a slice of toast and 'a wee spoonful of scrambled egg' for his breakfast, saying, 'I only eat the bare minimum, just enough to keep me going'. Neil Warnock, admittedly not needing to play later, takes the opposite view, admitting, 'I eat as much as I can. I have a cheese, ham and red onion omelette with four slices of brown toast.' It seems unlikely but he says, 'If there's toast over I have marmalade.' This final morsel of breakfast information marks the only similarity whatsoever between Neil Warnock and Paddington Bear. Ledley King meanwhile is having whatever he had the week before if Spurs won. Repetition on a winning run comes up a lot with our guys.

Terry Butcher is having a lie-in until his kids disturb him, ideally staying in bed until 10.15 specifically when his wife 'Rita brings me a cup of milky coffee, made in the microwave'. You heard. In the microwave. Why, Terry, why? This would have been the eighties when microwaves cost a small fortune and would have been cutting-edge technology. Maybe it came with a book that detailed all the wild possibilities that were now open to you with your new microwave and maybe coffee was in there as an option, but why it would be your preference, I don't know. Still, if it brings him luck, then who are we to judge?

Meanwhile, back at Chez Warnock, Neil's shaving with the same razor, washing and putting contact lenses in, to a strict pattern before getting stuck into five or six newspapers. This suggests that had Neil's team lost, he would have changed his razor after each defeat. Maybe that's why he's got no eyebrows. Perhaps he shaves them off to get maximum razor usage before he chucks it out after a bad result. Given some of the teams he has managed in the Premier League this must all mean that he's created a lot of shaving landfill over the years.

THE JOURNEY TO THE GROUND

Warnock is in the car now and on his way, taking the same route as last week if they didn't lose, also taking care to 'stop at the same lights' and ensuring that 'if I had a sweet or something similar last time we didn't lose I have one again'. This does, of course, suggest that he's stopping at lights whether they are green or not, and possibly ploughing on through red lights if he didn't stop there the previous week, which creates a nice cartoon image of Neil popping a sweet in as he drives along, oblivious to the carnage he's left at the junction behind him. On his way he might pass Pepe Reina at the garage because he always stops there to get fuel, regardless of whether he needs it or not, as 'one of countless rituals I have to perform to make sure I am in the right frame of mind to play for Liverpool'. I'd be interested to know if he's still doing it at today's prices. I know he was a professional footballer for many years, but he's not made of money. Meanwhile Ledley King reckons that John Terry 'counts lampposts on the way to the stadium'.

DRESSING ROOM

The pre-match dressing room is where it all happens. Stuart Pearce talks about having a very specific physical routine from 2.15 onwards which involves a lot of intricate stretching and kicking a ball against the wall. And given that Pearce played on until it felt he must have been about 53 years old, I would say it worked for him. Edgar Davids is another who kicks a ball against a wall, decreasing the distance until his shoulder is up against it. I really hope this isn't the same wall that Stuart Pearce is working at, as that much testosterone could bring the thing crumbling down. John Terry, meanwhile, wants nothing to do with a ball pre-match and refuses to touch them. England team-mate Peter Crouch says that if a ball rolled towards him, he'd be up off the floor 'like an old deer with a mouse'.

Bob Wilson, clearly a man after my own heart, has brought a copy of Bert Trautmann's book *Steppes to Wembley* with him to every game as a good luck charm, while Andy Morrison, Andy Gray and Stuart Pearce (between the stretching), stick to reading the programme. Amongst all this Wilson has a moment of clarity, saying, 'What is good preparation and what is superstition is too close to call,' although I would say a lucky book drifts away from meticulous preparation and into something else. Particularly if that book features a keeper sustaining a broken neck while playing.

Ledley King is here in his lucky trainers and pants, while Kenny Dalglish has arrived in 'a new shirt for a game to see if it brought luck' just in time to see Bruce Grobbelaar going through his routine of throwing a ball against a light switch to turn it off and on, which must have got a bit annoying for some of the others while they were trying to get changed. Wimbledon once tried to scupper him at Plough Lane by putting a cover over the switch, but sneaky Bobby Gould hadn't quite done as much research as he thought. When he stuck his head around the door to explain the measures he had taken, like a budget Bond villain, Dalglish looked calmly at him and said, 'You shouldn't have bothered. Bruce only does it at Anfield!' Gould closed the door and shook his fists at the sky outside I reckon.

Who's this ambling in, just about on time? It's notoriously unfussed footballer Benoit Assou-Ekotto. Ignoring the pre-match meal for everyone else, Peter Crouch says that at Spurs Assou-Ekotto would often arrive with 'a croissant, a hot chocolate, a full-fat Coke and a packet of crisps' in a Tesco carrier bag, which doesn't feel exactly like a breakfast of champions, but according to several sources Benoit did whatever he fancied. I'm dying to know what the lucky crisps were though. Eschewing the fat Coke for something a little stronger are Mike Phelan with an unspecified miniature and Norwich keeper Kevin Keelan who had 'a big tot of whisky', according to Ted MacDougall who once asked him if it did any good – 'he told me he didn't know, but he liked it', and you can't say fairer than that.

Bryan Robson is having his lucky pre-match shower, Viv Anderson his lucky pre-match bath while that other splashing sound you can hear is Ian Rush making his boots all nice and wet because 'after scoring five against Luton in the new (wet) boots, I took to soaking my boots in water before every game I played', which must have been freezing in winter, but again you can't argue with the results. That man scored a lot of soggy goals and he kept it up for the rest of his career, although by the end it must have been harder to get his leg up and in the sink.

Over there, Carlton Palmer has got his shoes 'aligned exactly in the same place on the same bench' and now we're ready to get stripped and changed. Of course, the order in which this happens is crucial to your team's success. Bob Wilson is strictly 'jockstrap, socks, shorts, boots, undershirt and, much later, goalkeeping jersey', Terry Butcher is 'left sock on before my right and put my shirt on last' and Ray Wilkins had to be the last player to put his shorts

George Best. Do not nick his date's chips.

Gazza with his unique brand of international diplomacy.

The Charity Shield, 1974. Bill Shankly has his biggest fan behind him. Brian Clough does not.

Pat Nevin,
Gregory's Girl *(1981)*

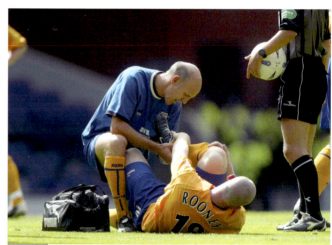

Mick 'Baz' Rathbone makes sure it isn't Thomas Gravesen before he starts treatment.

A classic bench. Bob 'Rats' Paisley, flanked by trusted assistant Joe Fagan (R) and Ronnie Moran (L) — bucket and sponge just out of shot. All you need.

Peter Crouch tries to break up the escalating 'Leather Jacket War' between Matthew Etherington and Jonathan Walters at Stoke.

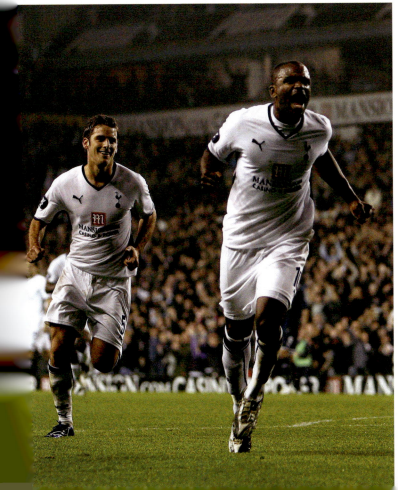

Bents and Benty, or Benty and Bents.

England in yellow? Bobby Moore and Pele playing for the USA? Gerry Francis not wearing stacked heels? The hotel ghost wasn't the only uncanny thing about this tour.

Greavsie packing for Milan and wondering if he is doing the right thing. He is. It would have taken him ages in that little car.

Ian Rush at Juventus. If you're not happy in a kit as nice as that, you may as well come home.

Keegan in Hamburg. Is he tiny or is that quadrant massive?

Nobby Solano, being made to feel at home at Newcastle.

Ivan Golac. Knows what he wants in a fire drill, if not in the butcher's.

Malcolm Allison – catnip for the ladies of the Directors' Lounge.

Jimmy Hill. No, it's true.

Deadly Doug and Big Ron pretend to get along for a few minutes.

Cuddly Ken Bates preparing for a cage match with Dennis Wise, possibly.

Stuart Pearce keeping his job options open. He could wire that fence up for Ken, you know.

Goalkeeper chums Corrigan, Shilton and Clemence. I've stared at this picture for hours and still can't work out whose jewellery is whose, or which of them is taking the photo.

Cech, Terry and Lampard – one of Chelsea's top five players, according to Didier Drogba.

on, which feels ripe for messing with, but maybe everyone is too nervous to bother.

Wilson likes to splash his face with cold water at the last minute, while Dean Windass must wash his face exactly three times, and Andy Morrison 'had so much aggression and adrenalin pumping around my system that before a game I'd go into the toilet and head butt a door'. And that's it. As the sound of the toilet door reverberating from that last lucky headbutt fades into nervy silence, everyone is ready to go out.

THE TUNNEL

Andy Gray insists on being the oddly specific fourth out of the tunnel while Carlton Palmer and Pepe Reina both want to be last, as do several others. This raises many questions that I have always wondered about. What happens at international level when two of these tail gunners come together? Who gets dibs on the last spot? What happens if you're given the captaincy? What happens if you join a new club where there's already someone taking your spot in the line-up, or even your favourite dressing room peg position or even your number? Does this sort of thing come up in contract negotiations? It's only fair that we're told.

Once we've emerged from the darkness and drank in the adoration of the crowd, there's still a bit more ritual to stick to. Ledley King, who seems to have so many things keeping him lucky that you wonder quite why he was so unlucky with injuries, must stub his toe on the touchline (oh, maybe that's why) and jump twice in the air before the whistle blows. Pepe Reina can't simply rest easy, safe in the knowledge that his car has got a full tank, he still needs to cross the white line with a very specific hop-scotch style routine before touching fists with each of his back four, apart from Jamie Carragher who wasn't into it and preferred a high-five instead. Given the lengths that Reina went through to harvest good luck throughout his career, from croissant club to forecourt foolishness to white line fever, it seems a mystery that he remains the only goalkeeper in history unlucky enough to concede a goal scored in off a beach ball.

THE TOSS

Finally, it's time for the toss. We've sent forward Terry Butcher as the captain's captain and he's got a lucky system. 'At the toss-up I always follow the motto 'Tails never fails' and it seems to work for me as I win 75%.' So 'tails fails about a quarter of the time' might be more accurate. The percentage also tantalisingly suggests that Terry kept a book full of notes on how often he won the toss. Which is nice as he doesn't seem the type, but I suppose you need to do something while you wait for your microwave coffee to cool down.

And that's it. We're away. Roaring into the game, where it becomes about ability and fitness and tactics and things like that rather than special breakfasts, lucky toilet trips and soggy boots. Good luck everyone.

* * *

Outside of the pre-match routines there are still those that have their own little quirks that they maintain in the name of not angering the footballing Gods. Robbie Savage reveals that his top soccer pal Roberto Mancini is particular about pepper pots and silly about salt cellars, saying that when the two were eating out 'I had to push the pot across the table as opposed to passing it, otherwise he would go spare'. Quite right too. He's a purist and wants to keep everything on the floor instead of in the air. Rodney Marsh says of his QPR and Fulham manager Alec Stock[72] that he wore one blue sock and carried a 'small bell in his pocket he turned over in his fingers' for good luck, as well as constantly repeating the phrase 'it's a funny old game' to his players, years before Greavsie monetised

---

72 Alec Stock, of course, has been identified as the inspiration for *The Fast Show*'s Ron Manager, so this must have all been a lot of fun. Marvellous.

it as a catchphrase. Mind you, Marsh himself was in no position to judge as his everyday business involved more medallions, lucky charms and cuddly toys than a seaside tat shop.

Harry Redknapp says that Steve Claridge was obsessed with lucky boots, and that 'he thought certain pairs were lucky and would just pick them and wear them, whatever the size, whoever the owner. It was superstition, not stealing.' Well, I mean, it's still stealing if they're other people's boots, Harry. Apparently, this led to problems on the pitch as these 'lucky boots' were sometimes a couple of sizes too small and Claridge would be forced to choose between the all-powerful unseen forces of fate and comfortable footwear. There's only one winner there. You can't put a price on comfy feet.

Andrea Pirlo says that his team-mate Alberto Gilardino was another boot obsessive, who would carry an 'ancient, ugly, tatty' pair around with him in his kitbag: 'He'd shine them up, caress them; sometimes he'd even talk to them and kiss them.' Pirlo goes so far as to say that Gilardino was a believer in witchcraft, which takes us beyond the veil and into 'The Twilight Zone', where football meets the supernatural, or at least meets the spooky.

Don Revie isn't the only manager to try to get what he thought was a gypsy curse lifted from his ground, but he might be the one that believed most in the power of it. I remember a news story about Barry Fry weeing in all four corners of St Andrew's when he was Birmingham boss, but that always felt like a bit of a publicity stunt. Norman Hunter[73] says that Revie was convinced that a gypsy curse, remaining from the time that a community was moved off the site to build Elland Road stadium, 'was preventing us from taking the top prizes and asked the gypsy to come and lift the curse'. That man really did think of everything. Between his famous dossiers, arranging for curses to be lifted and his well-documented pre-

---

73   Norman Hunter, who let me remind you, comes across in his book as a much nicer man than his on-the-pitch persona ever suggested.

match walk to his lucky lamppost and back, he had everything just about covered.

Dave Mackay doesn't strike us as a man to entertain too much nonsense, but he brings us a tale that clearly rattled him a bit, of Matt Busby apparently displaying magical powers. During Busby's spell as Scotland manager, he picked Mackay and made him captain for a game against Wales in 1958. Busby sent Mackay out telling him he wanted him on penalties but also with these very specific instructions: 'In the event of a penalty, I don't want you to side-foot it. I want you to blast it into the corner of the net. Is that understood?' He also told him that should goalkeeper Bill Brown get injured, he wanted Mackay to take over, again with the specific instructions that 'in the event that you have to deputise in goal and a ball comes over, do not rise to the temptation to punch the ball away. Catch it Davie. Catch it.'

Now this could be seen as Busby simply preparing for every eventuality, or, given what occurred next, could equally be seen as Busby being some sort of soothsayer. Firstly, Scotland were indeed awarded a penalty and in Mackay's words 'as I stepped up to take it, I puzzled even myself by side-footing it with the flat of my foot', and missed. 'I couldn't look over at Matt and to this day I have no idea why I ignored this instruction,' he says. Further freakiness came later when Bill Brown did indeed take a knock and Mackay went between the sticks. He started off well enough but as one ball came down towards him, he went to catch it only to see it sailing over him. 'My instinct had been to punch it, but I remembered Matt's words and stopped myself. The loss of those micro-seconds, though, caused me to miss it.'

Denis Law got him out of jail and cleared it off the line, but we're left wondering how Busby knew all this was going to happen. Mackay says, 'I strongly feel that Matt had somehow watched that match before it was played and had run through it in advance, 'and despite nailing my colours firmly to the sceptics' mast until now, I can only agree. I reckon Busby was involved in some kind of short-term *Back to the Future* style experiment and went back just a few hours to pass on his wisdom like a gruffer but more tactically astute Marty McFly. It's the only possible explanation.

Other unnerving shenanigans include Lomana LuaLua casually telling Shay Given, 'I once saw a man turn into a snake,' as he sat beside him in the Newcastle dressing room. Quite how he wanted Given to respond is unclear, but anybody who thinks the insistence that 'he was stood in front of me, and the next thing – he was a snake', might faze Shay has never seen that clip where the whole Sky Sports studio is in uproar at a Mo Salah goal while Given casually ploughs on with his dinner. The man is unflappable.

We must also consider the ghost that Mike Duxbury insists haunts the saunas at his local leisure centre, the spirits that came through Davie Wilson when he had 'the gift' and became a medium, and the UFO lights 'that appeared seemingly from nowhere in front of us, dancing against the backdrop of snowy fields laid before us', seen by Rodger Wylde and Chris Turner while staggering home drunk one night from a country pub. Although that one turned out to be a tractor, so we can stand the *Fortean Times* down and chalk that off as explained.

Before I go, just like Jacob Marley in *A Christmas Carol* I have news of three more ghosts to round off our tales of all things anomalous. First up we have Don 'The Revs' Revie and his England lads getting spooked in a haunted hotel, while in the USA for the Bicentennial tournament. As if playing in yellow and playing AGAINST Bobby Moore wasn't spooky enough for England, they were also upset by two reporters experiencing 'poltergeist activity' including one *Times* journalist called Norman Fox who endured what Kevin Keegan describes as 'the most sustained visitation'. Fox had things moved around his room while he was in the bath and came out to find nobody there and the chain on the door. This would surely have rattled Revie, a man prone to all kinds of voodoos and hoodoos. I would be tempted to say that a hotel full of footballers might have found a way to move things around and frighten the reporter, but as Keegan himself said, 'You can't disbelieve *The Times*', even when it comes to ghost stories.

Next up comes Mick Quinn who reports unearthly goings-on in his room when he was in digs as an aspiring young player. 'There was a chill in the room and my breath was leaving a vapour trail. I craned my neck over my shoulder and let out a shriek. Standing at my shoulder was a ghostly figure in human form.' In the morning Quinny was informed that a member of the family had died in that room. The episode might be the reason that Quinn seemingly tried his hardest to sleep with a barmaid every other night of his life, just so he wouldn't be left alone at the mercy of some spectre again. In an odd echo of the previously mentioned *A Christmas Carol*, Quinn as good as quotes Ebenezer Scrooge when he says that the whole episode 'really put the shits up me'.

Finally, it's Neil 'Razor' Ruddock with a tale that he freely admits we might think 'is a load of old bollocks', of a perverted ghost in his bedroom called George 'who had a bit of a thing for my missus'. Mrs Razor complained about feeling a presence when she was getting changed, and despite his understandable initial scepticism, Neil did the only thing a loving husband would do in those circumstances and got Derek Acorah in. Acorah identified the ghost as George, a military man who had been shot down during the Second World War. Now, Acorah's credentials for being able to communicate across the veil are hotly debated. All I'm saying is that he died a few years ago and we haven't heard a peep from him since. Whatever it was, before it left, Ruddock was asked to sit in the bedroom on his own with the lights on and he swears that 'somebody said "hello" in my left ear. I swear I'm not shitting you.' By his own admission, the previously doubtful Ruddock was suddenly convinced and his 'heart was going like a shithouse door when the plague's in town'.

I WANT TO BELIEVE

Well, what do you make of that? I confess that I've been slightly dubious about the whole gamut of external influences from lucky charms and pastries through pre-match rituals to full-blown spectral visitations, but now I'm not so sure. Perhaps there really is more than any of us can understand out there in the ether, controlling our destiny, guiding our path, or just shitting us up a bit. It certainly makes you think.

Sleep well everyone. Sleep well.

8.

Stranger in a Strange Land

'Debut Catastrophique'

IT'S GOOD to broaden our horizons with travel. Don't get me wrong, it suits me just fine if you've got your head in this book and looking down, not up, but if you're doing so while sitting by an infinity pool somewhere or riding on the back of an elephant rather than sat in the bath at home, then so much the better.

We can only dream of being as windswept and interesting as international man of mystery and referee Pat Partridge, who intoxicates us with his adventures as far afield as India and Malta and 'Corsica, the historic land of bandits where fireworks lit up the night sky in a display never bettered on November 5 and to Japan where Tokyo University made a graphic study of my every move'. We'll stop him there as he's starting to sound a bit like Rutger Hauer on the roof in *Blade Runner* – he's seen things you people wouldn't believe. Not everyone is as exotic as Uncle Travelling Pat, but let's take a moment to celebrate those that have given it a go.[74]

Ian Rush once famously said of his spell with Juventus in Italy that it was like 'living in a foreign country' – except he didn't say

---

74 Although if Pat's been to Tenerife, then Eddie Hapgood has been to Elevenerife, claiming, 'I've been in a shipwreck, a train crash, and inches short of a plane accident.'

it. He says that it was a joke line made up by Kenny Dalglish, upon his return, which stuck. Through gritted teeth Rushy describes it as 'another of Kenny's impish wind-ups'. I'm happy to set the record straight here as things can get lost in translation when players move abroad, and I think (almost) anybody who tries playing in a different country deserves our praise. Some move onwards and upwards to some of the planet's biggest clubs, others scratch around the minor leagues of the world hoping to squeeze the last drop of juice out of a career that hasn't turned out exactly as they might have hoped, while the rest go for a bit of a jolly-up between real seasons. So, let's go on a globe-hopping trip. Bring your passport and let's get going. And where better to start than in Ian Rush's different country.

ITALY

When Rush left Liverpool for Juventus he did so as arguably one of the deadliest strikers on the planet.[75] Once he arrived in Turin, less so. Then he returned to Liverpool and was pretty much deadly once more. If you squint a bit then his goalscoring figures in Italy are okay, but it's undeniable that, once upon a time, Italy was a tough place for Brits to go and play football, and he is not the only one to struggle.[76] Denis Law famously didn't have much fun at Torino and jumped at the chance when Matt Busby bumped into him and asked how things were going, telling him, 'I don't like it. Why don't you come and buy me?', which is a bit forward, but got the job done. Law, of course, went back to Manchester and made a little bit of a name for himself at Old Trafford.

---

75 It could have been different though. Rush casually drops in that he was Terry Venables' first choice for Barcelona before he turned to Gary Lineker.

76 More recently, of course, Fikayo Tomori, Tammy Abraham and Ashley Young must wonder what all the fuss was about, as they seem to have coped just fine.

FINAL THIRD

Jimmy Greaves was another who tried his luck in Italy, in his case in Milan, playing for the Rossoneri.[77] His stay was even shorter than Law's, describing conditions as 'more like a prison camp' under the legendary manager Nereo Rocco. The two never got on and Jimmy didn't thrive under the strict regime, being something of a free spirit who liked to choose his own food and things like that. Greaves says that 'Rocco used to order my food and then sit opposite me making sure I ate it. He allowed us only two cigarettes a day, one after lunch and one after dinner.' Who can live like that? Only two fags a day?

Shackled on the pitch by stifling tactics and physical defenders and shackled off the pitch by his over-zealous gaffer, it was only a matter of time before Jimmy's thoughts turned to escape – literally. At one point Jimmy's pal, singer Tommy Steele, genuinely offered to help smuggle Jimmy out of the country disguised as one of his musicians on a private plane, another time Greavsie risked death to get past Rocco. With the manager sat at the bottom of the hotel stairs to ensure that Greaves couldn't get out, Jimmy took the only course of action open to him when faced with such an affront to his professionalism and went out of the window, 'three storeys up and edged along a narrow ledge looking for an escape route'. Eventually he found one, to Spurs.

So, as Rush and his wife Tracey arrived at Turin Airport for his Juventus spell, mobbed by fans and press alike, he could have been forgiven for feeling a little trepidatious. His initial press conference, at the airport, because why wait, saw him field questions about the Falklands War, Charles and Diana, Thatcher's government, and Italian literature that made his head spin. He found an ally in Michel Platini but, unfortunately, he had already left Juventus and was just hanging around the place like David Brent. Showing the

---

77 Italian football club nicknames like Rossoneri or Nerazzurri until you realise it's just their colours, red and black or blue and black. I remember the crushing disappointment I felt when I worked that out, later than I care to admit to.

flair for diplomacy that surely pointed to a successful, unblemished administrative career in the future, he told Rush to 'tell the press what they want to hear' because 'Italians will always believe what they read or hear, rather than what they see'. However, it was all too little too late. Rush said that he did successfully adapt to some aspects of Italian life and learned enough of the language to get by, but rather cattily says that what he 'never did adapt to, was playing in a team where just about every player was playing for himself'. I bet he couldn't get back to the chocolate biscuits at Liverpool quick enough.

All these players trying and failing in Italy were like personal daggers to the heart of the big undisputed success among Brits abroad – John Charles. The man of many golden nicknames was sad and disappointed that the likes of Law, Greaves and Joe Baker thought ill of Italy, because he bloody loved the place. On the pitch Charles was big and strong and took his lumps in good grace, and off the field he didn't miss the boozy British culture because he never really drank beer in the first place – a genuine rarity. He settled quickly and 'had no problem switching from whisky and lemonade to red wine, and from roast beef and Yorkshire pudding to spaghetti', learnt Italian and became an icon at Juve. This is the spirit.

During his time away he won three titles, two cups and footballer of the year. In the early noughties Charles was voted 'Greatest Ever Foreign Player in Serie A' above the likes of Maradona, Van Basten, Zidane and Danny Dichio. He even found time to have a singing career, appearing on TV[78] and having hit singles. The man is an absolute legend and stands as a shining beacon among British players who have tried their luck abroad. The key seems to be embracing the lifestyle and throwing yourself into it. Committing.

---

78 You can find him on YouTube singing 'Sixteen Tons' if you're so inclined. He's bloody good.

Nobody ever accused Graeme Souness of lacking commitment and his move to Sampdoria was no different. His 1984 move may have taken Liverpool boss Joe Fagan by surprise and apparently given him the right hump, but Alan Hansen applauded his fellow Scot's honesty in saying he was going for the money and off he went. As we will see later, Souness has approached European travel like Michael Portillo with an Interrail pass but Italy was his first adventure. The biggest shock for him was the difference in the drinking culture. Stepping away from that early eighties Liverpool side might have left him thirsty but fluids were still taken on board, just in a different way.

Having lunch one day in the summer, a few hours before training, he was surprised when 'my new team-mates all ordered a bottle of wine each'. However, instead of necking it in one go and running it off like the boys back home did, the way of things in Genoa was for players to 'write their name on it, have a glass and hand it back. It was to last them for four or five days.' Very civilised, although why a few of them didn't just share a bottle and have a glass each there and then I don't know. But I'm not from round here. Souness also remembers his Sampdoria team-mates being giddy with excitement at the prospect of an away trip to Avelino, telling him 'Wait till you taste the coffee down there. The water was supposed to be special or something.' It's all a long way from the six pints and a careful drive home culture he had left behind.

Maybe it was the money or the whiff of the coffee in his distinguished nostrils, but Trevor Francis overcame an initial reluctance to go abroad, and soon joined Souness at Sampdoria and during the eighties and nineties we also saw the likes of Ray Wilkins, Mark Hateley, Joe Jordan, Luther Blissett and the multiple club enthusiasts Liam Brady and David Platt leave the English game for the Italian. But not everyone had the nerve to go. In Alan Shearer's *Diary of a Season*, that most English of English strikers is linked with a move to Juventus and says that he's going to learn Italian just in case. He then mentions at least five times in the book that he hasn't got around to starting yet so it's fair to say his heart wasn't in it, and he preferred the idea of a different, colder brand of black and white stripes instead. Malcolm Allison is another who flirted with the idea. He wants you to know that Juventus approached him to manage them once and he turned them down. In fact, he mentions it so many times that his enigmatically titled book *Colours of My Life* may as well be called 'I Could Have Managed Juventus, You Know'. Maybe they were worried about being discarded when they were no longer wanted, or as Joe Jordan forlornly puts it, 'the oldest truth in the game, which is nowhere more implicit than in Italy – for the great clubs, a footballer has his time and then he is gone like an old brown leaf in autumn'. Poor Joe. I feel a bit maudlin now. Anyone fancy a coffee? Ciao!

COLOMBIA

Colombia was pretty much the first country to tempt English players abroad way back in the fifties. The lure of riches beyond their dreams was enough to turn the heads of several players such as George Mountford, Charlie Mitten, Jack Hedley and Roy Paul. This 'Soccer caravan to Bogota' is described by contemporary striker Trevor Ford as the biggest scare that British football had received and was considered something of a scandal. Reactions among players seem to have been split though. Ford himself, who pushes constantly throughout his book *I Lead the Attack* for better wages in football, says good luck to those who went. He can see why they went having been 'driven out by the slave-drivers of British football', and he was tempted to go himself (although there is no record of him being asked). Stanley Matthews, on the other hand, who himself is no stranger to a pound note, was shocked and stunned by the moves. Considering he didn't even move house from Blackpool to Stoke when he re-signed for them, he may have considered uprooting to Bogota a bit of a stretch for the removals van.

The biggest figure in the Colombian saga was Matthews' Stoke team-mate Neil Franklin eschewing the chance to play for England at the 1950 World Cup in favour of moving to Santa Fe. Given England's disastrous performance in that tournament he might have considered himself well out of it. At least he would have done had he ever received the fabulous sums promised to him by his new employers. Instead, Franklin was back home two months later 'having received only one week's wages and no signing-on fee' and was subsequently 'ostracised by the FA and Stoke City'. The fact that Franklin and some of the others returned home from Colombia with little more than a tan, perhaps explains why there's hardly been a conveyor belt between the two countries since, give or take the odd Tino Asprilla visit to Darlington, before thinking better of it.

FRANCE

When Chris Waddle signed for Marseille for £4.25m in 1989 it left his Spurs team-mate Terry Fenwick gasping, 'I wonder if it will ever be beaten for a British player?', so the sums spent in recent years must have made his head fall off. The Waddle fee was money well spent though, as he became a much-loved character in France, with a Marseille highlights reel that not many could rival, as well as that pop single he did with Basile Boli.[79] Waddle's former singing partner before he split Glenn & Chris to go in a different musical direction with Boli, was, of course, Glenn Hoddle, another man who made his mark in France. Hoddle once wrote, rather sniffily, 'You do not have to be a football connoisseur to realise that my style is best suited to the Continental game. I have never really believed that I fit in here in England,' which seems an extraordinary thing to say given his legendary status at Spurs but here we are. Sorry if it wasn't all a bit more suave and sophisticated for you, Glenn. Hoddle duly went to Monaco, played under a young Arsène Wenger and

---

79   Oh yes, he did. Have a look on YouTube. The video is quite something.

STRANGER IN A STRANGE LAND

had the time of his life. Another silky midfielder, Ricky Hill, says he also very much enjoyed his French spell, with Le Havre, and says that perhaps he should have stayed longer, but not everybody had such a tres beau time.

US goalkeeping superstar Hope Solo says she found the language barrier a problem with her back line: 'I tried to learn the right French words, but in the pressure of a game I would resort to English. If I said "away" they thought I was saying "J'ai" – I have it.' You can see the problem and she says, 'At times it felt as though I was trapped in a Monty Python skit.' I mean it's hardly The Ministry of Silly Walks, but I take the point. A few more hours in the language lab needed for Hope maybe. A bit more ecoute et repete. Although she didn't hang around in Lyon long enough to worry about it.

A few more brief stays to consider now, or bref séjours, if you will. First up, it's the very definition of the 'much-travelled' footballer, Clive Allen. Clive moved so many times in his career that I imagine he always slept with a toothbrush and a railcard in his top pocket. Admittedly, much of the time he bounced around London like a black cab driver with insomnia, but he did momentarily give it a go in France with Bordeaux. Unfortunately, after only six weeks, the club president called him into his office where he sat in a big chair at a big desk, with Clive sat in a much smaller chair opposite for the classic power play and told him that he was a great player but 'you must go away'. Good of him to speak English at least. Even Hope Solo would have understood that. Once he was told to 'find a new team – England, anywhere. It doesn't matter,' Clive would have just shrugged this off, found one or two teams that he hadn't already played for yet and given them a try.

Another striker who has more than likely played for your club is Lee Chapman. Like Allen, he managed to take a short break from collecting as many English football shirts as he could to try his luck in France with Niort – a club which frankly I have only heard of because Lee Chapman played for them. You will have to forgive my ignorance as far as Niort are concerned, but as long as Chapman himself did his due diligence, I'm sure it was fine: 'I signed for Niort, a team I had never heard of.' Oh, right. Making a big career move to France seemingly on the basis that he quite liked wine turned out not to be such a smart move. Chappy found that his new team-mates didn't quite meet his exacting standards and he complains of a 'distinct lack of discipline', that 'many had a volatile temperament' and that they 'liked to wander from their given position whenever the mood took them'. After a particularly hairy away trip to Bastia on Corsica, after which Chapman needed to be rescued by a kindly gendarme, he decided enough was enough and came home. Having grown tired of the volatile temperaments around him he decided to sign for Brian Clough at Forest.

Sideways glance to camera.

Mick McCarthy was part of this late eighties French exchange too. Mick tried to broaden his horizons with a move to Lyon where, unfortunately, he had what the papers called a 'Debut Catastrophique' against Waddle's rampant Marseille. In case you were wondering, that's French for not very good. Mick stayed just long enough to pass on some English swear words to his team-mates and to note that in France 'they commit more fouls off the ball when the referee is not watching – pulling your hair, pinching you, things like that'. He decided to move on and pass on what he had learned to those shy retiring lads down at Millwall.

SWEDEN

The best of the Scandinavian countries[80] played host to a young Teddy Sheringham who had a loan spell at Djurgårdens from Millwall early on in his career. It must have been quite a culture shock, but Teddy seems to have really enjoyed it, saying, 'I had the

---

80   Face facts, Norway.

use of a nice apartment, an old BMW car, my basic meals paid for and a decent wage,' which is all any of us can ask for. He says he was never homesick, did a bit of growing up and euphemistically says 'I lost a bit of my innocence, but that was no bad thing'. All in all, it sounds like a decent Tripadvisor review – would recommend.

Also losing a fraction more of his innocence during a spell in Sweden with Mjällby AIF, was Frank Worthington. He recounts an adventure in *One Hump or Two* when he spent time with a couple in a nearby town who owned a clothes shop. 'I stayed over one night and next morning the lady of the house climbed into bed with me after he'd gone to open the shop. It was typical of the Swedish attitude to free love and added a whole new meaning to breakfast oats!' I think he means he had sex with her. That's what he usually means – to the extent that he could have said literally anything there and we would still have known what he was getting at.[81]

Jeremy Goss had no time for such sexual shenanigans when he spent a time on loan at Lulea. Instead, he was busy getting addicted to a local brand of sausage called Bullens Pilsnerkov. He became absolutely obsessed with it, telling us, 'You don't cook or grill the sausage though, the best and only way to enjoy it is to warm it in a hot broth, ideally the one that it comes with it in the jar.' See? For Norwich fans and team-mates, Goss is the man who scored a glory goal in Munich on their biggest European night. For the folk at Lulea, he's the sausage guy.

NORWAY

Sources of information about the experience of playing football in the truly best country in Scandinavia[82] are scarce, but we do have a note from Charlie Miller about his time spent in the very lovely Bergen, plying his trade for Brann. He says that he would frequently

---

81 'Added a whole new meaning to marmalade on toast / a bacon roll / smashed avocado' – see.

82 Face facts, Sweden.

receive text messages directly from fans 'telling me how much they loved me', which is either very friendly, or slightly creepy, depending on your own particular take on it. Miller says that somehow fans could get his number at will and 'wouldn't think twice about giving you a call or sending a text after a match'. I think it's something to be discouraged over here. Poor old Harry Maguire's phone would have more pings than the NHS Covid-19 app.

SPAIN

Rather than dive straight in with the playing experience in Spain, let's take a moment to examine that curious phenomenon of the British coach in Spain. In more recent years we've seen David Moyes and Chris Coleman both have a go at managing Real Sociedad,[83] but they have been rarities. There was a time in the 1980s when it felt like there were more British football managers than British armed robbers in Spain, and that's saying something. Terry Venables, Howard Kendall, John Toshack and Ron Atkinson all had a go. At managing Spanish football teams, not at robbing post offices – just to clarify.

Howard Kendall clearly didn't leave Everton for Athletic Bilbao for the glamour because he was housed in a 'small apartment with a bedroom and a bathroom' at the training ground when he got there. He passes it off as 'the logical thing to do because the alternative was to closet myself in a city-centre hotel where, I'm sure, I would have felt totally isolated', but surely a hotel in town or squatting at the training ground weren't the only options. If they had any faith he was going to stay for a while, surely the club would have found him a house exactly where he wanted and helped him pick out curtains. These arrangements smack of knowing it was going to be a brief spell in charge. They may as well have left the engine

---

83 'I'm going to manage Real.'
'Sociedad?'
'No, just me.'

STRANGER IN A STRANGE LAND

running on the car that brought him there from the airport. Mind you, he seems happy enough. Perhaps he had his head turned by that flat having both a bedroom AND a bathroom. The lucky sod.

Big Ron went to Atlético Madrid where his tenure was also brief but clearly made an impression on him. Ron says, 'To me, Madrid was full of stardust,' which is a bit of a kick in the face for the West Bromwich he left behind, but maybe he was just dazzled because he once saw Seve Ballesteros in the street.[84]

Atkinson really enjoyed the change of routine in Spain, but unfortunately for him, being at Atlético back then meant he was working for club president Jesús Gil, who went through managers like I go through tea bags. Atkinson had clearly met his match, saying that Gil was 'built like a fighting bull and with a larger-than-life personality – at times almost beyond the normal rules of sanity'. He was also known to say racist things from time to time, and you can do your own jokes about that. A clash between the two and an early away for Ron was as inevitable as it was messy. Ron's job was offered to his assistant Colin Addison and he took it, displaying 'disloyal behaviour' according to Ron, which 'did seriously strain relations' between the pair for years to come.[85] Inevitably, for a man with a sense of his self-worth the size of Ron's, he feels that he was cut off in his prime, saying 'without boasting too much, I am convinced if I had been left in charge for longer, Atlético would have been celebrating real achievements on the field even earlier'. I mean, that does sound a bit like boasting. If it's any consolation, Addo didn't hang about for long either before Gil gave him the Spanish Archer.

---

84 'I ran over the road shouting, "Seve, Seve," and shook hands with him.' It's not his best story

85 There is an edition of *Midweek Sport Special* from the time featuring a disgruntled Ron being interviewed at some ice-skating event by Elton Welsby. Welsby also had a phone interview with Colin Addison and got him to admit what had happened before Ron knew about it. It's delicious and I one day hope to make a six-part drama about it.

Where shall we go for a view on playing in Spain? To Gareth Bale, who has managed to win everything in sight, score spectacular goals while doing so, and simultaneously get on the wrong side of everyone at Real Madrid because he prefers Wales and golf? Or go back to the Galácticos era and drink in the achievements of David Beckham, Michael Owen and, er, Jonathan Woodgate? If you answered none of the above, you would be right because, of course, we're visiting Jermaine Pennant at Real Zaragoza for the real juice.

Pennant's stay in Spain was a real mixed bag, and so little of it has to do with football. On the plus side Jermaine found it easy enough to indulge his pursuit of any and all women, saying, 'The girls couldn't speak English, I couldn't speak Spanish, but I didn't need to say anything. I could just grab a girl, take her into my bedroom, close the door, draw the curtains and that was it. No conversation. Just sex.' However, on the negative side the opening times of shops frustrated him somewhat because they 'closed at twelve, open at five. It was crazy. It was a bit annoying after training, when you're starving and everything is closed. You couldn't even get a bun!' It's real swings and roundabouts stuff isn't it. I can see why he might want a bite to eat to keep his strength up but why does he specifically want a bun? He's not an elephant from the seventies.

Eventually Pennant ran out of women in Zaragoza to have wordless, meaningless sex with and set his agent to work to get him a move home. Before long 'Stoke came in, I was thinking, "You know what? Fuck it! I don't care who it is!" It could have been Bolton Wanderers for all I cared. I didn't give a shit.' I'll apologise on his behalf here to Bolton fans, as well as Stoke fans I suppose, although there's really no nice way to spin that.

Mark Hughes at Barcelona in the eighties always gave the impression he was having a lovely time, as part of a glamour couple up front with Gary Lineker, but while Lineker loved it, Hughes hated it. Old Lager Legs does say that he was able to leave his big drinking days behind him and learned to train much harder and better while he was there, which no doubt sustained him in his long and impressive career, but he describes his time at Barça as 'a full-blown, X-rated horror story' tempered only by money – 'bundles of it'.

Hughes's biggest problem was the press who slaughtered him and made life difficult: 'Because I got stuck in and tackled a few opponents, it seemed to infuriate the Spanish critics. All they wanted was the back of the net bulging.' He also feels he was targeted by referees for being a bit rough. If you are considered too rough for Spain at that time, when players such as 'The Butcher of Bilbao' Andoni Goikoetxea walked the streets, then you are really putting a shift in, frankly. With his Barcelona stay turning sour, Sparky was soon looking for somewhere else to wallop people, which leads us to …

GERMANY

Two incidents illustrate very well how the toughness of Mark Hughes found a more spiritual home once he'd moved on from Barcelona to Bayern Munich – one is that time he played two games in the same day (for Wales in Czechoslovakia during the day and for Bayern at home to Borussia Mönchengladbach in the evening),[86] and the second is that he found a worthy opponent to scrap with.

Hughes speaks with misty-eyed nostalgia about the running battles he had with Guido Buchwald, saying, 'He must have hated me.' Although, Sparky possibly overstates the case when he says that 'for the sake of Aryan pride, he was out to prove he could conquer the world or at the very least, put me in my place'. Of course, we can all well remember that time Hughes had a fist fight with a bare-chested Buchwald as that plane was going round and round,

---

86   Hughes well remembers zooming through the Czech countryside to a private airfield in a Lada with 'loose bolts flying, and exhaust just holding on', before transferring to a 'full-blown turbo Porsche'. Jeremy Clarkson would get a series out of recreating this day.

181

FINAL THIRD

before Buchwald eventually got chopped up in the propellers. Oh, my mistake that was Indiana Jones and Pat 'Bomber' Roach in *Raiders of the Lost Ark* wasn't it. Silly me. It's easy to tell the two apart because Buchwald isn't really fighting for Aryan pride is he, Mark? He's just an excellent German footballer who was as good at kicking people up the arse as you were. Their rivalry came to its natural conclusion in Hughes's final game for Bayern, with a few heavy hits from Buchwald, after the last of which, Hughes 'jack-knifed around and just booted him' and was sent off. Don't think I didn't notice how close together he put 'jack' and 'boot' in that sentence, either.

Hughes was merely continuing a fine tradition of British players getting into dust-ups for German clubs and following in the footsteps of the never knowingly under-scrapped Kevin Keegan. Keegan, who stands head and shoulders above all other UK exiles to Germany after his time in Hamburg, remembers getting frustrated with defender Erhard Preuss while playing a (not so) friendly against Lübeck. After one foul against him too many, Kev snapped and 'hit him flush on the jaw with a left hook and followed it with a right cross that stretched him out unconscious. No need to wait for the red card; I sent myself off,' though I think technically the ref sent him off, really. This quote is from early volume, *Kevin Keegan Against the World*. By the time he considered the flare-up again for his nineties *My Autobiography*[87] he went further, saying, 'For a split second I was afraid I might have killed him – it was the hardest I had hit anyone in my life.'

It wasn't all brawling and bratwurst for Keegan in Hamburg, and his success both on the pitch and off it (where he forged a pop career to rival John Charles) is not in doubt. However, one thing really rankles with him – the slightest suggestion that his move was motivated by money. He concedes that 'the financial side of

---

87 Presumably he felt he had conquered the world by then.

the move was a strong attraction' and blaming UK taxation for providing 'no incentive for me to go any further in England', but a few pages later he's arguing nose to nose with a chef at a London hotel who suggests that he went for the money. He's a complex character. But with British newspapers only available for 75p over there and usually that was just 'the Welsh editions', every penny counted for Keggy.

Keegan rather haughtily, but quite correctly, says that 'other internationals will follow me from the English League; my success at Hamburg guarantees it'. Dave Watson went, Mark McGhee went, Alan McInally went, Neville Southall says he fancied it because 'German efficiency struck a chord with me and my relentless perfectionism' but never got round to it, but Phil Neal was dead against it. Although he considered himself an admirer of 'German thoroughness' he concludes that 'the simple answer is that it is not for me'. He may have worried that he may not be able to get breadless toast over there or been put off by how tough Keegan initially found it. He says Kev told him 'it was so tough that he nearly chucked the whole thing in – and Kevin Keegan is no quitter'. Let me just stop you laughing there to point out that Phil Neal's book was written a long time ago before Keegan quit that job, and that job, and that other job in the toilets.

Tony Woodcock feels perhaps like the player who went most native, enjoying two spells with Cologne and settling in as a respected pundit on German TV to this day. Keegan claims that Woodcock has become so immersed in the life that he 'now speaks in broken English because he has lived there for so long and thinks in German rather than English'. I've heard Woodcock speak and his English is just fine. He hasn't just forgotten how to speak English. I do like the bit about thinking in German though, like Clint Eastwood in the film *Firefox* where he must think in Russian to fly the plane. What do you mean that's a bit niche?

Woodcock's ability with the language was nearly nipped in the bud, however. He was playing at Nottingham Forest under Brian Clough when he was approached about a possible move and fancied it. His keen wife Carole immediately went along to sign up for German lessons at an evening class but bumped into team-mate John McGovern's wife in the queue and had to sign up for something else instead to cover her tracks. Now, whether Brian Clough had an intricate network of spies on the Nottingham adult education scene or John McGovern's wife is simply a grass, we cannot know. What we do know is that Woodcock got hauled in to explain himself to Cloughie, and Carole Woodcock possibly ended up with a load of wonky ashtrays she made at 'Pottery for Beginners'.

TURKEY

Thinking about Turkish football, the word 'lively' springs to mind. Intimidating atmospheres, intense rivalries, and flares, lots and lots of flares, before they were banned, and only slightly fewer since. Given the nature of the game there, perhaps Graeme Souness was not the man to throw into the mix. The enduring image of a Brit abroad in Turkey is that of Souness defiantly planting a flag in the centre circle during a fiery derby between his Galatasaray team and Fenerbahçe – presumably because he thought things needed spicing up a bit.

Describing it as 'a moment of madness' the actions of Souness certainly made his route to the sanctuary of the dressing room a bit more difficult. He made it to the tunnel 'although I had to duck under the plastic shields of the police to do so unscathed', only to meet an irate Fenerbahçe fan in the corridor. Souness admits to 'having a bit of a stramash with him', which I believe means that the two shared a frank exchange of views about how appropriate that whole flag business had been. You would think that Souness wouldn't need to create more problems for himself at Galatasaray, bearing in mind that one episode saw his squad create a shooting gallery in the games room and fire live rounds into some cushions 30 metres away. As Souness says, 'Even in Istanbul, I had to discipline them for that.' Fair's fair.

In case the lure of live ammo at the training ground wasn't sufficient, it seems that Turkish clubs can be very persuasive in trying to sign and trying to keep players. Pat Nevin considered joining Galatasaray when he left Everton and was offered 'a beautiful flat overlooking the Bosphorus and a BMW' by his suitors. However, when Pat, not unreasonably, wanted to wait and discuss the terms with his wife at home, the chairman became more insistent, telling him, 'You cannot leave!' as 'two burly henchmen' barred the door. Eventually, Pat established that it wasn't quite a full kidnap, got out of there and signed for Tranmere Rovers instead, having probably decided that Istanbul might not be on the touring schedule for Aztec Camera.

Les Ferdinand was so popular during a loan spell at Beşiktaş in his younger days that the club petitioned Prime Minister Maggie Thatcher to urge her to intervene and let him stay. Though I'm not sure they thought that through. It's simply not how it works. Ferdinand knew he was popular because the good folk of Beşiktaş had not only slaughtered a lamb for him on arrival and dabbed the blood on his head and boots, they had also given him a pigeon to release as he ran out. This double animal ritual was only rolled out for special cases apparently, and although it put him off his lamb he says, 'It was very different to what I'd been used to at Loftus Road.' That's true – at Loftus Road they used to release a lamb and slaughter a pigeon. It's like a more brutal version of putting jam or cream on your scone first.

We'll conclude our slice of Turkey with a mention for Ralph Milne. In the twilight of his career, Milne seemed to dash around the world on a permanent holiday, chatting to clubs that might sign him, but usually didn't. He went to speak with Ankaragücü and says he was treated well during his stay: 'One of the young guys even brought a TV into my room. Unfortunately it was all in Turkish, but it was a nice gesture.' Sorry Ralph, there's not much they can do about that. They can't take it away and get you one with British programmes on it. Not back then anyway. As soon as he returned to the UK, Ralph got another call from Esbjerg in Denmark who wanted him to pop over for a trial. Being the absolute chancer that he is he says, 'I knew there was no way they'd want me but I wasn't passing up the chance of another jolly, especially to Scandinavia!' You want to be careful though Ralph, some of the telly over there is in foreign too.

PORTUGAL

After upsetting people in Turkey, Graeme Souness moved on to Portugal for a spell as Benfica manager. He quickly decided that while 'The Latins have that extra flair', what the situation really called for was a legion of mid-ranking British lads to make everything solid and stodgy. So, in came Brian Deane, Mark Pembridge, Michael Thomas, Scott Minto and Gary Charles to a collective underwhelmed sigh from the Estádio da Luz fanbase, with Souness conceding that at least a couple of his new recruits 'weren't deemed to be good players in Portugal', in stark contrast to their very high standing back home.

It seems like Souness wasn't really buying into the country as a whole – not like Rodger Wylde, who managed to maintain enthusiasm – for about a month. He describes his move to Sporting Lisbon as utopia, at least in prospect. A few weeks in, once 'the novelty of eating out four or five times a week and having a maid do the housework wore off, we were left with the reality that we were in a foreign country'. Boy oh boy. It really sneaks up on you, doesn't it? Rodger insists he might have been okay but with the sexist generalisation of 'women are completely lost when they have not got their friends and relatives to gossip with', he gave himself

NETHERLANDS

Apart from that conveyor belt of youngsters that Chelsea had running through Vitesse Arnhem a few years ago, and Lee Cattermole's surprising late turn at VVV-Venlo,[88] it's hard to find too many British players plying their trade in the Netherlands. Of course, that doesn't stop everyone having an opinion on the Dutch.

Stuart Pearce says that Dutch players 'will look for someone else to blame' after a defeat and Ron Atkinson implies there is a level of arrogance there by saying that Arnold Muhren 'was not a typical Dutch footballer' because 'there was no hint of arrogance about him'. As if to try and clarify the situation so that nobody is offended, Kevin Keegan wades in with 'there is an air about them, an arrogance that is not offensive'. So now you know. Well, you sort of do. What we need is for more people that have actually been and played there to write a book and give us their thoughts. I'm looking at you Ally Dick.

INDIA

In recent years, there have been a few British footballing exports to India, either as players or managers, with the likes of David James and John Gregory giving it a go. Who can forget that image of Gregory posing with a trophy in traditional Indian clothes after his success with Chennaiyin FC? Well not me, obviously.

Unfortunately, the only first-hand account from an autobiography covered here comes from former Rangers full-back, David Robertson – but believe me that's plenty. In a traditionally British approach to travelling abroad, Robertson accepted a job with Real Kashmir without ever looking anything up. Everything

---

88   A club which sounds like Arkwright in *Open All Hours* is saying it.

he knew about India was drawn from 'what I had seen on Karl Pilkington's *An Idiot Abroad* TV show' and it wasn't until he got there that he realised it was Kashmir he had agreed to coach, and not Lonestar, a completely different club.

Highlights of Robertson's time there include being casually asked by a supporter for a match to light his cigarette with, in the middle of a game, training at an 'indoor facility' that turned out to be somebody's front room with the furniture taken out and setting his bed on fire while he was in it. With an eye for a bargain, Robertson had bought a cheap electric blanket and awoke to find it on fire. Robertson did what anybody would do in that situation and phoned his wife, Kym, at home in Scotland to ask her what to do. He says, 'I eventually managed to put water on the bed and, as it was smouldering, I threw it out an open window. But as soon as it hit the fresh air, it burst into flames again.' Thankfully, nobody was hurt, not David out there alone in India, or indeed a bemused Kym, nearly four thousand miles away back home.

HONG KONG

It's difficult to find any players or managers from Britain that have been what you might call a success in Hong Kong, but some have certainly dabbled. And I don't just mean that infamous 'dentist chair' trip that England made before Euro 96. Unfortunately, it sometimes seems to bring out the lazy stereotypes from people. Alan Ball says that during his time coaching at Eastern AA with Bobby Moore, one of the Europeans in their squad brought bacon and eggs in for breakfast 'which completely baffled the Chinese, especially that one lad who was trying to eat a runny egg with chopsticks'. I'm not sure this really happened, are you?

The England duo invited a former team-mate of each of them (at Southampton and West Ham, respectively), Ted MacDougall out to play for them so he went for a look but got scared of the kung fu. Genuinely. He claims the game he watched 'looked more like kung fu than football with plenty of high tackling'. He tried to consult Micky Horswill, who was already playing there about a potential move 'but his jaw was wired up – yes he had been kung fu'd during a game out there!' Firstly, it seems like another lazy stereotype to suggest that everyone in Hong Kong is running around kicking each other in the face like a permanent immersive Jackie Chan movie experience. Secondly, how did he not notice Micky's wired-up jaw before he got as far as speaking to him. And finally, I'm not sure that you can use kung fu as a verb like that, can you? As in 'I'll bloody kung fu you in a minute'.

There are two further accounts of players returning from Hong Kong with their tails between their legs that we can call upon – but their reasons for leaving are very different. First up, it's Stoke legend Terry Conroy, who left Hong Kong club Bulova under a cloud after a row with his Triad-connected chairman, Mr Chim. Well, you would, wouldn't you? Conroy says that Chim questioned his commitment when he was injured and the two got into a row as all their issues 'boiled to the surface and broke out into the one major act of my life which I feel ashamed of. I pushed the chairman. He staggered back, but didn't fall. The look on his face said everything though.' Somewhat surprisingly, Conroy wasn't packed and on the next flight out before the chairman so much as recovered his composure. Aware that 'I'd made a very powerful man lose face', the end was inevitable. At a meeting the following day, Chim sat in his office 'like a Bond villain' and told a shaking Terry, 'You can no longer live a safe life in Hong Kong.' Given the two options that such a sentence left him with, Terry decided to sign for Crewe instead, where the Triad presence was far less pronounced.

Former Everton favourite Kevin Sheedy also left a short stay in Hong Kong after upsetting his chairman, but in less dramatic circumstances. Sheedy says that karaoke is a huge part of the culture in Hong Kong and claims that on a night out after his second game playing as a guest there, he was forced to sing, despite protestations that he was no good. Sure enough, he was no good. 'I can't remember what I attempted to sing. I tried a duet and all I know is that it was horrendous. The football club owner took my paltry attempt as an insult. I think he felt his honour and reputation had been damaged! He told me our agreement for me to guest in another match had been terminated.'

Exactly how bad do you need to be at Karaoke to get sacked for it? It feels like there may have been a bit more to this story, but if there is then Sheeds is not letting on. This wouldn't be too surprising – there are stories around booze with Sheedy front and centre within the books of several Everton team-mates, but precious few from Sheedy himself. He won't even tell us which song he sang, beyond it being a duet. I reckon if you had been forced to sing under such circumstances you would absolutely remember which song you did. If he won't tell us, then I'm just going to assume he tried to sing both parts to 'Islands in the Stream' until I hear otherwise.

LEBANON

Terry Yorath had a rich and varied career as both a player and a manager, but it's possible that nothing took him out of his comfort zone quite like his spell managing Lebanon in the mid-nineties. Overall, he did a great job and dragged them up the world rankings, gaining popularity along the way. However, a 5-3 defeat to Kuwait saw that all come crashing down. He remembers the aftermath being distinctly chilly as he popped out to his favourite local store for some comfort food: 'As soon as I walked into the delicatessen, all backs were immediately turned. Nobody would do anything for me and they started calling me a male prostitute in Arabic – not too loudly but just enough for me to hear.' It seems a shame that it all went sour. Not only had Terry done a great job up to that point, but he'd clearly made an effort to learn the language. If he knew what male prostitute was, he must have already been

AUSTRALIA

If you look for long enough, you might find a bad word said about playing in Australia, but you would have to search for longer than I did. It sounds terrific. Charlie Miller had a few personal problems while at Brisbane Roar but at least while he was having them he was two minutes away from the beach. Emile Heskey took a punt when he joined Newcastle Jets, admitting that he didn't even go over for a look or do much background research, but it paid off. He says, 'I was in an apartment overlooking the beach and the sea. It was beautiful. I was looked after very well.' Given that Heskey happily admits that he would 'lay down on the floor, staring at the ceiling' and be in tears, pining for Leicester when he moved up the road to Liverpool, the move to Australia was quite a leap of faith and I'm glad it paid off for him. The only downside for Emile was the sharks, which to be fair is a valid concern. It kept him out of the open water, unfortunately, but Heskey seems happy enough swimming in the rock pools or sitting on his balcony watching 'dolphins leaping while people were surfing'. The off chance that you might witness a live shark attack from a safe distance must have made this very exciting.

Dwight Yorke is another who had a wonderful time Down Under. Yorkie is very pleased with himself about his move to Sydney FC, boasting that they 'were the Manchester United of the A League', had broken their wage structure to sign him, and that the press had already christened him 'All Night Dwight' due to his off-the-pitch reputation. Yorke boasts that during his time there 'when I wasn't playing golf with the prime minister John Howard, I was hanging out with Jennifer Hawkins, Miss Australia', making friends with Ricky Ponting and being neighbours with Nicolas Cage. It says a great deal about the powers of persuasion of Roy

Keane, either by silver-tongued charm or pure intimidation in his phone voice, that when the call came, he left all this behind and moved to Sunderland, where, to the best of my knowledge, Nicolas Cage hasn't even got a place.

UNITED ARAB EMIRATES

John Burridge, the former goalkeeper for most clubs, sees himself as some sort of Lawrence of Arabia figure in terms of football in the Middle East. The man who in his own words has 'done more than anyone else in the Gulf' across coaching and television jobs in Oman and the UAE, can't get enough of the place. Yes, yes, if you ask him nicely, he'll tell you about that time he got knocked over by a car driven by 'somebody high-profile' that he mysteriously can't reveal – but the perks of the place far outweigh a little light running over as far as Budgie is concerned. Even after being sacked from a coaching job in Oman (where he discovered Ali Al-Habsi, Bolton fans), he dusted himself off and picked things up again across the border in the UAE.

One thing you can be sure of is that with Budgie firmly ensconced in his waterfront hammock, he is not coming back to Britain any time soon. His reasoning takes the form of a spectacular rant about the state of Britain taking in tax laws, the cost of filling his Hummer up, and my favourite gripe – a dentist's surgery 'giving me all the "are you registered, sir?"nonsense' when he waltzed into a surgery and demanded treatment back home. I'm sure this was a simple matter of filling out a few forms, but as we know, that's tricky with goalie gloves on so instead Budgie 'tried to tell them I'd paid millions of pounds in tax and played football for 32 years, but they weren't having it'. Honestly, a total stranger refusing to give any details can't even get a cap refitted these days despite having played professional football for far too long. What has the old country come to?

Warming to his theme he pretty much claims a full house on the *Daily Mail* bingo card, citing 'the rip-off nature of Britain', 'the government let anyone into the country and give them a house' and 'it's full of freeloaders'. Well, we all miss him dearly, don't we? The irony of a Brit sitting abroad, complaining about foreigners being let into Britain, will never get old for me, I have to say. And as he swings gently in the breeze coming off of the Indian Ocean, we can only hope that the waves deliver a moment of self-awareness to John Burridge.

SOUTH AFRICA

In a previous volume we covered in detail the experience of British footballers playing in South Africa under the apartheid regime. Some pleaded naivety and said they had their eyes opened by an experience they regretted, others defended their position, maintaining they did nothing wrong, while others fell between two stools, feeling uncomfortable but going anyway. So, in this chapter I won't dwell on it again and sit in judgement on people's actions. Except for Jimmy Hill.

You can tell that Jimmy knows he did wrong because he calls an entire chapter 'The South Africa Controversy'. The bones of the story are that Jimmy was invited to take charge of an all-star team to tour South Africa in the early 1980s. He claims that 'the word "manager" was the bait I fell for' but it's fair to say that the money didn't hurt either. In justifying the trip Hill says, 'I knew and believed in enough of the principles that lay behind Christianity to represent a firm view against apartheid's unacceptable face,' but 'I wanted to see at first hand and inquire for myself and make my own judgement,' and it's fair to say that the money didn't hurt either. Whatever wrestling Jimmy did with his conscience about undertaking the tour he managed to bury it quite deep while he enjoyed a six-a-side training match involving Mario Kempes and Ossie Ardiles, in which he scored the winning goal, and a lovely round at Kimberley Golf Club where he 'holed an enormous putt from off the green to win the hole and halve the match!' So, when the FA announced that they wouldn't sanction the tour and Jimmy came home chastened, at least he had his own special sporting memories to bring with him. In case you were thinking he might show a bit more contrition or embarrassment about his association with a tour that would have helped prop up an oppressive, racist regime, he's got an answer for you. 'On the following Saturday my other daughter, Alison, married an American – Chuck's a great guy. I just wish he'd been black.' So, there you are. Jimmy can't have had anything to do with racism because some of his best sons-in-law are black, or at least he wishes they were.

One man who seems like he tried to make a more honest living in South Africa is Graham Tutt, the former Charlton goalkeeper who suffered a horrific head injury in a game at Sunderland (more of which in 'Between the Sticks') and had to quit British football as a result. Tutt tried to bolster a meagre insurance payout by playing abroad and one of his stops was at Arcadia Shepherds.

During his time there, Tutt was coaching at a school as a sideline, when he heard a car crash outside. He phoned for an ambulance only to be asked by the operator 'if the people injured were white or black' because, of course, there were two types of emergency services. Thinking on his feet, Tutt said white in the hope that an ambulance would arrive quicker and indeed it did, but in a thoroughly depressing turn of events, the 'white' ambulance left empty 'when they found out there was no white person involved'.

Dealing with that sort of thing meant that Tutt didn't hang around long and moved on elsewhere, as we'll see – but he did stay long enough to experience an unusual away trip in Namibia. As Tutt stretched in his penalty area, 'a witch doctor jumped out from behind my goal', which it's fair to say he didn't expect. 'Staring intently at me, the witch doctor produced something from behind his back and held it high and triumphantly above him. It was a dead chicken. I knew it was dead because it was minus its head!'

Displaying some degree of cultural sensitivity, Tutt let the witch doctor get on with the dance he was performing and just politely tried to kick sand over the chicken blood he left in his goalmouth. But more strangeness was to come. The opposition number five (Tutt knew this because he had a big number 5 painted on the front of his shirt) brought someone down and conceded a penalty, but instead of accepting the decision or even pleading his case, he 'walked over to the referee and punched him on the side of the head. The poor ref went down like a sack of potatoes and was out like a light.' Unconscious for a few minutes, the referee eventually came round, sat up, gathered his whistle up and gave a corner instead. So, if you were there thinking that VAR is the only thing that can get a referee to change his mind, think again. A solid right-hander will, in some cases, also do it. Not really. Please don't punch referees, kids.

USA

Ah, the good old US of A. This is the stuff. Some will mock it for its gun laws, backward attitude to women's rights and that business with Trump, but deep down inside can we all just admit that we love it? It's the country that's in most of our favourite films, after all. It's the land of the free and was home to the NASL, which sounds like a right laugh. Let's stride into this section imagining James Brown playing us in with 'Living in America' like in *Rocky IV* before it all goes a bit sideways for Apollo Creed. Both Jimmy Hill and Graham Tutt of South Africa fame dabbled in the North American Soccer League, Jimmy ultimately failing to make Detroit Express a going concern, despite turning them into the Washington Diplomats and signing Johan Cruyff,[89] and Tutt rubbing shoulders with some of the greats on the pitch as a goalkeeper, and once as a striker, because let's face it, anything goes.

---

89 Paul Cannell played for Jimmy's Washington Diplomats and reckons that Jimmy stiffed many of the players on money and insurance. He also cryptically throws in, 'Did you ever wonder why Jimmy Hill never went to America during the World Cup which was held there???' I mean, I hadn't, but now it's all I can think about.

FINAL THIRD

His turn up front came for the Georgia Generals during an injury crisis. He claims he almost scored and displayed 'a decent touch for a tall player', which is perilously close to a good touch for a big man. He was, however, forced to play in a medium-sized shirt which was a bit tight and 'exposed my midriff and bellybutton'. I don't want to give you the impression that practices in the US at that time were not quite up to professional standard, but this sort of thing doesn't help. Tutt also was fined $100 per punch after a fight on a plane with team-mate David Byrne (not that one) while with Columbus Magic. The powers that be went easy on him, either because they thought Byrne[90] deserved it, or just because people are always more emotional on planes, aren't they? It's why you're more likely to cry at a film. Something to do with the altitude, apparently.

He also played with a team-mate who just might be the king of the shithouses. Daniel Mammana was an Argentine defender who Tutt roomed with, which was just as well because it sounds like you might want to keep on the right side of him. Tutt says that after bringing people down on the pitch, as a matter of course he would pull 'the guy to his feet with one hand, and would poke the player in the eye with his thumb on the other hand'. That's not even the worst bit. He also carried a large safety pin in his shorts and would jab people with it at corners. He seems nice.

Another eccentric South American was the Brazilian Tatu,[91] who played indoor 'soccer' with Howard Gayle at Dallas Sidekicks.[92] Gayle says that Tatu was quite an entertainer and had a gimmick of throwing his shirt into the crowd after every goal, adding, 'There

---

90 Son of Johnny 'Budgie' Byrne – former West Ham and England player. Byrne also dabbled abroad, in South Africa, where, as a coach, he once interviewed a non-plussed Pat Van Den Hauwe about coming to play for him. Of the encounter, Pat charmingly remembers, 'I had never heard of him, although within an hour I knew the ins and outs of his arsehole.'

91 Not to be confused with those Russian women that sang 'All the Things She Said'.

92 I love this name, and the fact that they played in a league containing Wichita Wings, Baltimore Blast and Los Angeles Lazers.

were some high scores and when I was there it was common for him to go through five or six shirts per match.' No wonder the finances of some of these clubs went through the floor. I'm sure Graham Tutt would have done the same had he scored, but he would have needed a shoehorn to get out of his.

Exotic team-mates are what playing in the NASL was all about. Dennis Tueart talks about playing alongside Franz Beckenbauer, Johann Neeskens and Carlos Alberto for New York Cosmos, while Steve Hunt who got there before him was a regular team-mate of Pelé. What I love most about Hunt's stories are the incongruity of Pelé shouting at Hunt for not passing and Hunt giving him the finger in return, or Pelé 'throwing haymakers' in the middle of a mass brawl, rather than just standing still and simply emanating greatness. When Pelé waded in, it was actually Hunt who got sent off, seemingly for not very much as the ref 'turned to me and then pointed to Pelé, "Well, I can't send him off, can I?"' Maybe it was at that point, as the unfortunate Hunt trudged past him contemplating the injustice of it all, that Pelé really did just stand there emanating greatness, and keeping his trap shut in case the ref changed his mind.

Turning out for the Cosmos also meant rubbing shoulders with some showbiz stars such as Mick Jagger, Peter Frampton and Robert Redford. Hunt didn't have any of that at Coventry. Alan Hudson, meanwhile, is surprisingly light on stories of his time with Seattle Sounders but is at least as pleased as punch to have met Tony Bennett.

The beauty of the North American football season seems to be that if you didn't want to fully commit to plying your trade there, you could just dip a toe in over the English summer, then return to your, dare I say it, proper club. Those players who gave it a go in one form or another include the never knowingly PC Frank Worthington, who took a turn in Philadelphia ('better known nowadays for wooftas, and as the back drop for the Rocky films'), Paul Cannell in several cities including Calgary ('I fuckin' hated it!'), Clyde Best in Portland (where he reveals that Portland Timbers fans called themselves 'fannies'), Gordon Hill in Montreal where he recalls a game being invaded by pigs and pigeons released from the crowd, and Rodney Marsh who was the king of Tampa Bay Rowdies. Marsh has a very high opinion of himself and his contribution to football in the USA so I'm loath to indulge it too much here. His opinion is less high of Gordon Jago who came over to coach the Rowdies. In whatever the American equivalent is of damning with faint praise, Marsh says, 'He was more of an administrative coach; he was brilliant with the travel arrangements for example.'

I'm going to leave the final word on the American experience to Harry Redknapp because, quite frankly, he makes his time at Seattle Sounders sound absolutely dreamy. Eating out as a family every night, either in restaurants or at 'barbecues down by the lake with all my team-mates and their families'. Counting Bobby Moore, Geoff Hurst and Mike England among his crew, he says, 'We'd have a swim and some food and sit by the lake until nine o'clock every night.' It all sounds like it should be gently narrated by Richard Dreyfuss, and my only concern about all this is that someone might have always been on the edge of getting a guitar out, but for how idyllic this sounds I think I could have suffered even that. As Harry says, 'It was like paradise.' God Bless America.

9.

Coming Over Here

'Manly Musks'

THE FLIPSIDE of all those intrepid travellers that leave these shores and try their luck abroad, are, of course, those that make the reverse journey to try their luck here. What started as a trickle, eventually became a flood in the baggy-shirted nineties and now the British game has become a glorious global village where we have had the fortune to witness the tactical and conditioning advances introduced by elite coaches from around the globe and appreciate some of the greatest players of all time playing on our doorstep such as Cristiano Ronaldo, Thierry Henry and Oumar Niasse.

Arsène Wenger is one of those great innovators, changing the English game when he arrived amid a chorus of derisive shouts of 'Arsène Who?' in 1996; but what we didn't know was that he already had the place in his heart from childhood. In his recent autobiography *My Life in Red and White* (so called because all of the teams he was associated with played in those colours, and because he spent three summer seasons as a Butlin's Redcoat),[93] Wenger remembers that in his childhood he would watch the FA Cup Final and be in awe of Wembley: 'Television was still in black and white

---

93 Not really, it was Pontins, but that messes up the colour consistency, so don't tell anybody.

in those days but the ball stood out brightly against the grass pitch that looked so beautiful.' He almost brings a tear to the eye as he calls it 'a dazzling memory: for me, it is the definitive image of football'. Imagine his pride when years later he got to lead his side out at the cathedral of football, again and again. The idea of the hallowed Wembley turf certainly gets overplayed, but here's a small boy from Alsace giving weight to the idea that it is somehow magical.

Given how privileged people like Wenger feel to become a part of the fabric of our game, you might expect everyone to welcome our foreign cousins with open arms. However, with the exception of Phil Neville, who is described by brother Gary as 'foreign daft',[94] it isn't always the case. Rather than seeing an influx of new ideas as a universally positive development, there are, believe it or not, some dissenting voices.

Neil Warnock maintains that 'you've got to keep a certain amount of English players', while Graeme Souness broadens the remit slightly, saying, 'We have to retain our Britishness,' before going into a reverie about how we all 'like to see young fit men challenging each other physically' as if he's talking about the beach volleyball scene in *Top Gun*.[95] He no doubt means good, honest, straight up and down, nine to five, pie and a pint, side-parted, British, young, fit men, though. David Batty complains dismissively that his Newcastle side signed 'mainly foreigners I had never heard of', which seems more like his problem than theirs, and David Seaman remembers being 'less than impressed' by a similar rash of signings at Arsenal, even if they eventually carried him to immortality. Terry Dyson grumbles that modern players 'do not have English as their native tongue'. Well, no Terry, some of them

---

94 Gary says that Phil and Jordi Cruyff used to hang out a lot and 'bored each other to death!', possibly discussing how they were both making a good living as professional footballers despite not even being the best player in their family.

95 Or the Touch Football game in *Top Gun: Maverick* if you prefer.

don't, but I don't think you can accuse too many of not learning the language. Many are multilingual in a way some of us could only dream of – or 'sognare' about, if you will.

John Toshack remembers Little Englander Tommy Smith talking about the arrival of Ricky Villa and Ossie Ardiles by saying that 'they had better get used to the idea of being tackled'. Because famously, Argentina don't have any tough-tackling players at all, ever, do they? Dean Windass's wife even joins in to say that at Middlesbrough 'they were mainly foreigners so I didn't really mix much' as if she had no option but to stay well out of it, so between them all it's clear to see that there isn't exactly a welcome in every hillside.

Warnock is back to grumble that the foreign managers don't have a post-match drink with him because 'it doesn't seem part of their culture to socialise with the opposition' – that's all of them, mind. All their cultures. It must be their cultures, because there's no other reason not to have a drink with Neil Warnock, right? Harry Redknapp, meanwhile, accuses Roman Pavlyuchenko of a 'failure of imagination to be frank' because when his Spurs squad indulged in the traditional pursuit of a visit to Cheltenham, the Russian striker didn't even look out on the balcony. Or maybe he just didn't like horse racing, Harry? Not everybody loves the gee-gees – it's hardly a red flag.

The situation at Liverpool seems complicated. It's always been a team that hasn't necessarily possessed an English core or needed one. In their Paisley and beyond dominance there was always a strong Scottish influence and plenty of Irish in the mix too, so you might not think that a few players from slightly further afield would prove to be too much of a culture shock, but here's Robbie Fowler saying that things were 'so disjointed because there were so many foreign players in the squad' which he claims led to a loss of 'identity and a bit of spirit', Jamie Carragher also complains that while some players assimilated just fine, the French contingent remained 'arrogant and aloof'. If there were any issues between the English and the foreign players, then Didi Hamann remained blissfully unaware of it, and absolutely loved his time with the club. He talks about enjoying the 'jaunty feeling' around the city, in which 'everyone seemed to be an apprentice comedian'. Didi spent a lot of time in various pubs, claiming he was on a research mission 'improving my grasp of the English language and I was seeing ordinary English life'. His pub commitment clearly earned him praise points from Carragher who describes Hamann as somebody who 'can enjoy a night out on a Friday and give a man of the match performance on a Saturday'.

Jens Lehmann was less keen on Liverpool, and quickly rejected a move there before he settled on Arsenal. It just goes to show you that one man's jaunty fun hub with a comic on every corner is another man's 'grey industrial town'. Lehmann was put off on his visit by 'torrential rain from all sides' and a hotel he didn't like, and instead high-tailed it to London and Arsenal, calling it 'one of the best decisions of my life'. Don't tell Didi. During his time in England, Lehmann was particularly impressed to meet the Queen at a reception for his Invincibles side, saying, 'When I finally shook her hand, I had been forced to think, awestruck, of the fact that I had been a touch away from Winston Churchill, Roosevelt, Kennedy, Nixon and Carter. It had been as if I had shaken hands with history incarnate.' It sounds like he must absolutely love *The Crown*. Maybe between Lehmann and Hamann this means that Germans find it easier to settle than anyone else – or maybe I'm indulging in a lazy sweeping statement about an entire nation of people based on one or two people. There's a lot of that about.

Stan Collymore says, 'The Norwegian lads are all very serious. Around the dressing room they have all got their white socks and their flip flops on. They read on the coach on away trips. They are low maintenance; a manager's dream,' which surely can't be true of everyone, while Peter Storey dismisses all Argentinian footballers as 'bitter and brutal whenever they're not getting their own way', and Alex Ferguson doesn't disagree with that too much. Fergie says, 'I confess I found working with Argentinian footballers quite difficult,' claiming that the few he managed 'didn't try particularly hard to speak English. With Verón it was just, 'Mister'. Isn't it possible that they were all just scared of him? Even with a rudimentary grasp of English they might have still been in the dark about what Sir Alex was saying to them. Learn Govan or there's no point.

Obviously, so far, I'm on the side of the imports, and painting a picture of dedicated pros doing their level best to fit in, while their English counterparts welcome them with the kind of warmth displayed by Nigel Farage on a boat in the channel, broadcasting live on whatever that horror show of a channel he's on is called. In doing so, I'm prepared to admit that I'm being simplistic, as it's not as if these players from abroad don't cause some of the problems themselves.

Harry Redknapp has a wealth of experience managing imports, from the briefest dalliance with Marco Boogers, who he bought after watching a VHS of him, and was gone before he had rewound the tape, to Niko Kranjčar, who seemed to travel everywhere with him like some sort of lucky Croatian charm – so he has seen it all. At West Ham, he had Javier Margas who got so homesick for Chile that he escaped from a first-floor hotel room, 'left all his clothes behind, his boots and all his kit; took his passport, his money, one small overnight bag and legged it'. He has also seen Sulley Muntari get paid so much money that he forgot about his house. Muntari was part of that Portsmouth FA Cup-winning side that lived the dream and left a large bill behind them. The Ghanaian only stayed on the south coast for one season but nevertheless bought himself a lovely house near Harry on the much sought-after Sandbanks. Redknapp says that when he 'upped sticks and moved to Italy' he left his house and his car 'to go to rack and ruin' and it wasn't sold until ten years later.

Now you can do your own jokes about Redknapp leaving Portsmouth and what happened after, but here he's cast in the role of a concerned neighbour, moaning that 'the garden was all overgrown, plants were climbing up the windows, and the Mercedes had gone all rusty and rotten'. Imagine having so much money that you could just disregard property you own in one of the most desirable locations in the country. I had never heard about this until Redknapp raised it in his book, and yet Jermaine Pennant leaves one little sports car behind in Spain and the tabloids are in uproar.

Other foreign lads causing their gaffers headaches include Sebastien Schemmel who booked himself and his family on a ferry to France before the season was over at West Ham, then copped the hump when Trevor Brooking pointed out that maybe he shouldn't have done so; Pascal Chimbonda, who famously handed Paul Jewell a transfer request while he was still in his Wigan kit on the last day of his season, and Tom Peeters at Sunderland, who enjoyed Howard Wilkinson's sacking a bit too much. Matt Piper remembers the day that Wilko gathered his squad together to solemnly tell them he had been sacked. Piper admits that Wilkinson perhaps hadn't been the most popular gaffer and that 'inside, I was having an absolute party'. The crucial part of that quote, for me, is 'inside'. Belgian midfielder Peeters wasn't nearly so discreet, standing up and shouting, 'YES! Get in there,' minding Wilko's grief not one jot. Even when Phil Babb told him to sit down and stop being unprofessional 'he just carried on whooping and clapping'. It's nice to know you're wanted, isn't it?

Players aren't usually so vocal, or quite so near, when they criticise their manager. However, a staple of the modern game is the interview given back home which finds its way to the English press. In recent times, Romelu Lukaku was caught speaking out of school about Chelsea, while the most famous example is perhaps Jaap Stam's book which caused Alex Ferguson to ship him out soon after. Stam and Lukaku might have been able to plead that any nuance had been stripped from their actual words by a newspaper keen to sensationalise them. However, Danish Rangers midfielder, Jan Bartram, left little to the imagination when he gave Copenhagen paper *Ekstra Bladet* the scoop about Graeme Souness under the headline 'My boss is a bastard'. Mark Walters says that Bartram told them that 'he had been instructed to kick opponents'. I think we can all imagine how well that went down with Souey.

Of course, Souness is the manager who presided over unquestionably the worst foreign signing in Premier League history, when he was duped into believing that Ali Dia was George Weah's cousin and gave him a game for Southampton. However, Souness refutes the legend, saying, 'The reality is we knew exactly, after 10 minutes of the first training session, that he wasn't very good, but circumstances dictated that he got a chance when he shouldn't have.' He blames an injury crisis for Dia making the bench and getting on and insists that 'nobody was being conned or tricked for a second'. Surely Southampton had a youth team at this point. Would it not have been better to have a youngster with a promising future on the bench, rather than signing somebody that bad for a month as cover? I know that Souey is trying to defend his position here but I'm not sure that 'we knew he was absolute shit but played him anyway' is quite the retort he thinks it is.[96]

Ali Dia was a high-profile case in the top division where nobody can hide, but Godfrey Odebo was a new name on me. Odebo was signed by Mick Rathbone for Halifax with the club in dire straits and willing to gamble on the word of a pushy agent who told him his client had been playing in Serie A. Rathbone is prepared to concede that it's possible that he misheard and the agent 'actually said Syria!', because what they got was a man who, when

---

96　Not to labour a point too much but Dia came on to replace an injured Matt Le Tissier after half an hour. Southampton also had Neil Maddison and Robbie Slater on the bench that day. They may not have had quite the creative spark of Le Tiss, but they were both, you know, actual footballers. It's not as if Souey was all out of options.

FINAL THIRD

asked to warm up, went into a virtuoso routine that fell somewhere between 'somebody performing a breakdance and somebody having a fucking seizure'. Once on the pitch things didn't go much better. He was introduced as a substitute when the ball was put out high above the stand, and it bounced back down from the roof as Odebo came on. Rathbone then describes the scene as Godfrey latched on to the wrong ball and headed towards Doncaster's goal while every other player was playing with the correct ball. Oh Godfrey. I bet for a fleeting moment there he thought he was a hero.

Ali Dia and Godfrey Odebo can be chalked up as honest mistakes. They do happen, even to the best. Alex Ferguson is happy to concede that Patrice Evra used to mock him for ever signing William Prunier for a start, and he's a man who might slot easily into a Worst Foreign Imports XI should we be cruel enough to jot one down.[97] Other notable failures include Frank Pingel at Newcastle, a man so bad that a precocious young Lee Clark refused to clean his boots anymore, because he was better than him;[98] Julien Brellier at Norwich who kept taking other options instead of pinging 25-yard balls out wide to Craig Bellamy because he told him 'I can't kick it that far'; and Milton Núñez, who Peter Reid spent £1.5m on at Sunderland before panicking on first sight that 'that's not the Milton Núñez I saw on the DVD. He was white and 6ft 4! He's black and 5ft 2!' This last tale comes from Lee Clark once again, who is clearly something of an expert in underwhelming imports to the North East. He would suit a job in customs if all else fails.

Occasionally, a club gets a chance to sign a player who might be considered by some to be above their level, and that always raises questions. Well, one question really – 'what's wrong with

---

97 Of course, you are. You're probably writing one already. And you might even have put another Fergie signing, Massimo Taibi, in goal.

98 A repentant Clark says of Pingel, 'Because he was such a nice guy, he let me get away with it! Anyone else would've given me a right hook. I was out of order.'

them?' One such 'too good to be true' deal was Emile Mpenza, once considered one of Europe's most promising strikers and a Belgian international, joining Plymouth. Paul Sturrock signed him and concedes that they didn't get much for their money, apart from a cracking story about an absence from training. Mpenza cried off one day and, when Luggy questioned it, he was told that 'Emile had taken Viagra the previous night and still had an erection and wouldn't be able to take part in training'. To be fair, it doesn't sound like something he would make up.

Perhaps we're being too harsh here. The previous chapter showed that some Brits struggled to fit in abroad, and it must be the same for anyone that comes here. They need all the help they can get. These days, clubs have a player liaison officer to help with everything from mortgage advice to finding your TV remote for you,[99] but it hasn't always been the case. In Alan Curbishley's *Game Changers* we hear from people from all aspects of the game and the PLO[100] he speaks to, Mark Maunders of Fulham, is very revealing. He says that Fulham have the advantage of being in London where there are all sorts of international communities to make people feel comfortable, which is an interesting point. He remembers signing Seol ki-Hyeon from Wolves and the local Korean population of New Malden being a real selling point for him. Evidently, he was already travelling down to buy his food there when he was at Reading and Wolves, so he jumped at the chance to join Fulham. That's not a funny story, but it's a nice one. Sure enough, when Seol eventually left south-west London, he moved back to Korea, where I sincerely hope his shopping was cheaper.

Maunders says it is within his remit to help a player 'find a house, find a car, get a bank account, sort out a mobile and maybe

---

99   It's down there between the sofa cushions. It's always between the sofa cushions. You're welcome.

100   That's player liaison officer not Palestine Liberation Organization. I said PLO to be quick, but now I've had to explain it down here, I wish I hadn't bothered.

look for schools for his kids', which is all a far cry from Ivan Golac joining Southampton from Partizan Belgrade in 1978. All he and Mrs Golac had to help them was Alan Ball's wife Lesley 'taking them to the butcher's shop and making mooing, flapping and grunting noises to help them identify the different meats'.

I remember Golac as a decent full-back who hung around for a long while with the Saints and played many games for Lawrie McMenemy, but the gaffer clearly had his doubts about him, saying, 'You judge people in football by imagining who would leave the room first when the fire bell goes. In my list Golac would now be near the top.' I do like his confident assertion that we all judge people in football by this same specific fire bell metric. I'm not sure we ALL do, do we? Even if we did, leaving the building quickly isn't necessarily a bad thing. If he does so in an orderly fashion and doesn't use the lift, I don't see the problem.

These doubts crept in because he felt Golac exaggerated an injury once which he perceives as a general weakness in foreign players. It's a theory that Jack Charlton might also subscribe to after his own experience with Ante Mirocevic at Sheffield Wednesday. Jack grumbles that the Yugoslav would 'turn up for training with gloves, a balaclava, two shirts, two sweaters and a tracksuit', and once refused to run through a frozen river when asked to do so. Honestly, some of these guys just don't want to fit in, or freeze to death, do they? On a similar theme, Rodney Marsh once went looking for South African trialist Eddie Abrahams on a winter's day and found him 'sitting, shrivelled up, arms wrapped round his body' in a 'drying oven'. Now then, I don't quite know what a drying oven is, and whether it's more like a dryer or an oven, but either way it sounds nice and warm, so good on Eddie.

Fitting in for Jan Mølby at Liverpool meant hitting the bar, of course. Doing their best to put Jan at his ease, Paul Walsh and John Wark offered him a drink when he greeted them. Mølby remembers that Wark 'appeared most upset when I asked for an orange juice and lemonade. He immediately ordered me a pint of lager instead. There was absolutely no point in asking him was there? Just get it down you.[101]

If it's not John Wark forcing lager down your throat, you've got to contend with Alan Hansen pranking you in training. Hansen cheerfully admits to telling newcomer Ronny Rosenthal that 'any player who managed to sit on the ball on the goal-line during a practice match would be awarded three goals'. With backroom legend Ronnie Moran in charge of the session, you can imagine how well it went down when the Israeli striker took a seat and waited for his reward only to be told, 'You've been talking to the wrong people,' presumably while Ronnie turned a raging shade of purple.

Bruce Grobbelaar, who always seemed happy enough, when he wasn't slapping Steve McManaman, found a bit of a hostile environment when he first arrived. After an aborted trial with West Brom for which Baggies boss Ron Atkinson 'never refunded the money for my air ticket!' Grobbelaar became a superstar on Merseyside, but he wasn't popular with everyone. He received letters from an elderly supporter who cheerily told him that 'if Tommy Smith had still been captain he would have already broken my legs three times. That was one of the more pleasant letters.' We saw earlier how Smith felt that these foreign types might need to get used to being tackled by him, but surely even he would have drawn the line at his own goalkeeper.

Another imported Anfield keeper, Pepe Reina, had a bigger and better support group during his time at Liverpool. He lived with Maxi Rodriguez, Luis Suárez, Martin Škrtel and Fabio Aurelio as neighbours. I know that you're already wondering which one you would go to if you found yourself short of milk, sugar or tea bags, and the correct answer is … 'Usually I go to Maxi. He never

---

101 Let's not forget that John Wark's favourite song is 'I Am What I Am'. What happened to letting Jan Mølby be what he is and have an orange juice?

FINAL THIRD

seems to run out of anything,' so now you know. You might need to whisper it, but it seems that it really was one big happy family round there, a regular Ramsey Street, with Reina thinking nothing of extending the hand of friendship across Stanley Park to the likes of Mikel Arteta, Tim Cahill and James Beattie as well. Whether Maxi was quite so accommodating when the Everton lads came knocking for a cup of semi-skimmed isn't known, but for the sake of a peaceful neighbourhood, let's hope so.

In addition to this community of Liverpool players from abroad, Luis Suárez could also count on the very progressive Glen Johnson, who he says is 'not your typical Englishman. He understands the Spanish and the Latin Americans, the way they are, the jokes we tell, the sense of humour, the character.' Johnson speaks Spanish and Suárez says that his children do too. Maybe Glen fancied a move to Spain himself at some point, or maybe he was just a nice guy 'always looking to improve', but either way it's nice to know that he was a great comfort to the Spanish lads for making the effort.

Shay Given says that Peruvian Nobby Solano picked the language up quickly and became 'a Geordie within about 10 days' when he joined Newcastle, and that he would always 'bring this trumpet with him everywhere' which is always going to ingratiate yourself with people – but not everyone settles so quickly without help. Unfortunately for Newcastle's Brazilian striker Mirandinha, he was given Gazza to help him with his English. Lee Clark, who would have been an apprentice at the time, remembers Mirandinha, under the influence of Gazza, rubbing his belly after a game and telling manager Willie McFaul, 'Mr Willie, I am fucking starving. Can I have fish and chips?' There was plenty of other filth being taught too with 'Wednesday' becoming 'Wankday' and 'can I have a coffee' becoming 'fuck off', which, in fairness, isn't far off. Especially if you want four of them.

The language barrier can be just as difficult for coaching staff. We all fondly remember Marcelo Bielsa's little mate helping him through his *Match of the Day* interviews, but it wasn't always such a formal arrangement. Graeme Le Saux remembers that in the early days of Claudio Ranieri's time at Chelsea, his English wasn't great, and he had to rely on Gus Poyet to be his translator: 'Gus would be in his kit at half-time, standing by the manager next to the board explaining what Ranieri was saying. When Ranieri started leaving him out of the team, Gus told him he could stick his translating service up his backside.' Was this in English, Spanish or Italian? Possibly all three if he felt strongly enough.

Poyet wasn't the only Chelsea player that Ranieri upset. Jimmy Floyd Hasselbaink claims that the Tinkerman tinkered with the pre-match routine by banning music in the dressing room and insisting on calm and quiet before a match. The strict teacher vibe continued on to the team coach where Jimmy sat at the back with the cool kids, away from the gaze of Claudio, but 'if we were laughing a little too loudly, Ranieri would turn around and look at us scornfully'. Honestly, he gave us such a look.

Over at Spurs, Ledley King says that Juande Ramos made the bus sad by banning sweets. The first journey after Harry Redknapp took over and reinstated the Haribo Tangfastics must have been wild. King says, 'Someone opened up their bag and put a pile of sweets on the coach table,' and with players diving face first into a mound of sherbet like a kind of sugary 'Scarface' he confirms that 'we felt that we could be ourselves again'. Blimey, they really liked those sweets. Evidently, Ramos felt that the Strawberry Laces were part of a bigger problem because, when he arrived, he told the whole squad they were overweight and 'made us feel as if we were fat English yobs eating chips and drinking beer all day'. Ramos introduced a new regime to get the weight off, but King sticks up for those hefty British boys, saying that it's different to Spain: 'You're not playing in the sun, and you need a bit of meat on your bones.' Meat on your bones, presumably added by eating a bus full of Fizzy Cola Bottles.

When Marco Negri came to Rangers from Italy, he was also slightly taken aback by the difference in refuelling methods. While he says that the Italian footballer 'follows a strict diet of strong doses of carbohydrates and proteins' he was stunned to find his Scottish counterparts 'scooping fried eggs, beans, toast soaked in butter, chicken and a couple of forkfuls of spaghetti into their mouths. And they were all together on the same plate!' There are some carbohydrates and proteins in amongst that lot, surely.

Robert Huth was another who was worried about the fitness of his team when he arrived at Stoke. Anxious that bluff old traditionalist Tony Pulis was concentrating too much on team shape and chucking the ball as far as you can instead of fitness, Huth took it upon himself to cycle 40 miles into training from Hale to Stoke every day. Peter Crouch says, 'I shall never forget him swooping into the car park on his carbon-fibre racer. Hugely impressive.'

After getting on his bike to Leicester to put a Premier League winners' medal in his pannier, Huth made new friends. Among them was Jamie Vardy who credits the big German with a dry sense of humour and 'this strange knack of rarely saying "yes" to a question. Instead, he'll say something like, "Does Rambo carry a knife?"' I haven't heard that one. Pope in the woods, by all means, but not this Rambo one.

Other characters that the British game has been blessed with include Sandro, who, according to Peter Crouch, sound-proofed his entire house, so that he 'could party later, longer and louder' (well those darts nights can get rowdy), and Tugay, who smoked so much, so Robbie Savage says, that you might even glance around on the training ground 'and he would have one on the go'; and Maurizio Gaudino, who Brian Horton says that Man City were able to sign because 'he had been implicated in a stolen car racket'. However, one that made a genuinely lasting impression on all who saw him, played with him, or partied with him, was Tino Asprilla at Newcastle.

Asprilla was a Colombian striker who briefly lit up St James' Park in the nineties. There are a few references in the autobiographies of team-mates detailing what a good player he was – but there are significantly more talking about his love of the nightlife off the pitch. Keith Gillespie was a huge admirer of Asprilla's technique, with women that is. Not letting his limited English hold him back, he would 'just say to the girl "You come home with me, yes?" and, often, it worked'. Lee Clark remembers knocking for Tino to come out one Sunday and finding him lounging in his bedroom and urging them to grab a drink from his 'enormous fridge in his en-suite full of beer', while his dad played bongos in the living room.

On a night out Clark says that Asprilla would secrete a bottle of tequila inside his jacket pocket and 'take sneaky swigs'. When Clark got to taste it, he says, 'It was like rocket fuel, about 90 per cent proof and he'd be necking it like pop!' The Colombian's commitment to having a good time in Newcastle was clearly impressive, with Shay Given in awe of his party policy: 'He would just rent houses, enjoy himself, then lock up and move somewhere else when the mess inside became too bad to handle.' That is certainly one way to live your life.

When Asprilla arrived at Newcastle, he had been part of a very exciting Parma side, was a superstar, and quite a coup for Kevin Keegan. It was an exciting time for English football with new stars arriving on practically every flight. This does lead to the odd claim of 'I nearly signed …' though. Some of which seem legit, while others need to be taken with a pinch of salt. Here are a few of the 'could have beens' – make your own judgement on how likely they were, or just shut your eyes and try to imagine them in the shirt.

ROBERTO CARLOS – MIDDLESBROUGH

Bryan Robson says that when he signed Juninho for Middlesbrough, he also asked the agent about Roberto Carlos but was told that they had just missed him as he had signed for Inter. Given what Middlesbrough were up to at the time, this one seems plausible. He also says that when they came back from a meeting with Juventus with cult hero Fabrizio Ravanelli in tow, they had originally gone to talk about Gianluca Vialli.

Sometimes it's important to improvise when you're out shopping isn't it?

ZLATAN IBRAHIMOVIĆ – SUNDERLAND

Matt Piper tells us that the summer he signed for Sunderland, 'I know Peter Reid tried hard to get a rising Ajax striker called Zlatan Ibrahimović before I came in.' Reidy may have tried, but I would say that once Zlatan was at Ajax he was already looking towards bigger and better things. Although he doesn't talk directly about Sunderland, the Swedish egomaniac does say he was told on one occasion, by his agent, that Southampton were interested, only to react with, 'What the fuck! Southampton! Is that my level?' Southampton! Unless it's the Isle of Wight ferry he particularly objects to, or he'd heard about that Ali Dia business, I think this rather suggests that Sunderland wouldn't have been his dream move either.

LUÍS FIGO – MAN CITY

In recent times we're more than used to oil-rich City routinely signing the likes of Erling Haaland and pretty much whoever they want to sign, but back in 1994 it was all a bit Carl Griffiths. However, Brian Horton brings us news that, on the say so of Malcolm Allison, new chairman Francis Lee tried to sign Luís Figo from Sporting Lisbon. Now Figo wasn't quite the superstar he later became, but he was a very promising rising star, so how likely does it seem that he would have come to Maine Road? A year later he signed for Barcelona, but it could all have been so different if this is to be believed.

EDINSON CAVANI – HULL

Cavani eventually did come to the Premier League, of course, coming to Manchester United in his later years to show us all that he still had it. However, back in 2009, Hull tried their luck at getting their hands on a bit of prime Cavani. Brian Horton (again) says that he 'nearly came' and that the club offered Palermo £2.5m for him, which doesn't seem like it would have been enough. Hull signed Jan Vennegoor of Hesselink on a free instead. Which would at least have earned them more in shirt sales if they charged for printing by the letter.

One superstar who did make an unlikely cameo in the English game was George Weah. The man who went on to become president of Liberia, (and might well be the most famous person ever to come from Liberia, apart from that girl that Michael Jackson sang about, or Ali Dia), decided to dip a toe into the Premier League after scoring all the goals for Milan. Initially he had a brief spell with Chelsea, which seemed a bit more in keeping with what was going on at Stamford Bridge back then. However, he then had a Man City cameo, which left an impression on those he left behind. As Weah was leaving, Shaun Goater caught up with him and 'asked whether he had any boots or something to keep as a memento. I knew he had about ten pairs, but he said he didn't have anything left – the lads had cleared his locker out!' Stand easy everyone, I'm almost certain this was done from love and affection for a legend of the game, rather than an act of spite. And it's lovely that even a City hero like Goater is in awe of having such a great player alongside him.

Weah's last day at City was very different to Karel Poborský's up the road at United. Having signed for Benfica, 'all the lads were moaning that he hadn't bothered to say goodbye', according to Gary Neville's season diary; however, the entry for the next day brings a small tear to the eye, as Karel came in to say goodbye after all, only to find that 'the first team had been given the day off so only the injured players, me Roy, Denis and Maysie, were in. Karel was disappointed, but everyone there shook his hand and wished him well.' It's got a whiff of *The Littlest Hobo* about it, this, and should probably be accompanied by the end title theme from that most heartbreaking of shows.

What have we learned from all of this? While this chapter has obviously focused on the odd stories and occasionally the less successful imports, I'd like to think that we can all agree that the arrival of players from abroad has been a good thing. People may grumble about young homegrown kids getting a chance but look at the academies now and you'll see that even they are fairly multi-national. If kids are good enough, they will make it, wherever they're from. In my view, the influx of great players from overseas will have improved those fine young British boys that Graeme Souness likes so much, as they get to play alongside them. Phil Foden might agree.

Rob Lee has a very clear idea about the whole 'playing abroad' situation. He says that 'all the best foreign players want to come and play here' because it's the best league in the world, while any British players that have gone to play abroad are 'all motivated by money'. Lee is pretty sure about all of this, though he seems so close to an epiphany about the money thing and may even have got there by now.

One unexpected side effect of the rise in the number of foreign players in English dressing rooms is a slight alteration to the actual smell of football. That's right. I told you that Mick Rathbone's book is called *The Smell of Football* and, though you might think he is talking figuratively, at times he is concerned with the actual smell of football – you know, Deep Heat, Brut, that kind of thing. However, Rathbone says, 'The foreigners imported their own exotic aromas to add to the traditional heady mix. Spices from deepest Africa, herbal rubs from the southern Mediterranean and manly musks from our former colonies. All welcome, all embraced.' Admit it, you'd never thought about the exotic smells before, had you?

10.

Board Games

'Strutting in the Super-Glory Zone'

PAUL PARKER once deliberately whacked a golf ball straight into Jimmy Hill's house. That's your headline for this chapter. Ever since I read about the incident, I've been bursting to tell you about it and here is as good a place as any. This chapter examines The Board, that amorphous mass of largely faceless people that own or run your football club and make the decisions, hand out the transfer war chests, tighten the purse strings, issue dreaded votes of confidence and all sorts of other clichés. I will write thousands of words about the symbiotic relationship between players and those folk that sit above them like Roman emperors at the Colosseum with their futures in their hands, but almost nothing will distil the fragile nature of that relationship into one handy image quite like an angry little Paul Parker walloping a golf ball through Jimmy's French windows.

The incident came about when Hill was chairman of Fulham and Parker was both captain and the most promising player at the club. He was also the most viable asset and looking for a move. Obviously, there are two ways to look at that from Jimmy's perspective; either Parker is most likely to bring some much-needed money into the club or he's a potential traitor to the noble Fulham cause. Whatever Jim's innermost thoughts at the time, it's clear that Parker was getting a bad vibe from him. Things came to a head when Jimmy invited the whole Fulham squad down to his Brighton home for the day for a bit of a do, in what Parker calls 'a typically flamboyant gesture' through gritted teeth. Activities involved music, listening to Jimmy going on about stuff and helping yourself to the golf practice netting he had at the end of the garden.

The vol-au-vents were flowing as Jimmy schmoozed around the place, but Parker says that 'he spoke to every member of the staff except me, the club captain. I don't know why he was so rude.' Parker assumes that it was because he was about to be sold and then casually drops the bombshell that 'in a fit of pique, I drove a golf ball the other way through his patio window'. And that's as much as he mentions it. As if it were a tiny incident, but this must have caused quite a scene – he could have killed someone, or at least left someone with a cartoon bump on their head as they came out to shake an angry fist at him. Relations didn't improve between the two and Parker was soon off to QPR, ironically little more than a spectacularly well hit drive away up the road from Fulham.

Chairman is, of course, just one of Jimmy Hill's many football hats, but it's one he wore very jauntily, becoming one of the early celebrity chairmen back in the days before it all changed upstairs. These days we're used to the elite clubs in the land being run by oligarchs and representatives from oil-rich countries with questionable human rights records. Supporters are regularly having to check their moral compass to see if they're okay with the owners of their club peddling sweat shop clothing, dildos, porn, and gambling or representing oppressive regimes. Back in the day it was all local business owners, and your only concern was the possibility of an unscrupulous butcher or shifty car dealer worming their way into owning a few shares.

We wouldn't let just anybody look after our family. We wouldn't let just anybody look after our car. Some wouldn't even let just anybody look after their pint while they nipped to the pub toilet. And yet, all football fans are saddled with the situation where they have to let just anybody, and I mean anybody, look after the love of our lives – the football club. Teddy Sheringham warns that people 'become directors of football clubs as a way of fulfilling their own secret dreams through others', and maybe there's some truth in that. He feels that their love of the game blinds them and affects their usual judgement, saying 'most of them, probably, are successful in their business lives, and yet they routinely make the sort of decisions in the club boardroom that would result in a lynch mob being raised by shareholders of their companies'. Dennis Tueart echoes the sentiment, confirming that 'too many directors believe themselves to be the heroes of the show'. Alex Stepney refers to directors as 'faceless amateurs', Jimmy Greaves quotes Shakespeare in saying, 'There's little choice in rotten apples,' when it comes to the board, and Viv Anderson claims that 'in my experience, most chairmen hate their manager. The feeling is generally mutual.' Although it's possible that Viv's statement is clouded by the time he spent playing for Brian Clough. Cloughie always insisted that he and his brave boys travelled on a separate coach from the committee members at Forest. Steve Hodge recalls one occasion when they pulled out of the City Ground car park and Clough instructed his players to get up and give the executive bus a wave through the windows, saying, 'Keep smiling while they have their smoked salmon dinners. Keep smiling at the shithouses, every last one of them!' The disparity is echoed by Trevor Ford who complains that 'directors' wives are entertained to gin-and-limes in the Boardroom after the game; and poor Soccer wives are mighty lucky to get a cup of tea'.[102]

Malcolm Allison is someone who knows all about directors' wives and shares enough gossip for a Jackie Collins novel on the subject. He claims that 'in my time I have had to take evasive action

---

102 For the record, if you're getting them in, I'd rather have a brew.

against the wives of some rich and powerful football directors', before going into detail about times he did indeed take evasive action: 'She said that if I made love to her I could forget about my money worries,' and another time in which he didn't exactly take evasive action. Without naming any names again (the spoilsport), he recounts being pursued by the wife of a different director at a different club to the woman who suggested he prostitute himself. This time he admits, 'I buckled. I spent an afternoon at her girl friend's cottage. We made love. I wasn't pleased with myself, I sensed that I was letting myself in for some unnecessary trouble. But it was a diverting way to spend the afternoon.' Well, what else are you supposed to do when there's no game on?

It seems that Big Mal was catnip to the bored wives of any number of football directors but, when he wasn't beating them off with a City stick, he found time to pontificate about the 'pettiness' of their husbands, saying that the boardroom became 'a playground for their second childhood', and he may have been right. Simon Jordan, who happily concedes that he only got involved initially with Crystal Palace because of their 'extremely pretty marketing manager', has a book full of tales of one-upmanship and name-calling. He remembers Freddy Shepherd and Douglas Hall slagging off Roman Abramovich within earshot at a Newcastle vs Chelsea game, oblivious to the fact that he spoke English and could understand them, as well as Charlton rival Richard Murray telling him, 'Enjoy the Championship, tosser!' as Palace got relegated. And that was before their feud escalated over Charlton's appointment of Iain Dowie.[103] Honestly, with the way some of them behave, it's only a matter of time before one director is caught chalking a cock and balls on to the back of another's suit.

These squabbles between chairmen are often about getting a new manager in. As soon as one is nearing the exit door, the search

---

103 It's sobering to remember that there was once a time when people fought bitterly for the services of Iain Dowie. Football clubs, of course, not modelling agencies.

is surely already on for the next one. And if they covet another team's gaffer, it can cause friction. Ron Atkinson, who knows a thing or two about chairmen, says, 'I'm not going to deceive the world that the tapping routine has not gone on in my case' which is an elaborate way of saying that he has indeed been tapped up. Although he's coy about it here, he's not shy of naming names elsewhere, putting Franny Lee firmly in the frame. Big Ron claims that Little Franny wanted him at Man City when he took over, presumably offering a king's ransom and all the toilet roll he could use to leave Coventry and join him. When Ron said he couldn't do it to his Highfield Road chairman Bryan Richardson as he had only just started there, he claims that Lee told him it was a waste, 'like Sinatra playing Wigan Pier', which is a line that will have done Ron's already rampant ego no harm at all.

Francis Lee is, of course, that rare example of an actual player that went on to become a chairman. We all know his background – City legend, had that hilarious fight with Norman Hunter at Derby, went off to make a fortune in the bum wad game, and arrived triumphantly in the City directors' box;[104] but who are those others up there in the good seats? Gorging on chicken goujons and free booze in the lounge before sticking a head out to see what effect their money and decision-making, for good or ill, has had on the lives of thousands in the stands. Let's imagine them all sat around one huge boardroom table as we go around and meet some of the noteworthy members of the great big board in the sky. Just to clarify, several of these people are still alive; I just like to imagine it in the sky.

---

104 Before we get all misty-eyed about him though, let's remember that Brian Horton found out that he had sacked him from City when he picked up a newspaper and read it while he was at the League Managers' Association annual dinner in St Albans. Which must have been awkward as presumably he was no longer allowed in.

Bobby Charlton – Manchester United

While never taking the big chair at Manchester United, Sir Bobby Charlton is another former club legend who has enjoyed more than the odd tray of expensive sandwiches in the boardroom. He was a close confidante and supporter of Sir Alex Ferguson but was less popular with his predecessor. Ron 'Big Ron' Atkinson describes Bobby as 'hardly a soulmate' and 'a relentless boardroom adversary', painting him as a kind of malevolent figure, working in the shadows and hinting that he was partly responsible for his sacking. If you close your eyes and think of it, it is difficult to see them getting along famously, and so it proved.

Ron remembers a disagreement with Charlton over the potential signing of Terry Butcher. Atkinson wanted Butcher when he eventually ended up going to Rangers. In Charlton's considered opinion, Butcher wasn't better than United already had at centre-back (Paul McGrath and Kevin Moran, so he may have had a point), while Atkinson felt that anyone in their right mind would want England's first choice.

Atkinson's books are full of *esprit de l'escalier* and situations he always got the better of. In this case, in a comment that he claims 'ricocheted around the room like a sniper's bullet', he told Bobby in a crowded boardroom that Butcher might just have been good enough 'to have kept Preston up when you were briefly there as manager'. Atkinson feigns contrition at his words, but he is clearly very proud of his burn. However, given that the England stalwart had just been relegated with Ipswich that very summer, that wasn't necessarily a (Shay) given, and ignores the fact that Butcher would have been 15 when Bobby managed Preston to relegation in 1974, so he may not have done the business there either. I'm not sure this is the burn Ron thinks it is. Besides which, are snipers' bullets famous for ricocheting around a place? Surely the good ones get it in first time.

What we can say for certainty about Bobby, is that he has a bit of pull. Ryan Giggs remembers sitting next to him at an away

BOARD GAMES

match v Fenerbahçe, and the home PA system was pumping in loud music just in case the atmosphere wasn't quite intimidating enough. It was all a bit loud for Charlton and he managed to get them to switch it off. Whether he spoke Turkish, or simply banged on the wall or ceiling with a broom handle isn't clear, but either way he got what he wanted. And in a stadium containing thousands of people at fever pitch, that's some clout.

Michael Knighton – Manchester United

It seems that whatever Bobby Charlton says goes in terms of stadium etiquette. Not content with getting the music changed in Turkey, he also ruled the roost at Wembley, which he may have considered his own stomping ground, as our next contender found out.

Michael Knighton had a much-coveted access-all-areas pass for the 1990 FA Cup Final against Crystal Palace and fancied a stroll on the pitch, as we all would. Unfortunately, he bumped into Bobby, who had clearly appointed himself as some sort of guardian of the hallowed turf. He told Knighton that it wasn't for the likes of him but rather it was 'reserved, Michael, for people like me, players and ex-players'. This is patently nonsense, as I've seen Prince William, Bruce Forsyth, Ian Beale from *EastEnders*, at least one referee per final and loads of those soldiers in daft hats on there before now. Confronted with this scenario, I like to think I'd have tried to dart round him and do a quick knee slide, but Knighton accepted Charlton's word, perhaps feeling that he had made a tit of himself on a pitch once before.

In his whirlwind attempt to buy United, he ruffled Martin Edwards' feathers and convinced him that he had the plan[105] and the means to have the club 'strutting in the super-glory zone', which, admittedly, sounds brilliant. However, the absolute highlight of his

---

105 His blueprint for Manchester United's world domination is included as an appendix in his book, in case you're interested in how things could have gone. As if they could have gone much better than they did in the nineties anyway.

223

association with Manchester United was the bet which he almost put on himself to get picked for United and play in a cup final. He got as far as being quoted odds of 100,000-1 and genuinely thinks that 'Fergie would have agreed if he had been told the proceeds were all going to charity'. Agree to disagree, Michael. Agree to disagree.

Thaksin Shinawatra – Man City

The big money before the BIG MONEY at Man City, Thaksin was a big fan of karaoke and drowned out accusations of human rights abuses in his role as prime minister of Thailand by singing 'Should I Stay or Should I Go' at manager Sven-Göran Eriksson on a night out in Bangkok once. His insistence on drinking tequila may have made the evening slightly less awkward. Sven even says, 'Thaksin was a good singer. He fancied himself as Frank Sinatra.' You know, Frank Sinatra from Wigan Pier.

Jimmy Hill – Coventry, Fulham, Charlton

Jimmy Hill gains entry to the literary boardroom by virtue of his spells among the suits at Coventry City, Fulham and Charlton, but, frankly, he could have fitted in anywhere. The man is a polymath who in his time has been a player, a manager, an owner, a chairman, a director, a TV pundit, a TV presenter, a linesman and a PFA chairman. He came up with the idea of three points for a win, wrote club songs for both Coventry and Arsenal, designed club shirts to incorporate sponsorship (even wanting to change Coventry City to Coventry Talbot at one stage), ran a chimney sweeping business (see False '9 to 5' chapter), was employed as a technical advisor on a television drama, became the most unpopular man in Scotland since the Duke of Cumberland, took on a property consultancy, led an FA tour to the West Indies and a less right-on tour to South Africa, developed the Tinder app and appeared third on the bill at Live Aid. Now I might have made a couple of those up, which is entirely fitting as I'm talking about a man whose chin has become synonymous with telling whoppers, but even if you take those ones out it's been a busy old life.

Jimmy does confess to being a little too busy while at Fulham, involving himself in team affairs and being so annoyed by a bad first half against Orient under Don Mackay that he 'went into the dressing-room, asked Don to take a back seat and then extracted honest answers from miserable players', which is not on, miserable or otherwise. I can't see how much Jimmy turning up for a motivational chinwag would have cheered them up. Unless he'd written another one of his songs.

At Coventry, Hill always had one eye on innovation, and one of his ideas was to release a massive firework after each goal 'which would explode high in the sky and let the whole city know that Coventry had scored'.[106] His vision was thwarted because the local council wouldn't let him release a big enough firework to be seen in daylight: 'Such a device was contained in something which looked like half a coconut shell and a spent firework like that falling from the sky would clearly do some damage.' Oh okay, let's leave it then. You can't have people finding out that Coventry have scored because Uncle Harry's been knocked out by a falling coconut while mowing the lawn. Also, this would be impossible to do in the age of VAR. With decisions being reviewed left, right and centre, there's a danger of releasing your firework too early. See, VAR and falling coconuts ruin everything – I've always said so.

Despite everybody loving fireworks, Jimmy was not universally popular. Steve Hunt is very critical of him for announcing over the PA system on a matchday that 'it took our board only 20 seconds today to reject unanimously Steve Hunt's request for a transfer. He must honour his contract,' which stitched him up a bit. There's also that Coventry name proposal, and don't even mention his name around Sunderland fans.

---

106 Some readers might remember that Bobby Gould's grandad had a pigeon-based system to do the same job.

In 1977, Sunderland were in the relegation mire along with Hill's Coventry who were hosting Bristol City. If Sunderland lost, then a draw at Highfield Road kept both Coventry and Bristol up. The kick-off was delayed at Coventry to get the crowd in, which Hill insists was entirely the referee's decision; however, that's not the worst bit. With the Sunderland match finishing early in defeat for the Mackems and Coventry and Bristol drawing 2-2, Jimmy took 'action in pressing the Radio Sky Blues' host to deliver the vital result to the whole stadium'. Jimmy Hill claims that the players already knew the score from the crowd and had already slowed down accordingly; Jimmy Hill claims that it was Radio Sky Blue policy to broadcast 'relevant football news during matches'; Jimmy Hill says he feels no guilt 'whatsoever either legal or moral'; Jimmy Hill gets drunk on Sunderland tears. You be the judge, but please do remember what I said earlier about what Jimmy Hill is synonymous with.

Sam Hammam – Wimbledon

Sam Hammam was so much more than just a spell-checker's nightmare. He is the man who bankrolled the Wimbledon self-styled Crazy Gang as they hoofed their way up the leagues and into our hearts. They lived the dream when they won the FA Cup in 1988, and within a few days Hammam decided to cash in and announce to the press that every single player was up for sale – the old romantic. Maybe Sam couldn't be blamed, as money had always been tight. Dave Bassett, who put in most of the hard yards for several years before Bobby Gould stole his cup final thunder, remembers that smooth-talking Sam had at one time persuaded him to 'put my house up as a guarantee for a bank loan of £100,000' to put some funds into the club. Bassett says that 'Sam seemed quite happy to sit back and let me take the risk', Mrs Bassett less so. Although he rather cryptically says, 'If you really want to know the details of her reaction and what she said to me, I'll have to send them to you – preferably in a plain brown envelope.' Now I know this shouldn't be the thing to get hung up on here, but what on earth does he mean? Just put it in the book, or don't, Dave. Is he suggesting that every utterance was so filthy that it could only be written down and sealed away? Confusing.

Where was I? Sam Hammam, right? Between getting you in debt, insisting on being able to change your team line-up an hour before kick-off and the ever-present fear of the sack, Hammam must have been a nightmare to be a manager under, but the players seemed to love him. Cup final hero Dave Beasant remembers many pleasant nights out on the chairman's expenses as well as antics down at the training ground. Sam would evidently come down to the pitches in his suit and slippy shoes[107] and try to have a kickabout or take some penalties against Beasant for a cash bet.

Beasant also says he used to insist on races to one end of the pitch, with the players starting at the other goal line and himself starting on halfway. Wally Downes was allowed to start on the 18-yard box but that might be another story. Beasant, somewhat reassuringly, says that players 'would pass the pair of them with ease but what Sam didn't realise was that while his back was turned we were creeping forward. He would be sliding all over the place as we ate up the ground in our boots.' You would like to think there was no need to cheat but there we are. Bobby Gould recalls one such race in which Hammam put up £3,000 in spending money for a day at the races if anyone beat him, which they did. Gould remembers, 'He had a huge start but Terry Phelan pissed it, so did Keith Curle and the players were whooping around as they got their hands on their betting money.' A small part of me hopes he is misremembering this and that Curle finished in front of Phelan, because a couple of years later Keith Curle took part in the Rumbelows Sprint Challenge[108] and Phelan didn't, and I want

---

107 Not another one.
108 Look it up kids and imagine it now. Pick your own winners.

with all my heart to believe that everyone took that as seriously as it deserved.

Jack Walker – Blackburn Rovers

Jack Walker lived the dream. With a football landscape strewn with club owners with little or no previous attachment to a club, Walker represents a bygone age. A boyhood Rovers fan, he made a fortune in steel and poured it into his football club, turning them into what, in hindsight, looks like some modestly priced champions, but at the time they were splashing the cash all over the place on global superstars like Paul Warhurst. Just in case you were looking for his story to be any more wholesome, Graeme Le Saux reveals that Jack used to play 'Penny Up the Wall' with his players, 'where you bounce a penny against a wall and the person who gets the penny to stay closest to the wall wins. Jack was unbelievable at that game. He used to play it with all the lads and he always won.' A dedicated player, it is estimated (by me) that up to £117m of Jack Walker's £300m was earned through his penny-up-the-wall winnings.

George Reynolds – Darlington

George Reynolds is someone who might euphemistically be called a 'colourful character' and his book *My Wicked Life* is a wild ride, taking in impoverished childhood, harsh Catholic schooling, the Merchant Navy, safe-cracking, peanut scams, ice cream wars and bare-knuckle fighting, before he got anywhere near Darlo. It really is worth a read. He also found time to own a nightclub, be a neighbour to both Baby and Sporty Spice and have a contract taken out on his life. He must have been exhausted.

Reynolds was drawn into Darlington when he tried to buy a car from a local businessman who got him interested in buying the club instead. The club was looking for a saviour, having had, in the words of Reynolds, 'more ups and downs than a tart's knickers during its 116-year history'. George was greeted with a standing ovation when he first set foot on the pitch, but before long there were recriminations and public meetings at which his wife took centre stage to defend her husband and accuse the players of not trying.

Reynolds complains bitterly that his criminal past was constantly referred to in the press, saying that stories 'always referred to my safe-cracking days' rather than just as a legitimate chairman. It's a fair point he makes. If we believe in justice and our prison system, and the idea of rehabilitation and second chances, then why should George Reynolds forever be reminded of his criminal past? What's that you say? He posed with a prison ball and chain in both the team photo and his wedding pictures. As you were.

Peter Stroud – Chelmsford City

Stroud must have made sure he had the golf clubs firmly under lock and key in the shed before offering the Chelmsford City job to Paul Parker when his top-level playing career was at an end. Parker was in two minds about taking the job until Stroud used the tried and trusted negotiating tool of telling him, 'If you don't take it, I will see you as a s**t-out merchant,' and before he knew it, Bob was his uncle, Fanny was his aunt and bad boy of golf Paul Parker was his manager. He's pretty much dared him to take the job there.

Alderman Harry Booth – Stoke City

Described by Stanley Matthews as 'a tactful chairman' who didn't exactly rule with a rod of iron, the Alderman once caught two young players smoking cigarettes at the ground. Instead of reprimanding them, Stan recalls him producing two cigars from his pocket and gently suggesting that he would appreciate it if they smoked them away from the ground. Apparently one of his favoured sayings was 'let's not use a guillotine to cure dandruff' and here he is putting the gentle approach into practice.

Mohamed Al-Fayed – Fulham

Al-Fayed certainly brought a bit of glamour to the banks of the Thames during his spell in charge of Fulham, with a splash of showbiz and a dash of the daft thrown in. Lee Clark remembers being lavished with gifts from Harrods including a gold bullion bar made of Belgian chocolate after every home game, which is nice. He also recalls conducting his medical in Harrods and it being interrupted by an appearance from Sophia Loren, brought in by the chairman to show his athlete off to.[109] If you think that's playing fast and loose with his Harrods brand, he also asked Chris Kamara to be 'the media face of the Harrods business empire, and also director of football at Fulham FC!'. Now we all know that both would have been interesting, had they come to pass, but I think Harrods has the edge. You can see an advert involving his 'Unbelievable' catchphrase in there somewhere. Unbelievable prices can mean high as well as low, right?

Well, we've got this far without talking about that Michael Jackson statue, but we can't really put it off any longer. It's been there, looming over us the whole time, hasn't it? Al-Fayed was, of course, great friends with Jackson,[110] and invited the singer along to a game at Craven Cottage once. I mean, he was probably going anyway, but the chairman offered him the guest of honour treatment. Lee Clark remembers rose petals being strewn in front of the 'Speed Demon' star's feet 'exactly like *Coming to America*', and the chairman saying, 'Hide your cocks lads, Michael's coming,' which seems a little less 'guest of honour' to my untrained ear. Geri Halliwell also paid a visit but presumably didn't make as big an impact as Jacko, as she didn't warrant an awful statue outside the ground. Which is a shame for her, and Fulham.

---

109 Unless he wanted a second medical opinion from her as she sang on the very dodgy 'Goodness, Gracious Me' with Peter Sellers.

110 Those two were also friends with Uri Geller and David Blaine, which could have produced one or two cracking stag dos.

Jim Gregory – QPR

You know that things are lively when you need to deny allegations that your chairman was the mastermind behind the Great Train Robbery, as Terry Venables does. We can be pretty sure that he wasn't, but El Tel does concede that Gregory once flattened a journalist at the Football Writers' Awards do, so he wasn't exactly an angel. Stan Bowles loved him though: 'He liked roguish people and I think he saw a lot of himself in me. A Jack the Lad character, he always used to come into the dressing room before a game and have a laugh with us.' So keen was he to ingratiate himself with the players that Gregory would invite them into the lounge after a game and flaunt his laddish credentials in front of his opposite number. Bowles tells us, 'We would be larking around with Jim, who would pour us champagne in front of the opposing chairman and say to us: "Don't worry about that ****!"' An absolute charmer.

Peter Storrie – Portsmouth

Close associate of Harry Redknapp, Peter Storrie is a colourful character, rubbing people up the wrong way throughout his time as some sort of chief executive at both West Ham and Portsmouth. Tony Adams claims that Storrie once tried to insist that he take Giovani dos Santos off Harry's hands at Tottenham, saying, 'I told Peter the player was not for me. Peter insisted the deal had to be done, even putting Sven-Göran Eriksson, then Mexico manager, on the phone to tell me what a good player he was.' Adams acquiesced to a bleep test for Dos Santos but when he only scored 9 compared to the 12 that Adams himself could score, he managed to stand his ground.

Adams also claims that he once got so furious with Storrie that he forgot where he was and stormed out of his own office, leaving himself stood in the corridor with nowhere to go, with Storrie presumably just as awkwardly sitting inside. I have no idea how you

John Ryan – Doncaster Rovers

We've already seen that it takes all sorts to make up our overflowing boardroom, but John Ryan might be the most unusual of all. Before he came to the rescue of Doncaster Rovers and moved them on from the chaotic regime of Ken Richardson,[111] Ryan had made his name as a Boob Job Baron. Claiming to be all about boosting the confidence of women, this feminist of sorts says, 'It's amazing what bigger breasts will do.' One customer became a poster girl for Ryan's brand and the 'Girl of the Thrillennium',[112] – Melinda Messenger. Ryan describes the former Page 3 model and television presenter as being 'armed with two impressively approved assets, courtesy of one of our clinics' (I think he means her knockers) and says that 'at one stage we were bracketed in the same sentence so often that you'd have thought something was going on – and I played along to the full'. Well, of course he did, but I don't ever remember hearing their names together.

When he wasn't selling new boobs to famous women then trying to stand near them for attention, Ryan indulged in all the usual egomaniac chairman behaviour, like registering as a player so he could get on in a Conference game towards the end of a season. Quite rightly, Ryan's disrespectful act saw him trot on and be greeted by a Hereford defender telling him, 'If you touch that f---ing ball, I'll break your f---ing leg.' Completely fair enough, I say. However, just in case the football distracts you from his real passion in life, Ryan artificially enhances his book by including a chapter called 'Simply the Breast', which is no more

---

111 Now Ken Richardson's is an autobiography I would have liked to have read.
112 You remember, 'Girl of the Thrillennium'. It's all any of us were talking about, right?

than a load of testimonials[113] from satisfied boob job customers like Emma Champion, who tells us, 'After the operation I was a 32C and very pleased with what I saw. My friends at the bank were very impressed.' As far as I can work out, she doesn't even work in a bank.

Peter Swales – Manchester City

Years before Man City knew the fabulous riches of Abu Dhabi, before Thaksin 'Frank Sinatra' Shinawatra, even before Franny 'Two Ply' Lee, the Maine Road roost was ruled by Peter Swales. Swales was a singular-looking man with a sort of painted Shredded Wheat hairdo that fascinated Paul Lake, who would spend time injured in the stand during the less riveting games 'gawping at the City chairman's black, matted hairdo, trying to fathom out whether or not it was a wig'. Let's not judge a man simply by his hair, though, Lake doesn't like his actions either, saying that Swales habitually ignored him throughout his horrific injury problems and refused to pay for decent medical treatment for him.

When Lake spoke to a newspaper about his situation, Swales accused him of disrespect and the pair had a flare-up, with Lake telling him, 'I've lost count of the times that you've walked past me without even a good morning or kiss my arse,' – either one would have done. Rodney Marsh is also critical of Swales, but most of the mudslinging comes from the disgruntled Lake. However, I'm inclined to believe it all because his book is so very good. Where else would you get the takeover battle between Swales and Franny 'Soft, Strong and Not Very Long' Lee being compared in detail to 'Coronation Street's classic Ken, Mike and Deirdrie love triangle'? Not enough places, by my reckoning.

---

113 Chestimonials, more like.

Ron Noades – Crystal Palace

There's probably a lot to say about Ron Noades, but even just sticking to what is revealed in the autobiographies of those that crossed his path shows him in a sufficiently poor light. Vince Hilaire remembers him signing Steve Wicks for big money who then immediately sustained a back injury after a British gymnast was brought in 'to teach us how to vault a pommel horse!' I know what you're thinking, but we haven't got time for that now. Let's just accept that it happened. This unusual injury may have been more the fault of manager Dario Gradi, but Noades certainly leaned into it, 'walking around with a badge for the last two months that Steve was out injured with "I saw Steve Wicks play – once" on it. He wore it to half a dozen home games and it didn't do much for team morale.' Poor old Steve. I'm betting he didn't even want to find out how to vault a pommel horse.

As a saving grace for Ron, Andy Woodman says that his wife, the gloriously named Novello Noades, was a 'fantastic laugh' who 'could do this trick with a sachet of sugar. She would place it on her eye and then manoeuvre it down into her mouth.' I have seen such things done with an After Eight mint, but never by a football chairman's wife. Novello did unfortunately take things too far once and lead our Queen of Hearts, Gareth Southgate, astray by getting him so drunk on tequila slammers that he got battered and 'spewed up all over Ron' in a lift. 'Jacket, shirt, tie, trousers, shoes, the lot.' Reports that Ron subsequently went around with a badge saying 'Gareth Southgate Spewed All Over Me' are sadly unconfirmed.

John Deacon – Portsmouth

To clarify, this isn't the John Deacon who played bass in Queen, this is John Deacon the Portsmouth chairman; you know, Dolly's husband. I mention Dolly because it seems that she was front and centre in the big decisions at the club. Ian St John says that the pair of them arrived at his Motherwell home in a Rolls-Royce with lots of 'exciting talk' about grand plans for the club, including money to spend and a new out-of-town stadium, and charmed him into accepting the manager's job on the south coast.

Pompey fans will already know that such promises were not kept, and Saint was left to struggle as the money dried up. The final straw for the gaffer was when he tried to sell Peter Marinello to Motherwell to raise some much-needed funds, but when he told the chairman, 'Dolly Deacon chipped in, saying, "Oh no, John, we can't sell Peter – I like Peter". Peter was a kind of Lidl George Best and popular with the ladies – and Dolly's only human. St John complains about her influence and gives it as one of the reasons he eventually walked away from the club and into the showbiz life, but the records show that Marinello did indeed get sold to Motherwell so it can't have been that much of a problem. That said, maybe Dolly, without an official role at the club, should have stuck to vibes rather than sticking her oar in. What we can conclude is that it's better to be a Novello Noades than a Dolly Deacon. If you take one thing from this book, let it be that.

Mike Bamber – Brighton

In the late seventies and early eighties, Brighton earned promotion from Third Division to the First Division, which you might think had something to do with the job done by manager Alan Mullery. It seems that wasn't entirely how it was seen within chairman Mike Bamber's inner circle. At the promotion celebrations, a friend 'stood up and called for silence. She told us that when Mike took over as chairman he said Brighton would be a top club in five years. Now he's done it.' It was greeted by cheers among the circle, as if Bamber had carried the club uphill on his own, while the players and Mullery looked on, wondering what they had been doing with themselves while Bamber's solo efforts were taking place. 'The woman nodded to the organist in the corner and started to sing her own version of the old Ritchie Valens hit "La Bamba", only she called it "Mike Bamber" and the words were all in praise of the chairman.' Alan says it was all very embarrassing as he was expecting Bamber to give credit to the players instead of lapping it up. The only shame is that Steve Winwood classic 'Valerie'[114] was yet to be released as Mullers could have fought fire with fire and got someone to sing 'Mullery' to the tune.

Robert Maxwell – Oxford United / Derby County / Thames Valley Royals (nearly)

We might not even think of Robert Maxwell as the worst Maxwell anymore, given what certain relatives have got up to, but back in his heyday before he took his fateful dip, he was an absolute rotter. Books have been written and documentaries have been made detailing his crimes and misdemeanours, so we don't need to dwell too much here – instead we can just enjoy a few of his choice moments through the eyes of the football folk who crossed his path.

Maxwell tried to sign Lee Chapman when he was looking to return from his French nightmare. Big Bob rang him and tried to charm him by insisting he could tell that he wasn't a 'typical thicky footballer' and offering him all sorts of incentives including lots of money, a BMW of his choosing and spots on MTV and in his *Sunday Mirror* Magazine for his wife, Leslie Ash, from *Quadrophenia* and *Men Behaving Badly* fame. It still didn't work, Chapman joined Nottingham Forest instead, and that's why we never saw those Leslie Ash *Sunday Mirror Magazine* features in case you were wondering.

At one point Maxwell owned both Oxford and Derby and, although he initially had his fun with Oxford, winning the Milk Cup, in later years he favoured Derby and quite happily shifted players from one to the other, such as Dean Saunders and Paul Simpson. He installed his son, Kevin, at the Manor Ground, as a

---

114 Or the Zutons / Amy Winehouse one. I don't really mind. I just want Mullery to get a song if Mike Bamber's got one.

chairman who wouldn't mind too much. Mark Lawrenson resigned because of it and Brian Horton found the going tough as well, claiming that Derby boss Arthur Cox just rang him up whenever he fancied an Oxford player, saying, 'Jim Magilton, £750,000 – and if you don't tell Kevin, I will!'[115] like a school bully threatening to nick his dinner money. It's no way to live your life.

John Cobbold – Ipswich

Kevin Beattie describes John Cobbold as 'one of the boys', saying, 'On away trips he always arranged for beer to be put on the bus,' and that 'in the summer he always wore old khaki shorts and sandals with odd socks'. This combination of beer, ill-advised summer clothes and dicking about with the players led to an incident at a party he held at his Glenham Hall home.

Cobbold, Beattie and Allan Hunter wandered the grounds to have a cigarette (yep!) and passed three donkeys. Cobbold insisted that the three of them ride a donkey each and have a race. Cobbold's donkey, perhaps picking up on a certain sense of entitlement from its rider, bolted, jumped a low wall and sent him crashing into the drum kit of the band that were providing entertainment. Obviously, if you have money, this kind of thing gets passed off as eccentric, and it wasn't even Cobbold's most notorious moment at a club gathering.

Both Beattie and John Wark relate a tale from a party thrown when Ipswich won the 1973 FA Youth Cup which clearly mortified the pair of them, as well as all the parents in attendance. Wark remembers Cobbold's speech like this: 'In his own inimitable style he congratulated the players and then virtually ordered the parents to retire immediately. His actual words were, "I want you to go to bed straight away, f*** like rabbits and make us another FA Youth Cup-winning team for about 18 years from now."' It didn't work,

---

115 It wasn't Jim Magilton every time, obviously. That would be weird. This is just illustrative.

unless Millwall were having a do next door and overheard him because they won it in 1991.

Elton John – Watford

Elton John's love affair with Watford is very enjoyable. In his superb book *Me*, he devotes plenty of words in between the sex and drugs and rock and roll to the Hornets, about whom he says, 'I didn't care about the ground, or the hopelessness of the team, or the freezing cold. I loved it all straight away.' You might not think that a worldwide megastar would be quite so relatable, but this is surely familiar to all of us as he continues, 'It was like taking a drug to which you instantly become addicted.' Addiction is, of course, something he knows all about, but thankfully Watford seem to have outlasted his other vices.

Elton first got involved when he offered to play a benefit gig for the club at Vicarage Road and brought pop chum Rod Stewart along, because he bloody loves the football too. The club invited Elton to buy shares, so he did, and eventually became chairman, formulating a ten-year plan with manager Graham Taylor to get Watford into the First Division – which they achieved in five. He obviously gives a lot of the credit for that to Taylor, who became a great friend, was best man at his wedding and had the balls to tell him off once for turning up at the club with a hangover after a coke binge, telling him, 'What the fuck do you think you're doing? You're letting yourself down and you're letting the club down.' Does he not like his chairman turning up worse for wear on the sniff.

Elton was clearly an asset in transfer negotiations, schmoozing players at top hotels and handing out concert tickets and albums. It must have been a joy to play for him, even if at times he says himself that 'there was no glamour, no luxury, no limousines, no Starship. You got on the train to Grimsby with the players, you watched the game, listened to the opposition supporters sing about your allegedly insatiable desire to stick your penis up the arse of anyone nearby, and then you got the train home.' Still, the fish and chips would have been nice.

Although his association with the club is 'dill dandin' hafta hall dis time', the pinnacle of Elton's support must have been the 1984 FA Cup Final when he turned up in a daft hat and sobbed his heart out when the band struck up 'Abide with Me'. As he says, he had endured 'years of addiction and unhappiness, failed relationships, bad business deals, court cases, unending turmoil. Through all of that, Watford were a constant source of happiness to me.' It really is just lovely, apart from those rotten sods at Grimsby, of course.

Geoffrey Richmond – Bradford City

For a team to be successful, a good chairman needs to know how to handle his players. Dissent in the ranks can spread fast and it pays to be able to handle any unrest with tact and diplomacy. It will come as a surprise to nobody that this is an elaborate set-up for the complete opposite happening. Chris Kamara worked under Richmond at Bradford and, alongside a lot of interference on team selection and signings, he found that the chairman fell slightly short when it came to delicate negotiations. Upon reaching Wembley for a play-off final, the Bradford players had noticed the amount of merchandise being shifted in the club shop to keen fans and were angling for a slice of it. Richmond listened intently as they put their case before, according to Kammy, turning bright red, threatening to play the youth team instead and raising 'two fingers to the entire squad, triumphantly taking his right hand from behind his back and brandishing it to all of them'.

A tempestuous relationship between Richmond and Kamara wasn't helped at a promotion party Kammy held, when he inevitably got the karaoke machine out and had a sing-song. Instead of sticking to his tried and trusted classics (which he has somehow turned into a blossoming new career avenue), the manager went rogue and made up his own words to the Gershwin classic, 'Summertime'. So, while the other guests were by his own admission 'flinching uncomfortably', Kamara sang something that goes a little something like this: 'Summertime, working for Geoffrey ain't easy, he wants to pick the team and sign the players as well, but until that morning when he comes in and sacks me, all I can say is Geoffrey, please don't pry.'

Now look, we can all waste time worrying about whether this scanned or not, and for the life of me I can't see how it did, but the main point is that it won't have done Kammy's job prospects much good, and indeed the axe came before too long. Inappropriate song or not, surely only a monster could sack such a bubbly borderline national treasure.

Peter Ridsdale – Leeds United and too many others

It's easy to laugh at Peter Ridsdale. Go on take a minute. The tales of his profligacy while in charge at Leeds are legendary. Figures for Seth Johnson's wages go up with each retelling, as does the price of the tropical fish he kept.[116] It may not all be true but what we do know is that when David O'Leary fashioned a team of babies which went close to European glory, they were flying too close to the sun, with wings made of crisp £50 notes.

Understandably, Ridsdale is keen not to take all the blame and says that Leeds were chucking silly money around way before he was in charge, pointing the finger at Bill Fotherby. Fotherby, he says, told Alex Ferguson and Martin Edwards that he wouldn't 'pay over the odds' for Lee Sharpe, but while the Manchester United would have been happy to take £1m for him, the Leeds man defiantly said, 'I'll pay no more than four million.' Edwards kept a straight face long enough to cheekily push him to £4.5m and then presumably started the car as quickly as possible. Ridsdale clearly learned from a master.

---

116 Ridsdale says that in the Far East fish are considered good luck 'so when the poor run started under Venables, I felt the fish could do no harm, and ordered two tanks for Elland Road'. Or maybe he could have saved the money they spent on both the fish and Paul Okon and been better off all around.

In his book *United We Fall* Ridsdale has excuses for pretty much everything, from the fish to the private jets, which were only ever used for expediency, so that's alright then. He makes fun of the 'battered Montego'[117] that Robbie Fowler arrived in to seal his £11m signing, drops Rio Ferdinand right in it by saying he laughed about saying he wanted to stay at the club, while telling him, 'You know that was for the supporters ... me and you both know I'm off!', boasts about teasing Peter Kenyon and revels in the fans singing his name, saying that 'hairs on the back of my neck stood on end'.

Man of the people Pete says he was in it more to rub shoulders with the players in the dressing room, with the 'laughter and banter among the steam from the showers' and with the management, relaxing, post-match, with 'a glass of cold white wine and some scampi'. Sounds lovely, but unfortunately when the wheels came off, it was a bit less about scampi and having his name sung, and a bit more about sitting at home, drinking too much wine in his conservatory and 'looking out into the darkness of the fields that stretch out from our house'. At times he sounds like a brooding detective, desperately trying to crack a case, rather than a man who is simply paying Michael Duberry far too much money.

Ken Bates – Chelsea / Leeds

Nobody has ever looked more and acted less like Father Christmas than former Chelsea and Leeds chairman Ken Bates. Unless Santa has ever suggested putting an electric fence up to keep kids away from the Christmas tree before 25 December. There are those that will tell you that everyone is now jealous of Chelsea, and that Roman Abramovich's money made them unpopular with fans of other clubs. Well let me confirm that Chelsea have been unpopular for a lot longer than that, and Ken Bates should take a lot of the credit.

---

117 I assume he means 'battered' as in beaten up rather than being rich, golden, fried, and crunchy, but you never know with the excess at Leeds United at that time.

FINAL THIRD

A young Gary Neville, writing in his 1998 diary, says that he was often motivated to beat Bates who had called United 'just a club from the slum side of Manchester'; Graeme Le Saux says that he would order expensive wine then let you pay for it; Pat Nevin says that Bates made you sit in a smaller chair during negotiations in 'basic Reggie Perrin cod psychology to make me you feel intimidated'; and Graham Roberts says that he 'told him to stick the club up his arse' after the chairman said that Roberts' wife reminded him of a prize dairy cow while she was pregnant with twins. Maybe we'll let him off the wine as Le Saux's alright for a few quid himself, but the rest of it isn't on. Bates didn't turn the charm dial up any further once he arrived at Leeds, either. In what must have been a tempestuous relationship that you could have sold tickets to watch, Neil Warnock says that the two disagreed about transfers and that Leeds missed out on a bargain £400,000 Joel Ward transfer because Bates told him, 'If you want him so much why don't you pay it yourself?' Because that's not how it works, Ken. Mel Sterland says that the first time he met him, after a Leeds game he had gone back to watch as a former title-winner with the club, 'Bates just took one look at me and said, "Fucking hell, you're a fat cunt now, aren't you?!"'

For all the evidence stacked against him, however, he does have people that like him. At a chairman's annual meeting, which sounds like something out of *The Simpson*'s Stonecutters episode, David Gold says that Bates 'made me feel very welcome'; while Jimmy Floyd Hasselbaink says, 'I've always got along very well with him,' while Kerry Dixon is his biggest fan. It's worth mentioning that Dixon's love of Bates may come from the fact that he helped him out financially once or twice when he ran up gambling debts, but the love is real. Dixon says that Bates mucked in with the players, and even went as far as throwing himself into the big bath after a promotion once, as he knew that tradition dictated that he would end up wet anyway. The Chelsea scoring legend describes

242

BOARD GAMES

Cuddly Ken as 'not so much an ogre as a mischievous old rascal'. Fair enough – maybe Bates was just being mischievous when he suggested that barbed-wire-topped electric fence in the eighties. The cheeky scamp.

Roman Abramovich – Chelsea

Cards on the table – if you paid me millions of pounds, surrounded me with players to assist my rise to world-class level and let me have a few goes on your yacht, I would probably write nice things about you. So it proves with Frank Lampard on Roman Abramovich, back in the days before he was forced out of the country in disgrace for being a close confidant of Vladimir Putin. If Frank has any qualms about Roman's ill-gotten gains or shady associations, he's able to bury them deep and instead wax lyrical about how warm and nervous Roman was at their first meeting, when sparks flew between them.

Lampard says that as he greeted his new oligarch guvnor, 'he looked directly at me and very fleetingly I caught sight of the determination in his gaze'. Determination, initially at least to get 'rid of this shithole' that was Chelsea's old and shabby Harlington training ground. Lampard continues to eulogise Abramovich, says he admires his 'candour',[118] talks about fabulous evenings out they have shared with partners, recalls holidays on his big boat and says that Abramovich's cold, dead-eyed goal celebration is 'actually quite beautiful because it's so simple'. Good grief. Friend, Roman, Chairman – lend me your yacht and I'll say nice things about you.

David Gold, David Sullivan & Karren Brady – Birmingham City & West Ham United

'I Found Face of Jesus on My Fish Finger', 'Double Decker Bus Found in Iceberg at South Pole' and 'Aliens Have Eaten My Son' are

---

118 Although elsewhere Didier Drogba says he happily went behind Big Phil Scolari's back to Abramovich, so it wasn't all up-front honesty down at the Bridge.

just some of the *Sunday Sport* headlines that made David Sullivan famous. Charming the nation with its tried and trusted formula of daft stories and boobs, it represented the more mainstream end of his publishing empire, the proceeds of which he eventually decided to pour into football. And yet it could have all been so different. Karren Brady, known these days as much for being one of Lord Sugar's grasses on *The Apprentice* as she is for her London Stadium work, has long been the brains behind David Sullivan's grubby operations, and she suggests that the little man wanted a racecourse at first, before being diverted towards football, Birmingham City and Barry Fry.

Getting Fry in as their manager of choice proved a challenge, as he was firmly ensconced among the cockles and candy floss at Southend. But Brady and the Dildo Brothers drive a hard bargain, and eventually, after a protracted commission hearing, they got their man, and a tempestuous reign began. The relationship between Fry and the bongo merchants[119] was admittedly strained and ended acrimoniously, when they sent somebody else to sack him, but it can't have been all bad. Karren Brady reveals that Baz was best man at her wedding to Blues player Paul Peschisolido, and David Gold says, 'He is always the first man on my list when I have a dinner party,' which is nice because most people say Stephen Fry rather than Barry Fry when they're asked about fantasy dinner party guests.

Sullivan hasn't written his autobiography yet, but Gold's book is an extraordinary affair. His is an inspiring tale of rising from abject poverty to fabulous riches through the fairytale story of flogging mucky books and saucy undies. Along the way he tells of catching his wife and his best mate at it in a swimming pool, his own sexual liaisons, endless legal battles, Nazis, and the Kray twins. It's a real rollercoaster, but if you take anything away from it, please let it be

---

119 Or as David Gold prefers to call it, 'erotica or girlie magazines'.

that he was poor. He's very keen for you to know that he was poor. If I had a pound for every time he mentions being poor, I'd ... well I wouldn't be poor, that's for sure.

With an air of *The Fast Show*'s Swiss Toni about him, he says things like, 'Nowadays a typical lad of sixteen or seventeen can be over six feet tall and wise to the world. He has probably already been to America for his holidays and is well versed in women, sex and designer beers.' He seems oddly specific about the holidays and the beers here, doesn't he? Who has he got this impression from?

The famous GSB are now at West Ham, of course, at time of writing, which was Gold's first love, although he does say of Birmingham, 'They say you cannot change your allegiance, it doesn't happen. I am living proof that it does,' which he perhaps regrets now, if he uncrosses his 'Hammer' arms long enough.

Doug Ellis – Aston Villa

Growing up, I always thought that 'Deadly' Doug Ellis got his nickname because he was forever sacking managers. Not so. He insists that all 'contracts are carefully honoured', has an excuse for at least four or five of the bosses he worked his way through, and says that he actually got the nickname for clubbing a salmon to death with a 'priest' while out fishing with Jimmy Greaves. So, I hope that settles any nerves among you. Phew.

Ellis lives by two rules: Firstly, that 'the chairman–manager relationship has to be very close, both pulling in the same direction' and secondly, 'if a manager fails he pays the price with his job.' It's a fine line between those two. There's a need to pull in the same direction but if we pull in the same direction and fail, you're sacked. Oh, and if we pull in different directions, you're also sacked.

One gaffer that Ellis famously butted heads with over a few successful years before sacking him was Ron Atkinson (coming up a lot, isn't he?). The two each spend a lot of time in their books moaning about one another. Ellis says that Atkinson often wasn't available when he should have been (which he claims cost Villa signings like Andy Cole), moved his matchday office away from the players' lounge against the chairman's wishes and went to Gary Newbon's Christmas party with Jasper Carrott instead of going to a staff do. Ron says, 'I worked for the club in spite of the chairman,' complains about 'Deadly's tedious, never-ending fishing stories' and says, 'He is a classic case of a man full of his own self-importance to a degree you could barely believe.' Self-importance is never something you would accuse Ron Atkinson of. Sorry, I mean self-awareness is never something you would accuse Ron Atkinson of.[120]

On managers that got away, Ellis claims that he got close to appointing Franz Beckenbauer in the summer of 1990, immediately after he had won the World Cup. Now, you may find that as difficult to believe as I did, but Doug swears by it, saying that he and Mrs Doug had previously spent time with Franz and Mrs Franz on a skiing holiday in Kitzbühel and got on famously. When Ellis made the job offer call and recalled their previous meeting, however, he found himself talking to a new Mrs Franz, or 'the wrong wife' as he puts it. He seems convinced in his book that she didn't pass on the message and that's why Beckenbauer was never to be found at Villa Park. Seems like it might have been worth a follow-up call, doesn't it?

Ellis also claims that he came close to nabbing Clough and Taylor on two occasions. Once when he propositioned Clough, and a second when he claims that they shut the door during the 1972 John Robson transfer negotiations and whispered, 'Look, Mr Ellis … fetch us.' Despite telling him, 'We'll come and make you the most successful chairman in the country,' Ellis had a moment of integrity and decided to stand by his incumbent manager, Vic

---

120 One further note on the Big Ron sacking. His dad Fred retained his invitation to the boardroom and saw absolutely nothing wrong with maintaining regular appearances, saying, 'They sacked you, not me.'

Crowe, while Clough and Taylor went on to win the league and two European Cups with Nottingham Forest.

The smarter among you might point out that Aston Villa also won the title and a European Cup just after the success of Forest, but here's the rub – those were nothing to do with Doug Ellis. Ellis was involved with Villa from 1968 until 2006, apart from a few years in the middle during which the club actually won things. He insists he's not bitter and insists that he's 'rather proud of them', claiming that the success was built on the very solid foundations he put in place. That's right, the solid foundations are the real quiz.

Alan Sugar – Tottenham Hotspur

Alan. Sir Alan. Lord Sugar. Call him what you will. You may know him from the telly or from being really daft on Twitter, but we're here to talk about his time owning Tottenham. It was a time which saw Spurs win the FA Cup in 1991, but a time blighted by a bitter row between Sugar and Terry Venables. The players, by and large, took El Tel's side, with Neil Ruddock making his feelings clear and Teddy Sheringham saying of Sugar, 'He was used to getting his own way, and it did not seem to matter to him whose feelings he hurt in the process.' Anyone who has seen his stilted delivery of scathing one-liners on *The Apprentice* might agree. Sheringham's first impression of Sugar was gleaned from a motivational speech he gave in which he used a baseball bat as a visual aid, like Robert De Niro in *The Untouchables*, and clearly it never recovered. Sheringham says that when he left Spurs for Man United, the tiny chairman told him, 'I don't want to see any shit in the papers about me or Tottenham, or I'll be after you.' Well, it might not have gone in the papers, but Teddy devotes a fair chunk of his book to dishing the dirt on him, so he clearly wasn't too intimidated. Sugar boasts about selling Sheringham for the same amount they bought him for years previously and tries to sell it as some sort of victory, despite Teddy going off and winning a treble and Footballer of the Year in greener pastures, before coming back to Spurs once Sugar was out of the way.

Sugar's book is called *What You See is What You Get*, and if what you see is an angry, little man, then he's spot on. It's one of those sayings like 'plain-speaking', 'doesn't suffer fools gladly' and 'you know where you stand' which are sometimes shorthand for just not being very nice, isn't it? He says about his feud with the manager that 'Venables was totally out of his depth' and that he 'was very distrustful of me' and talks about being painted as the villain of the piece when he sacked 'The Adonis of football, God's gift to the game, the chirpy chappy'. Just to be clear, this isn't three people, these are all Venables.

It really is a mystery why more managers didn't succeed under Sugar, because even when they fail, they seem to go to great lengths to make it clear that none of it was the chairman's fault. According to Sugar, when Gerry Francis felt it was time to throw the towel in, he told Sugar 'he was grateful for the support I'd tried to give him – in particular for purchasing players such as Ferdinand, Ginola and others. He said he couldn't have asked for any more support from his chairman.' It feels like this might not have happened exactly like that. This is like breaking up with a partner who says you were the greatest lover they ever had, too good if anything, and that it's all their fault.

After Francis came Travelcard brandisher Christian Gross, who Sugar says he knew was 'dead meat' from that first embarrassing press conference – and then George Graham. Graham, of course, was famously close to a pound note, and Sugar says he had problems with him chasing up the club finance director for his bonus the day after they won the Worthington Cup. He describes Graham as not being 'the type of person I would socialise with' and claims that he 'had a lot of arse-lickers in the media'. Coming from a man who is in what might be the 327th series of a prime-time TV show in which everyone has to call him Lord Sugar and says 'thank you for the opportunity' at the very moment he crushes their dreams, is a bit rich.

* * *

There you have it. Please select your own personal eight-strong boardroom from the rogues' gallery above and try to imagine working for them for more than two hours without resigning. Even the nice ones either try to take your pennies from you or turn up for work off their nut on gear. There's no helping them. Maybe those managers do have it tough after all.

The dream #RelationshipGoals partnership may have been Arsène Wenger and his buddy upstairs at Arsenal, David Dein. The pair always seemed genuinely close, Dein was instrumental in getting the virtually unknown Wenger into the club and they had unimaginable success together. Wenger is full of compliments about Dein, describing him as 'an innovator, a highly sociable man with incredible tenacity and unparalleled generosity'. Let's skirt over the fact that, 'when he left, he sold his shares to the Russian oligarch Alisher Usmanov', and just enjoy the simpatico working relationship, as Wenger reminisces about how they 'had so many adventures together' as if they met 'The Folk of The Faraway Tree' once a week.

The seeds of the partnership were sown seven years before the Frenchman arrived at Arsenal when Wenger was a Monaco manager indulging his curiosity about the English game. He came along to see Arsenal beat Norwich at Highbury and was invited back to Dein's house for a do. Wenger recalls 'a very sociable evening with a lot of laughter and games, a kind of charades' in which he had to mime *A Midsummer Night's Dream*, which I would have paid good money to see.

It's easy to see why Wenger found Dein's house so intoxicating – Theo Walcott went there for transfer negotiations and describes it as 'like something out of an Austin Powers movie' with 'a lot of

FINAL THIRD

leopard print'. Walcott signed his shagadelic contract immediately. It sounds like an altogether less awkward story than when Alan Smith signed for Arsenal. He was also smuggled into a director's house, this time Ken Friar, and ended up stuck in the toilet because 'the lock on the knob was playing up'. Whether they got him out, or simply slipped the contract under the door, I can't quite remember but I do know that he got out eventually because I've seen him on the telly since.

Whether the salubrious surroundings of the Arsenal power men compare to the plush 'JR Ewing out of *Dallas*' office of Dave Whelan, or Freddy Shepherd's house 'full of memorabilia, equipped with a fine solid-oak bar', I'll leave it to Lee McCulloch and Andy Cole to duke it out (perhaps with a little help from Dion Dublin as he knows so much about property these days). However, Cole's assertion that Shepherd's gaff 'was a splendid place for a bollocking', swings it for me.

Asserting your authority in your rich mahogany office, in your leopard print home or through a broken toilet door is one thing, or three things, but being the lord of the dressing room is quite another. The dressing room is the domain of the players and a bit of a bear pit for anybody else, whether you own the ground, or have the nearest parking space to it; but some chairmen are brave enough to try. Shaun Goater says that John Madejski was one such brave soul, but he had the brass balls to name Reading's ground after himself, so maybe we shouldn't be surprised. Goater says that players would listen intently to Madejski's air-punching motivational speech and then 'turn and laugh, asking each other, "What was all that about?"' as soon as the door shut behind him.[121]

Brian Clough used to insist that his Forest chairman Maurice Roworth knocked before coming in his dressing room, on one

---

121 Goater says that his Reading team were 'all singing from the same team sheet', which is a bit confusing as it's generally a song or a hymn sheet, right? But let's assume it's still a good thing.

BOARD GAMES

occasion insisting he even went back out and knocked as he forgot to do it in the first place. The mind boggles at what would have happened if Clough had ever worked under Ken Bates. We've already learned about that time Bates threw himself into the big bath to save his players the job, but on another occasion he ended up wrestling on the floor. In an incident which might explain why Clive Allen didn't stay long at Stamford Bridge, as the much-travelled striker was clearly traumatised by the incident.

Allen remembers Bates bowling into the Chelsea inner sanctum in a big fur coat and being asked, 'What the fucking hell have you got on?' by feisty fashionista Dennis Wise. Bates responded in a perfectly reasonable and level-headed way by calling Wise a 'little shit', which few of us would argue with, and threatening that 'I could still knock you out'. In Allen's words, 'a scrap ensued' as little Dennis grappled with Ken in his big fur coat, in a battle for the ages that must have looked a bit like that bit with Leonardo Di Caprio and that bear in *The Revenant*. Allen was alarmed but was reassured by Kerry Dixon that this was something that happened often, and Bates felt it was just Wisey showing him a unique brand of respect.

Things were altogether more friendly at Liverpool, where Didi Hamann seems to spend a lot more time in his book on the cigarette he enjoyed in the shower room with David Moores after the 2005 Champions League Final, than he does on the 2005 Champions League Final. In what was clearly a special moment for both, Hamann says, 'For a long time he looked at me and I looked at him. Nothing was said. The look between us said everything. Not a word was spoken. Because there were no words that could describe what it was that we were feeling.' It's all very intoxicating – 'a feeling that defies description' that was taking place a safe distance away from the smoke alarms. But for something that defies description, he spends an awful lot of time describing it.

Despite this touching scene, the dressing room I would most like to have been in when the chairman came knocking was Luton

Town when Eric Morecambe was in charge. Both Ricky Hill and Brian Horton have very fond memories of him popping in for a motivational word. Horton says that 'he would come into the dressing room, make us laugh, try to relax us', which sounds like a dream. I think I'd run through a brick wall for an Eric Morecambe joke. Hill even remembers getting a warm smile and a 'good luck sunshine' from Morecambe before he ran out for his debut. As a send-off it certainly beats watching Ken Bates rolling around the floor trying to get Dennis Wise out of his furry pockets. I'll give you that, sunshine, I'll give you that.

11.

False 9 to 5

'Friendly Fish Man'

AS CHILDREN we were all constantly asked by curious, or nosey, relatives the perennial question, 'What do you want to be when you grow up?' And, while sometimes I feel like I'm still trying to decide,[122] back then I knew for sure that I hoped to be a footballer. Obviously, that hasn't worked out so far and deep into my forties I'm prepared to concede that I might not make it after all. I've had to move on and do something else instead. For those exceptional few that achieve their dreams and make it, you might think that they've never needed to countenance the wider world of work – but you would be wrong. Whether it's teenage jobs before their dream became reality, post-career jobs from a time before the big money came into the game or sometimes a little side-hustle, those jobs find room in their memoirs for a mention. That's right kids. It might be the case that a few years playing on Premier League wages these days means that you can not only retire comfortably, but maybe buy your own private island somewhere and a helicopter to buzz around above it, but it wasn't always the case. There was a time when ex-footballers walked the streets among us, running pubs, selling cars,

---

122 You don't want to hear my problems.

or working in insurance. It used to be a standard question in certain old football magazines to ask players what they would be doing for a living if they weren't a footballer[123] and it has clearly bled through to their books. Their answers peek through the cracks like alternative timelines. These days everything is all about multiverses, and if we buy into the idea perpetuated by big-budget Marvel films that all things possible are happening concurrently somewhere in alternate dimensions, then we must accept that somewhere out there Lionel Messi is a bus driver.

Among those to stare into the abyss and imagine a world where their football skills went unappreciated and were lost to the world include:

Rio Ferdinand – 'a community youth worker', which is all very commendable.

Brian McClair – 'if I hadn't pulled on a football shirt, I would now be a mathematics teacher'. A good one too, no doubt.

Clyde Best – 'quite possibly a panel beater' despite reservations about 'too much banging!' which would admittedly be an issue to contend with.

None of these men had to genuinely consider these choices as an option, but some do, as football wages haven't always been what they are now. For one or two players, there was better money to be made elsewhere. When Brian Horton was offered professional terms by Port Vale on £23 a week in 1970, he had to give it serious consideration because he was already earning more than that by combining part-time football at Hednesford with being a self-employed builder. Luckily for him, his wife was earning well as

---

123 There is a particularly grumpy Derek 'Pigeon Killer' Hales Q&A which does the rounds on social media from time to time, which might be the high watermark of not caring what anyone thinks of you. It's brilliant.

a computer programmer and was able to balance their wages and allow him to follow a dream; but it was a close-run thing. This is no longer a problem for players at Port Vale as I've heard that some of them earn as much as £60 a week these days. Eddie Hapgood and Rodger Wylde both considered returning to their former jobs as milkmen, or at least threatening to do so until a more viable deal was on the table from Arsenal and Sheffield Wednesday respectively. Both came perilously close to a life on the float before common sense prevailed.

According to John Wark, Eric Gates returned to potato-picking for a living when he got frustrated by a lack of early first-team chances at Ipswich, before turning things around, becoming a club legend and England international.[124] And Tony Woodcock reckons that very dapper Forest team-mate, Garry Birtles, simply wasn't that bothered about football at all and at one point considered a return to laying carpets.[125]

Had Nobby Stiles not made the grade as a box-to-box midfielder, he would have almost certainly had a career among different sorts of boxes – coffins, to be exact. Nobby's family were in the undertaking business, and he was being schooled to join them before the big leagues came calling. You might think it's quite a solemn job, but it had its perks. One day young Norbert was taken along on a visit to a bereaved family only to find that they were related to former Manchester United winger Jimmy Delaney. 'At an appropriate moment,' claims Nob, his father explained that his boy was crackers about the football and asked if he might be allowed to put on the Delaney shirt that was displayed on the wall for a minute. 'The lady of the house, who was Jimmy Delaney's niece, took the shirt down from the wall, put it on me and patted my head.' Nobby seems confident here that there actually was an appropriate moment for this business

---

124 They really unearthed a good one there.
125 Something about underlaying issues? Anyone?

to take place. I'm inclined to disagree, but I suppose so long as he didn't do his World Cup dance all around the front room, they might have got away without stepping on the family's grief too much.

Fellow beloved World Cup winner, Jack Charlton, had a more traditional teenage job in the shape of his paper round – until brother Bobby went and ruined it. When Jack went off to Leeds as an apprentice, he was hoping to have the paper round to fall back on in case things didn't work out, so he left young Bobby Charlton in charge of it, only to find when he came home that 'not only had he wrecked the bike I gave him, but he'd given away the bloody round. He just wasn't interested.' This might be the only instance in which a World Cup winner has had his paper round wrecked by another and I like to think this is what led to their famously frosty relationship over the years.

Others who earned a teenage crust any which way they could include Pat Jennings who put his massive hands to work picking blackberries and chopping wood to sell, Mark Bright who cleaned caravan toilets on weekends and took on an apprenticeship at a hydraulics company, Viv Anderson who was briefly in the silk-screen printing game, and unlikeliest of all, Neil Warnock who worked at a bowling alley where he 'oiled the lanes, repaired the mechanisms ... and made the frothy coffees'. I just can't picture it.

Alan Hansen worked in motor insurance and, aside from the messing around with people's lunchboxes and general tomfoolery, found it all a bit boring, saying, 'I saw all the years stretching away in front of me and I couldn't visualise myself sitting at a desk doing the same kind of thing day after day, week after week, month after month and year after year.' At least it wasn't a dangerous job, Alan. Think yourself lucky. It seems like we could have lost one or two of our stars before they had so much as laced up a professional boot.

PAT JENNINGS – Got his trousers caught in a crate while working with a milkman and pulled many broken milk bottles over with him. The milkman for whom he was riding shotgun 'didn't ask if I was hurt, he just called me all the names that sprang to his mind'. Calm down Mr Milkman, there's no use crying over it.

GORDON BANKS – Worked on a building site and was once struck a glancing blow on the head by a falling brick, which you would like to think he would have caught on a good day. As blood streamed from his temple, his East Midlands co-worker told him, 'What an effing scene ower nowt. Yon brick was only on yer head for a second!'

PAT JENNINGS (Again) – Worked in a timber yard where he was let loose with a hatchet or saw far too often and almost froze to death on the back of an open lorry from time to time. However, the biggest danger came when the huge three-ton trees would sometimes slip their chains and come crashing down nearby. A cheerful Jennings, who really does seem to take the positive out of any situation says that 'I can only think my positional sense kept me out of trouble'. You've got to learn positional play somewhere, and it might as well be with heavy things suspended precariously above your head. That's what I say.

BRUCE GROBBELAAR – A life in uniform beckoned for the likes of Steve Ogrizovic (policeman) and Chris Kamara (Navy), but nobody took it as far as Bruce Grobbelaar who spent time in the army in Zimbabwe. The seemingly happy-go-lucky Bruce was in the thick of the fighting and thankfully says, 'I never did get used to killing other men,' although he is clearly traumatised by the 'horrific screams that still ring in my ears when I have those awful dreams'. Bloody hell Bruce, keep it light.

NICK TANNER – The closest that Bruce's Liverpool team-mate, Nick Tanner, came to the armed forces was his time working for British Aerospace. It all seems very civilised on the surface, but it seems that he was working with some of the worst colleagues anybody has ever had and claims that 'at my leaving do, I drank so much booze I nearly died'. Before heading off to a career with Bristol Rovers, Tanner was thrown a parting bash at which he was forced to drink everything in sight, including a pint containing every spirit in the optics. So far, so standard perhaps, but then he was put in some stocks in a pub garden[126] while a colleague was pulling on gloves, 'dipping them in marking blue and shoving his finger up my arse'. He then had to go back to work[127] where he fell against the machinery and almost knocked himself out. When he eventually got home, his parents were so worried that they consulted an emergency doctor who insisted they stay up with him and keep him awake to keep him out of danger. You might think that players such as Tanner who come into the game a bit later might be spared all that hazing and initiation business that club apprentices got, but if the guys at British Aerospace are aggressively putting fingers up each other's bums too, I don't know where that leaves us.

Tanner would surely have been overjoyed to be out of the clutches of the British Aerospace gang once he was firmly ensconced in the professional ranks, but there are other players who felt the need to supplement their meagre income as footballers with a bit or work on the side.

Stuart Pearce is famously a qualified electrician and used to advertise his services in the Nottingham Forest matchday programme to drum up business. Brian Clough either took advantage of the situation or patronised a local business by bringing in his iron and kettle to be repaired. Terry Butcher, meanwhile, went further by touting his insurance business to opposing captains at the

---

126 You know, just some standard pub garden stocks, like they all have.
127 Presumably once the finger was out.

pre-match coin toss. He recalls asking a bemused Phil Thompson if he had any insurance: 'Then I whipped out a calling card from the company and said: "Give me a call if you need any – the phone number's on the card".' What on earth Phil did with the card I don't know? Tucked it down his sock or nestled it in his perm for safekeeping, perhaps. Imagine this now – Conor Coady hassling everyone in the centre-circle, trying to sell them financial advice or a new kitchen worktop.

Neil Warnock is a qualified chiropodist and still dabbled throughout his management career, treating his own players but also satisfying old ladies with his reassuringly expensive sessions, insisting that 'every one of them came back for more'. There were complaints about his prices, but I like to think he threw in a frothy coffee while he was giving their bunions a seeing to.

Other moonlighters include Bob Wilson who taught history and PE at a London school while playing in the first team as an amateur with Arsenal; John Gorman, who had a painting and decorating business while playing in America; and Peter Storey, who is one of many that had a pub on the go. All of which might have stood them in good stead when their playing days were done, had they not instead chosen to go into television, coaching and crime respectively.

Some had lofty ambitions for when their career was all done. Adebayo Akinfenwa harbours ambitions to be in a Marvel film, which surely all of us will do at some stage, while according to Clive Allen, the enigmatic Benoit Assou-Ekotto fancied something a bit more adult within the same industry, telling him, 'I think I'm going to be a porn star.' Allen insists that he was serious, but we can't be sure. He also says that Assou-Ekotto didn't know who Spurs were playing from week to week, so all bets are off with him.[128]

---

128 If any readers have chanced upon BAE in a bongo flick, please do let us know.

FINAL THIRD

Lee Chapman says that the end of a player's career is something that everyone knows is coming, but you can never quite prepare yourself for – a bit like a Julian Dicks tackle. Chapman wistfully says, 'For many players it is something to be pushed to the back of their minds in the hope that it may never happen.' Brian Horton knew the gig was up after becoming enraged with a referee when he was player-manager at Hull and getting himself sent off in what turned out to be his final game. After the game he found the referee and told him 'that because he had failed to spot something so blatant I had lost control and was packing it in'. The ref had apparently missed a flying elbow to Horton's face, but exactly how bad does a decision need to be to make you retire on the spot? Pretty bad. It didn't take a bad referee for Mark Bright to feel the icy hand of retirement on his shoulder, just young upstart Kevin Lisbie telling him to 'fucking shut up!' as Bright chided him for not passing to him, during a sparsely attended reserve game for Charlton. He says, 'It stunned me a bit,' and that was him done. Not even Olga Stringfellow could save him.

When the time comes it makes sense to have a plan. Paul Weller (not that one) points out that 'in no way is being a footballer a proper day's work' and that 'it doesn't prepare you for anything else that is "normal", and it's fair to say that some do struggle. Mel Sterland tried selling fish door to door, very briefly.[129] He explains, 'You had to knock and say "I'm your friendly fish man, what fish would you like today?"' but after seeing his partner get knocked back twice he immediately walked off the job without trying – which isn't that friendly and suggests he may not have been cut out for it.[130] Mel moved on to a call centre job with a firm that sold photocopiers and communication systems. Things started okay until he called a Sheffield United fan up who wanted nothing to do with anything

---

129 A surprising turn of events given Mel's troubled back story with a goldfish, as seen in 'Second Yellow'.

130 You thought I was going to do a fish pun there didn't you? Be honest.

the Wednesday legend was selling. Showing a flair for sales and handling people, and skilfully riffing on the call protocols that had no doubt been drilled into him and his colleagues, Sterland rang the customer back and shouted, 'D'ya know you, you're nowt but a fucking wanker!' and slammed the phone down. Mel's career in telesales lasted only marginally longer than the door-to-door fish business.

Others fare much better. Phil Thompson went into 'Phil Thompson Pine DIY' shops in the years before Jeff Stelling came calling, even saying that 'at times I might have even enjoyed it more than the football', while Steve Hunt, who played with Pelé remember, says that after working in a hardware store and as surely one of the country's coolest school caretakers, 'that I realised I was much happier making a living outside of football'.

Players can react differently to suddenly having the sociable side of the game taken away from them. We always hear about the craic and the banter and missing the lads. Bryan Gunn reacted by taking things up a notch and entering high society as the Sheriff of Norwich, clanking around in the chains and robes pressing the flesh and representing the city in any number of social situations, while Stanley Matthews tells us that Blackpool keeper George Farm took the opposite view and became a lighthouse keeper. That man could not get far enough away from other people, could he?

George Farm's bright future away from the pack sounds ideal for some. You're removed from the general public and the only risk of a social interaction is the occasional hair-raising visit from a *Blue Peter* presenter. But some players enjoy staying in the cut and thrust of it all and having a little dabble in a business venture every now and then. For those with a bit of spare cash and a bit of time on their hands, why not. It's just a matter of choosing your projects carefully and investing your money wisely. Unlike Johan Cruyff who admits to losing loads of his money in a 'pig-breeding venture'. We've all been there. Terry Curran played it a bit safer with a roadside café offering 'the best back bacon, Nescafe and "bottomless' tea" and duly turned a profit. Dave Mackay put his name to 'Dave Mackay's Ties' and regrets that he 'agreed to a lifetime's supply of neckwear for me and my family rather than negotiate a financial interest'[131] and Nobby Stiles had a tile company called 'Nobby's Tiles'. That last one isn't true, but wouldn't it be good if it was.

Dave Mackay certainly wasn't the only one to take a foray into the fashion business. It's a popular choice, with various degrees of legitimacy. Tim Cahill spends more time than is seemly in his book punting his own clothing line, while Rio Ferdinand isn't far behind when he boasts that your Tinie Tempahs and your Olly Murses of this world chase him up for his clothing line #5 (always with the hashtags, Rio).

At the slightly more Del Boy end of Hooky Street are Andy Woodman and, would you believe, Gareth Southgate. Team-mates at Crystal Palace, the pair set up a joint enterprise which involved buying Nike tracksuits and other sportswear directly from the warehouse and selling them on to the lads at the club. Lovely jubbly! Jack Charlton was at it as well, buying 'off-cuts and seconds, any kind of leftovers' from people in the rag trade and 'started making a few quid on the side by selling on cloth lengths, mainly to other players'. What these players were doing with these cloth lengths is anyone's guess. Could they all make their own suits? Was that a thing in the sixties and seventies? Is it a lost art now or are they all still at it without telling us? Is Jack Grealish spending most evenings slaving over a sewing machine, trying to get the cut just right around his impressive calves? Canny Jackie Charlton could not sell them enough, reckoning at one point that he was making more money from this than from football, and later expanded to take in a souvenir shop at Elland Road. No wonder he stayed there for his whole career.

---

131 A spectacular error of judgement from Mackay here. By all means, take a lifetime's supply in comestibles, but ties last a very long time. A lifetime's supply of ties is about seven ties. What was he thinking? Still, looking on the bright side, he said, 'in a good year, I do get silk ones.'

While Big Jack went legit, John Burridge found out the hard way that you've got to be careful. In the middle of his thriving sports shop business, he came into possession of some fake (some say snide, some say moody) sports gear and got his collar felt. Budgie was fined £16,000 for his involvement, which he swears was unintentional, and left the court which had declared him a convicted criminal, complaining of 'being treated like a criminal'. He would have got away with it if those fake tracksuit makers hadn't put an extra E in Reeebok, I reckon.

Perhaps the most surprising business venture I came across was one involving Jimmy Hill. A man with one eye apparently always on making a buck, he went in with occasional partner Ossie Noble on the 'Immaculate Chimney Sweeping Company'. Missing a trick by not calling the company 'Chinny Chimneys', the pair went door to door offering the service, then following up with some kind of revolutionary vacuum to do the deed. Jimmy wasn't restricted to the doorstep charm; on occasions he even mucked in and grafted in the fireplaces himself, 'equipped naturally with the essential white coat. The philosophy was that a chimney sweep in a pristine overall was incapable of blackening his reputation.' It's a theory, at least. The business was seemingly a success up to a point, but presumably not enough for him to give up on all the other strings to his bow.

* * *

The factory whistle blows, the office clock ticks round to 6pm, the van is parked back at the depot, and our quick look at the world of work is at an end. Apart from one final image that your body will want to reject but might just stay with you forever. Between the football, the chiropody and the bowling alley, Neil Warnock also found time at one point to work for the Combined Insurance Company of America. Nothing too remarkable about that you might think, until you hear that employees were forced to stand together in the office singing children's classic 'If You're Happy and

You Know it, Clap Your Hands'. Apparently, 'it was the manager's idea of motivation'. I like to think it's a motivational tool that Warnock might have carried over into his own team talks, but I just can't see it, can you?

12.

What Happens on Tour, Doesn't Necessarily Stay on Tour

'Foam Parties'

WE'VE ALL heard the phrase 'what happens on tour, stays on tour'. It's either a code of considerable honour, or a coward's charter, depending on your point of view. Regardless, I'm here to tell you that it's simply not true. Overwhelmingly, a more accurate phrase would be 'what happens on tour goes straight in a book', and we're all the better for it. Football tours can provide elite athletes with a chance to unwind, a chance to take the foot off the gas on their 100mph drive for sporting excellence, a chance to build international relations and reputations, and a chance to go somewhere hot and get drunk. All of which are valid reasons for going, and one of which is certainly true.

However, I wouldn't want you to think it's all sex and drugs and rock & roll. Some of these trips are very gentle and not the least bit raucous. It's a sliding scale you see, from the pensioners bus trip to the seaside, to Ozzy Osbourne snorting ants; and I'm here to hold your hand through everything in between.

In this chapter I want to present a wide variety of these trips away as a kind of holiday brochure, or trip advisor. As we dip a sun-tanned big toe into the tourist trade, I invite you to select the one

FINAL THIRD

you would most like to have been on, based on the company, the location and the events that took place. Whether it's the pyramids, the Great Wall of China, or Jim Smith's bare bum, the very best that the world has to offer is here to behold. But before we bomb off the top board into our holiday pool, let's wash our feet in that shallow trough they make you go through first,[132] with a quick rundown of some on tour antics. Just to help you find your level before committing.

We have:

- Neil Warnock's traditional pre-season tour of Cornwall, taken on with several of his clubs because it's very close to where he lives. He takes players to his local and has a barbecue at his house, which all sounds very gentle and lovely. You might even get a cream tea out of it, though I bet Neil has strong, intransigent views about whether the jam or the cream goes on first, and whether it's pronounced scone like gone or scone like moan. I'll stop you there – it's scone.

- Manchester United's sixties vintage travelling to Australia. Alex Stepney says, 'We did everything together,' which no doubt included surfing, beach barbecues and a bit more surfing, right? Not really. Instead, we have 'Bobby Charlton loving every moment he spent in arranging one crib championship after another'. Stepney doesn't even say if they played outdoors, but good on them. I love crib, me.[133] Unfortunately, the lads ran a forfeit system with the losers carrying the bags of the winners – which was fine until 'Nobby dropped the carrier containing Bobby's duty-free drinks and camera'. Oh, Nobby.

- John Sitton and Terry Howard inventing a game called 'Sharks' in the hotel room, in which 'the floor is shark-

132 You know the one – I think it's to wash your feet, or something to do with a verruca. Does that make this an actual footnote?
133 'Fifteen two, fifteen four, one for his knob. Your box' and all that.

266

infested water and you have to move around the room staying off the floor'. This sounds a bit like a game that most kids in the world have played at some point in their life, and whether they called the floor 'lava', 'shark-infested water' or 'Glastonbury toilets', I'm not sure they can lay claim to inventing it. However, believe me when I say that considerably worse has gone on in the hotel rooms of footballers and this all seems like harmless fun, so long as the lads have a bit of a tidy up afterwards.[134]

- Nick Tanner revealing that Mike Hooper once got his name up on the board at a restaurant on holiday in Majorca by eating six English breakfasts in one go. Well, when else is he going to eat six English breakfasts in one go? I wonder if this was an honours board for people who eat six, as if for a century at Lord's, or a leaderboard. The latter raises the tantalising prospect of István Kozma going in and trumping him with seven.

- Matt Piper joining Mansfield on loan and going on a mid-November[135] break to Portugal which involved 'sunbathing, daytime drinking, turning up to foam parties' and, of course, 'a Liam Lawrence special'. For those of you, like me, who were blissfully unaware of what a Liam Lawrence special is, Piper confirms that it involves finding a 'shit in the bath'. In case that puts you off a little bit, Piper also reassures us that 'otherwise, it was a great tour'. You know, apart from the shit in the bath.

There's your taster, so to speak, and hopefully you've found your level. If it's the Liam Lawrence special then let's never speak again, but I'll try not to be too judgmental about anything else. Here then, are the top ten football holidays available for you to choose from.

---

134 Though Sitton did later famously sack Howard at half-time of a Leyton Orient match so maybe the 'Sharks' game did get out of hand from time to time.

135 You wonder why this took place in mid-November, and then you remember how much cheaper things are outside the school holidays.

Pick your favourite, or your top three. You can do what you like, really; it's your book now.

ARSENAL IN EGYPT

Few countries in the world can fill you with the same sense of wonder as Egypt. It's difficult to fathom the history and the feats of architecture on display when considering the pyramids. Lee Chapman reports that most of the Arsenal squad he went there with were so awestruck that they decided not to bother even going for a look. Despite the thoughtful club laying on transport to go and see the pyramids and the Sphinx, only four players could be bothered to go, while 'those remaining formed card schools or watched television'. Chapman says that this ambivalence to the world's wonders is quite common among players, despite their chosen trade often taking them all over the globe. I reckon somebody should have told them there was a free bar at the Sphinx, but in the absence of such creative salesmanship, at least you know that on this holiday it will be easy enough to book places on the excursions.

STOKE IN GREECE

In contrast to Chapman's wilfully ignorant Arsenal team-mates, he reckons that his buddies at Stoke were quite the culture vultures and very keen to visit the Acropolis when in Athens. Unfortunately, in their naivety, they got lost and were told by the 'owner of a seedy bar' that 'the Acropolis is closed'. Believing him and seeking alternative entertainment, they followed the bar owner into his far from salubrious establishment where ... well, you're probably way ahead of me here aren't you? There were girls, and the Stoke lads were encouraged to buy them drinks and let them sit on their laps, but 'it was only when their hands disappeared down our trousers that we realised they were on the game. We quickly asked for the bill.' The bill was quite literally extortionate, but I won't print it here, because with the distance of time, it looks like a cheap round now. Suffice to say that Chapman and the lads were out of pocket, all revved up and no nearer to seeing the Acropolis.

It's possible to think that he's made this story up and that, of course, they went to the bar on purpose with no intention of brushing up on their classical antiquity. However, I've read the other things he reveals in *More Than a Match* and I see no reason why he would have held back if that was the case.

This one seems like a good trip, but it's probably worth paying for a proper tour guide to show you the right kind of sights.

ENGLAND IN PORTUGAL

Those of a delicate disposition should look away now, as Stanley Matthews brings us news of a trip to Estoril in Portugal which brought shame on the nation and its football team. Firstly, the lads got in trouble for only wearing trunks on the beach when local rules stated vests and trunks. Secondly, some were arrested for jaywalking. And if that absolute mayhem wasn't enough to leave you ashamed on their behalf, later that day Phil Taylor (not that one) and Laurie Scott got nicked for lighting a cigarette in public. A shocked Matthews says, 'We were all slack-jawed to discover it was against the law to use a cigarette lighter on the street without a licence because it was deemed detrimental to the government-controlled match-making industry.' What a pair of bastards. I have no idea how Matthews went on to receive a knighthood after being involved with such shenanigans. It turns your stomach to think of it all doesn't it?

In terms of this trip, Portugal always seems very nice, but it seems like it might be worth reading the small print on the flight over.

BLACKPOOL IN MAJORCA

You might wonder why there was any need to go to Majorca when these guys were already in the seaside utopia of Blackpool and, well, maybe they shouldn't have gone. Andy Morrison has a tale from the trip involving a bit of destruction, but for once it wasn't down to him. Not really, anyway. Blackpool went there in winter so at one point some players were huddled near a fire in the hotel bar.

Unfortunately for the hotel owners, their fireplace was a good size for a five-a-side goal, so nature took its course and centre-half Dave Linighan soon found himself as a goalkeeper, trying to keep the cushions being thrown in his direction out of the flames. Despite the bombardment, Linighan receives praise from Morrison for his 'reflex stops' as he kept 'tipping those cushions round the corner'. In the centuries-old tradition of children around the world, however, these lads played a game until something bad happened, and as one missile headed for the top corner of the fireplace, Linighan 'dived full length and pushed that cushion round the fire, smashing a table full of glasses in the process'. This scenario strikes me as like the psychological ethics test 'The Trolley Problem', with Linighan having to make the tough choice between letting the soft furnishings go up in smoke or smashing the place up. I can't quite decide if he made the right choice, but I understand his reasoning in making it. In many respects the man is a hero for not letting the fire cause any more damage than necessary. Wait, what's that you say Andy Morrison? 'Linny's heroics were in vain because, during the course of the evening, we still managed to set the carpet on fire in two places and caused damage to the tune of £3,500.' Oh, well that gives things a slightly different perspective.

If you do go on this holiday, guests are reminded to respect other residents while in the bar area. As a rule, I would just recommend heading to Majorca in the summer, where it's a bit more of a poolside drinks vibe than a fire and glass flying everywhere vibe.

BIRMINGHAM IN SPAIN

Football folk have an odd record with other people's weddings when away from home. Lest we forget, we have Neil Warnock's

WHAT HAPPENS ON TOUR, DOESN'T NECESSARILY STAY ON TOUR

harmless superstition of wanting to see one before an away game and Brian Clough being overfamiliar with a groom already in the bank. There's also John Burridge happily boasting about tipping a bucket of water out of a hotel window on to an unsuspecting bride and groom below for no good reason,[136] and now we go international with surely the only nuptials in history to be interrupted by a 'stark-bollock-naked' Jim Smith, apart from, possibly, his own.

Jim 'Bald Eagle' Smith took his Birmingham boys to Portugal for a break in Albufeira, and as the squad walked back along a cliff edge from a day's solid boozing, midfielder Tony Towers dropped his watch over the side. Being the diligent boss, and supporting his player, Jim helped Towers to dangle over the side to reach the fallen watch, but unfortunately, according to Roy McDonough, 'both of them lost their balance and tumbled down the cliff'. What could have been the end for the pair of them, luckily wasn't so bad as they only fell a few feet – but it was enough to leave Smith with cuts all over his body while his 'shoulders were all bleeding, and his hairless, red bonce was criss-crossed with scratches'.

Smith staggered back to the hotel to find a scene complete with the rest of the Birmingham squad sat peacefully around the pool, a number of what McDonough eloquently describes as 'surgically enhanced buoyant American goddesses' having a swim and a couple enjoying their wedding ceremony up on a balcony. This idyllic tableau was shattered by Smith's next decision as he surveyed the scene, dropped his shorts and dived into the pool completely in the nip and began doing 'an aggressive breast stroke'.

The women scattered as if Godzilla was emerging from the deep with his Godzuki out, the Blues boys were naturally doubled-up with laughter, while the wedding completely stopped as 'the

---

136 Budgie blames Andy Gray for egging him on and admits it was an awful thing to do. I'm not sure his excuse of being 'working-class boys' over-excited at 'being in a big five-star hotel'. I hate this argument. Most footballers tend to be working-class boys, unless they're Patrick Bamford, and they don't all go around ruining weddings for the sake of it. Well, alright, some of them do.

wedding couple, priest and guests all pushed to the front of the balcony to look down at this bald head and white backside lapping backwards and forwards in the pool'. Smith climbed out, leaving most of the blood in the pool,[137] retrieved his shorts and presumably went off to find some Savlon while he waited for the hotel staff to knock on his door about all the complaints they had received – not least from the couple whose special day he had ruined – or improved, if that's your kind of thing.

I'm not made of stone and have no doubt that this would have been hilariously funny, but I would need to mark the facilities down for having a pool full of blood and a naked football manager rampaging through the complex.

PORTSMOUTH IN JERSEY

More managerial misbehaviour here as Vince Hilaire recalls the adventures of Pompey boss Alan Ball in the Channel Islands. It's a rare story that begins with the players minding their own business in their hotel room while their gaffer causes the carnage.

Hilaire was sharing with Alan Knight and the two were possibly waiting for their tiny kettle to boil when a worse for wear Bally came down the corridor bellowing 'The Greatest Love of All' at the top of his voice. As the pair instantly regretted leaving their door ajar, Ball came bursting in from an evening on the pop, 'sat on the edge of my bed and started talking in a language that, even to this day, I could not understand'. After a bit of gabbling and giggling, Ball fell off the bed, and 'began pulling his trousers up', (from the bottom, he hadn't dropped them), before leaving again. Hilaire and Knight remained confused until another player, Eamonn Collins, came in looking for the gaffer and explained everything.[138]

---

137 I bet Jim was the sort of kid that used to wee in the pool too, when he was little.

138 Incidentally, Collins is one of those curious characters that follows a manager around. Collins started at Blackpool under Ball, where he made his professional debut at 14 years old (I know, right) and then followed him to Southampton, Portsmouth and Exeter. Barely played a game, mind.

WHAT HAPPENS ON TOUR, DOESN'T NECESSARILY STAY ON TOUR

Collins revealed that while queuing for a night club somebody recognised the gaffer. Ball was a World Cup winner, only recently retired, always wore a flat cap and possibly a big puffer jacket with AB on it, so this sort of thing must have happened from time to time, but on this occasion Joe Public overstepped the mark by telling little Alan that he had put on some weight. This is just plain rude, and Ball reacted the only way any well-adjusted man, comfortable in his own skin would and 'offered to race him over 100 yards for £50'. As a chunky lad myself I prefer the 'put on a brave face then go home and cry into a Pot Noodle' approach, but I guess that's what separates me from the World Cup winners. The race was quickly set up and watched by a small crowd who saw Ball take a commanding lead before disaster struck. Ball pulled away and 'was looking back at him when, all of a sudden, he'd run into a bollard and hit the floor'. Only at that point in the story did everything become clear to Vince Hilaire – Ball had been doing a running motion when he came into his room and had been dragging his trouser leg up to show the horrifically scraped knees he sustained in the fall. Of course, this doesn't explain 'The Greatest Love of All' but we can't have everything.

Whether this does or doesn't make you want to go to Jersey I can't tell. It always looked nice in *Bergerac* so don't let it put you off, at least.

LEICESTER IN FINLAND

This one is quite infamous and involves a violent flashpoint involving Dennis Wise – which I appreciate doesn't narrow things down too much. On this occasion the Leicester squad were playing cards on a pre-season tour in Finland when Callum Davidson accused Wise of cheating.[139] Matt Piper is our witness for this one as Wise escalated the row beyond all reasonable measure. Piper

---

139 There is no word on which card game they were playing when the row started but I like to think it was Twizzle, Chase the Ace, or Shithead as they are the best three.

heard shouting and screaming in the corridor and went out to find Matt Elliott and Gerry Taggart taking Wise to task and telling him, 'That little bastard has gone into Callum's room and knocked him out while he's asleep'. Wise had attacked Davidson, fractured his cheekbone, then ran away to his room, got sent home and left the club soon after.

Two things are true about this incident. Firstly, this is appalling behaviour, completely unacceptable and worthy of criminal investigation. Secondly, this might not even make the top five worst things that have happened on a Leicester tour.

HULL IN BULGARIA

Peter Swan brings us a very grotty tale of Hull's 1990 trip to Bulgaria, which was captured in a Yorkshire Television documentary called *A Kick Up the Balkans*.[140] Swan auditions for his own travelogue series by telling us that Sofia is 'an absolute dump', where 'all the women looked like men, with huge, hairy armpits' and then tells a very sordid tale about the prostitutes he sorted out for the lads in his role as 'entertainments manager'. Based on a hunch, Swan approached the hotel lift man and after 'using a bit of graphic sign language' in due course two women arrived with a minder in tow. Swan says he negotiated a price list, presumably with some more graphic sign language that doesn't bear thinking about, and some, but crucially not all, of the players got involved. Swan does preserve the anonymity of the team-mates that took part but he does say that the first two customers refused to leave the room while others waited their turn, so instead the rest just went back to drinking the local beer at 3p a pint. The entertainments manager, who clearly felt that timekeeping was beyond his remit, says that they each enjoyed 15p worth of the beer before heading off to bed. After all, 'we had

---

140 Obviously, I've watched this documentary because I leave no stone unturned. My conclusions are firstly that it would have been a far better documentary if they had included some of the stuff that Swanny describes, and that it would have been far better to call it 'Hullgaria'. I think we can all agree on that.

WHAT HAPPENS ON TOUR, DOESN'T NECESSARILY STAY ON TOUR

a game the following afternoon, so we didn't want to overdo it'. Quite right too. It's important to maintain professional standards on these tours.

Swan's scathing review of everything except the cheap beer might put holidaymakers off a trip to Bulgaria, but I'd like to think that much has improved since then, as it seems to have become very popular. Although the beer is probably a bit more expensive.

WEST BROM IN CHINA

This is another tour covered by a documentary and it is well worth a watch if you can get hold of it. It was a tour made famous by John Trewick's comment about the Great Wall of China that 'if you've seen one wall, you've seen them all', and I'm here to tell you that he was joking. It is often trotted out as an example of the stereotypical thick footballer, but the man was making a joke, and a pretty good one in my opinion, so let's put that to bed.

We're not short of witnesses for this tour with Alistair Robertson, Ron Atkinson and Bryan Robson all discussing it and giving it mixed reviews. Robertson describes it as 'the tour of all tours', and Robson says it gave him 'an insight into a society and culture I could never have imagined', while the less culturally sensitive Atkinson is a bit more dismissive. He talks about people 'clad in those grey boiler suits, obeying orders, doing what the system demanded' and unforgivably says that they are able to control the population there because 'in place is the finest contraception on the planet – ugly women!' Come on, Ron. That's not nice.

Robertson, who confusingly was nicknamed Robbo, despite Bryan Robson being around, does admit that the team were confined to their hotels for much of the time and went a little stir-crazy, as cards will only get you so far. Water fights became the order of the day, with players throwing buckets over each other at any given moment. Robbo (Robertson, not Robson – you can see the confusion) was often the aggressor and at one point found

275

himself naked in a corridor and accidentally throwing a spittoon full of 'fag ends and spit' over chairman Bert Millichip. These things escalate, don't they?

Bryan Robson fondly remembers a rare night they were allowed out to attend the Shanghai Circus, which is possibly where Robertson got the idea of throwing buckets of stuff all over people. The future England captain says that 'the acts were fantastic, but for some reason they wouldn't allow the cameras in'. Why he would say this I simply do not know. Not only were the cameras certainly allowed in, but the documentary crew captured an act which involved a panda playing a trumpet while being pulled around the ring in a cart by dogs. Believe me, I've seen the programme, and it's not the sort of thing you forget in a hurry.

To be honest, China remains something of a mystery to me as a destination, with only this and my sister's *Wham! In China* VHS to go on, so I don't feel able to advise too much on this one.

SHEFFIELD WEDNESDAY IN THAILAND

I can't decide whether you would be surprised or totally unsurprised by the fact that so many stories of footballers in Thailand involve what Alan Partridge would describe as 'Bangkok Ladyboys'. Ian Snodin says that a recently divorced and emotionally fragile Neil Pointon was encouraged to spend time with an attractive woman in a Bangkok bar by his sensitive team-mates before they told him, 'Neil, it's a fucking man that's been sat on your lap for the last half-an-hour.' Possibly on the same Everton tour, Pat Van Den Hauwe got chatting to 'what I believe was a transvestite' who wanted to take things further. A confused Pat insisted that his companion went to the toilet 'for a check out' before inviting them back to the hotel. Pat admits the alarm bells were ringing when he was led into the gents but 'off came the knickers and, although there was no visible problem as there was not a cock in sight, I was still unsure'. Discretion got the better part of valour here and Pat called it a night,

WHAT HAPPENS ON TOUR, DOESN'T NECESSARILY STAY ON TOUR

but fair play to him for negotiating that difficult social situation that we've all surely been in, where you're flirting with somebody and then invite them to the toilet so that you can see whether they have a penis or not. Of course, these things are so much easier in the modern age as mobile phones have torches on them.

Our main focus here, however, is the trip Sheffield Wednesday took to play Watford in a friendly in Bangkok in the mid-eighties. Exactly how much of a clamour there was in Thailand for a friendly between these two sides is debatable, but nevertheless they went, and, naturally, chaos ensued.

Sterland describes the eye-opening scene that he and his Wednesday buddies found, with 'transsexuals everywhere'. Startled Sterland says, 'They'd be playing with your cock under the table and it was like living in a different world.' Two unnamed but apparently well-known players succumbed to temptation and took two suitors back to their hotel room before one of them realised they were dealing with men at a crucial and intimate moment. A misunderstanding led to a row, which led to a fight in a short space of time. A knife was pulled and one player got slashed across the chest, badly enough to leave a mark, before it all calmed down. Sterland says, 'When the player in question got home, I think he told his wife that the scar on his chest was as a result of being caught by a high tackle during the match in Thailand!' This is a tough sell, in my opinion. It was only a friendly after all, who on earth is going in with studs at chest height? It's all well and good, Sterland keeping mum about the players involved, but somebody's wife and family out there have just been able to narrow it down quite a bit.

Lee Chapman was also on the tour, and it strikes me that between this and Stoke's adventures in Greece, that man was travelling the world at one point desperately trying to keep everyone's hands out of his trousers. Chapman remembers that the Watford team on that trip were on a tighter leash under Graham Taylor and 'were not allowed to enjoy themselves, even though the

FINAL THIRD

season was over'. On the plus side of that, though, Lee, none of them ended up with a knife wound at an orgy and a difficult story to tell their wife, so it really is swings and roundabouts.

* * *

There you have it. Ten tours to choose from. Take your pick, pack well, bring your flip-flops, sun cream, Harold Robbins paperback, toothbrush, and an open mind and away you go. Happy travels.

13.

Between the Sticks

'Like Highlander'

THERE'S A lot of fuss talked about the first name on the teamsheet. It's an idiom used to mark out an individual player as the driving force in the XI, the star and best player. Well, I'm here to tell you, it's nonsense. The first name on the teamsheet should always be the goalkeeper. Even if they're no good. You start at the back of the team from the top of your Post-it Note, envelope or fag packet for the very old school, and you start with the goalie. Anything else is just anarchy. If people have made a living and risen to prominence doing the one job nobody in the school playground wanted to do, then the least we can do is stick to the form and jot their names down first.

Goalies. Keepers. Custodians. The Last Line of Defence. They're a different breed, apparently, aren't they? Whether it's John Burridge sitting on the crossbar, David James throwing VHS tapes at a hotel room wall, or David Icke going on TV to tell everyone he's the second coming of Christ, they all seem to have just the right amount of daftness to do the job – and they love to tell you about it. Bruce Grobbelaar says, 'Aren't we all supposed to be crazy?' but rather than being a flippant remark, it's part of his bigger, oddly specific justification for becoming a keeper. He says,

'So many of my family have had legs amputated that they used to call us the "Hopping Grobbelaars" back in South Africa. My great-grandparents had fought on opposite sides in the Boer War and my grandfather had played saxophone in a circus band. With a background like mine is it any wonder that I was attracted to the art of goalkeeping.' I don't know mate. There's a lot going on here, possibly enough for a three-parter on *Who Do You Think You Are?*, but I'm not sure how much of it specifically made playing in goal for Southampton inevitable.

So, what really makes them different? Other than not being quite as good at football as the rest of the team. What makes them tick? What on earth do they keep in those tiny bags they always used to have in the goal with them, but that you don't see so much anymore?

Jens Lehman talks about a particular shot coming at him 'like a bat pissed out of its mind', which, though it sounds like it might be a Meat Loaf song, is in fact just an accurate description of what goalkeepers have to put up with all the time, and therefore what makes them special. They're out on a limb in a team game, frequently exposed before the baying crowd, and subject to the vagaries of whatever whip, curl or milk-curdling power has been put on the ball that flies towards them. Embarrassment and ridicule are never more than a fumble away. With this in mind, I can forgive things like Tim Flowers answering the phone to Alan Shearer with a cheeky 'safest hands in soccer'. They are, after all, as we're so often told, characters. And maybe they've earned their bit of fun and rest. Alan Rough certainly thought so.

Rough was Scotland's goalkeeper at a time when 'Scottish goalkeeper' was a bit of a running gag in certain quarters. After being on the front line for early exits in 1978 and 1982, by the Mexico World Cup of 1986, Rough clearly felt he had paid his dues, and was enjoying being second, possibly third choice. Steve Nicol says that he went to take a throw-in for Scotland against West

Germany in the searing heat only to find behind the hoardings, 'Roughie, lying on the ground covered in Ambre Solaire with his shorts tucked up as high as he could get them. He had a big smile on his face and gave me a wink.' Let's assume he was third choice then. Seeing the goalie trying to get rid of the tan lines created by his gloves must have been quite a distraction for Nicol. Firstly, because he's representing his country on the greatest stage and trying to give of his very best, and secondly, because he's a pale, red-headed gentleman who might have been worried sick that Roughie was using all the Factor 50.

Other goalkeepers driving their team-mates to distraction include Tony Burns, a Plymouth keeper who used to frighten a young Lee Chapman by lying 'in wait inside wardrobes or behind half-closed doors and leap out at unsuspecting victims uttering a piercing scream as he did so', and Stephen Bywater, who would tell defenders at corners that 'I'm coming for this cross like a train', which he accompanied with 'choo, choo' noises, according to Michael Carrick.

The king of the distracting keeper though, is, of course, John 'Budgie' Burridge. The man who may well have had a 'You Don't Have to Be Mad to Work Here, But it Helps' sticker on his crossbar. Neil Ruddock says of their time together at Southampton, 'I'd heard a few stories about him being a bit of a nutter, and I wasn't disappointed.' Ruddock played at centre-half just in front of Burridge and recalls that 'he used to do a running commentary of the game'. That's right. To maintain his concentration, he would come out with the likes of 'Burridge, rolls it out to Ruddock, who slips the ball through to Le Tissier' and 'that's another magnificent save by Burridge'. I suppose we've all done this in the back garden – who are we to judge?

Off the pitch, Burridge was no less unusual. His self-improvement regime included wearing a big combat jacket with sand in every pocket in training, so that he felt lighter when playing

FINAL THIRD

in matches, waking up room mate Steve Hunt by doing sit-ups at 4am, and getting anyone and everyone to throw things at him to keep his reflexes sharp. Hunt says that those dead-of-night workouts were followed by a request to throw oranges across the room 'as he practised his diving on the full length of his bed'. This routine is also remembered by Andy Gray, who shared a house with him at one time, and says that on Friday nights Budgie would sit watching TV with his gloves on and it was Gray's job to throw pieces of fruit at him when he wasn't expecting it: 'There'd be apples and bananas whizzing around and all the while Budgie would apparently be concentrating all his attention on *Bruce Forsyth's Play Your Cards Right*. Unfortunately, we can't know if Gray was throwing them just right or if they needed to be higher, higher, or lower, lower. Or if he got anything for a pear.

Burridge was still at it years later at Man City, where Paul Walsh remembers being asked to throw bread rolls at him over lunch. He must have been slowing down by that stage, though, because Walsh reckons that some 'caught him plum in the face'. Oh, and while we're discussing the way he finessed his game, it's worth mentioning that Steve Hunt also remembers being invited to Budgie's house one day and 'arrived to see him leaping off the garage as some kind of training for his goalkeeping dives'. Kids, please do not try any of this at home – not the fruit, because it will bruise it and you might get told off, and not the garage roof business because it's really dangerous and will also bruise any fruit you might have in your pockets at the time.

Danger, it appears, was Burridge's middle name, because Ruddock has another story of the goalkeeper putting self-improvement way out in front of any consideration for safety. Razor describes another day at Southampton when Budgie arrived for training with a three-foot steel pole and some nails, with the intention of nailing it up to do pull-ups on. Pampered Premier League stars of today have probably got people to nail up their random bits of metal for them, but back then it was every man for himself. Up it went without so much as a cursory glance at a stud finder, or a quick check to see if it would take his weight.

Burridge 'decided to just jump up, grab hold and hope for the best'. It took his weight well enough because he'd nailed it up well. Unfortunately, he hadn't checked what he'd nailed it into, and he had hit some wiring. Unsurprisingly, 'he let out a scream that would have woken the dead' and 'started shaking violently and screaming at the top of his voice'. One keen-eyed coach spotted the problem and shouted, 'Fuck me, he's being electrocuted,' and sure enough, he was. Once it was off at the mains, Budgie was restored to his former, normal self – though what that was exactly remained difficult to tell. My only hope is that somebody had the wherewithal to throw a plum at him while he was fizzing away up there to see just how committed he was to his craft.

Goalkeeping is dangerous enough, without shocking DIY stories. Shay Given reports that Lionel Peréz used to wear a cricket box in training to protect himself when he practised his big starfish jumps, and David Seaman had occasion to wish he'd done the same. The man his affectionate Arsenal team-mates call 'Goalie' remembers Lee Chapman leaving his foot in as he went down for a cross once and leaving 'two red stud marks at the top of my leg and into my groin'. While Chapman's Leeds team-mate Gordon Strachan stood over him insisting that he was faking it, the attending physio 'looked closer and found that studs had ripped into my balls as well and I needed a couple of stitches in them'. There was, evidently, a lot of blood, and a lot of apologising for Strachan to do later once Seamo had counted them and got some ice on them.

A more serious injury was sustained at Sunderland by Charlton keeper Graham 'Buster' Tutt of witch doctor and US adventures fame. The injury that prematurely finished his career in England happened when he was caught badly in the head by an onrushing forward as he went down for the ball. Tutt says that as he lay

FINAL THIRD

there cradling the ball 'I became aware that blood was starting to pool on the mud below my head'. The injury was horrific, and the description is startling. I won't go into it too much detail here (please read Tutt's book), but let's just say, that at one point, along with the blood, he threw up a large part of his cheekbone into a kidney bowl. You heard.

The only upside of Tutt's awful injury nightmare is that he got a benefit match that I would dearly love to have been at between an All-Star Celebrity XI (including Dennis Waterman and Bill Oddie) and a Goalkeepers' XI. That's right, a whole team of goalkeepers including the great and the good of the time like Pat Jennings, Bob Wilson and Jimmy Rimmer playing as outfield players. Ever since I read about this, I've divided my time between wishing I'd been at The Valley to see it, trying to find footage of it, and deciding who would play where if a Goalkeepers' XI were put together now.[141]

Dave Beasant may have had one or two knocks on the pitch but it's fair to say there's a funnier one off the pitch. No, no, not the salad cream drop – that's more route one than his Wimbledon days – I mean the one he sustained on a lap of honour at Stamford Bridge. When Beasant moved to Chelsea it was halfway through a season in which they won promotion from the Second Division. To celebrate, the players took a turn around the old gravel track at Stamford Bridge where the parked cars always sat. Beasant recalls that at one point he thought it would be funny to dive into a huge puddle: 'With a majestic belly-flop I took the plunge to the delight of the fans. Unfortunately for me I didn't realise that the hole was full of gravel and when I emerged from the water my knees were cut to ribbons, blood pouring down my legs.' Ouch. Of course, the way some Chelsea fans speak these days, you would think that the words 'Second Division', 'gravel track', 'Beasant' or even 'puddle'

---

141 There you go, a bit more homework for you. Pickford at left-back, Ederson in midfield and Alisson up front might be a useful start though.

had never been a part of their history – but Big Dave's scabby knees tell the real story.

* * *

One feature that comes up again and again when writing about goalkeepers, is a pathological hatred of being chipped in training. Why this is any worse than being beaten at their near post or being nutmegged, you would have to ask them, but it's something that has traumatised one or two team-mates. Ben Thornley recalls how 'wonderful character' Les Sealey would chase you if you tried to chip him in a training session, adding with a chill, 'God knows what he'd have done,' if the chase had been successful.

Neville Southall, by his own admission, suffered from the same condition. Nev says that all the Everton lads knew that chipping him was a guaranteed way to wind him up, and that if anybody did so, 'I'd respond by booting the training balls out of Bellefield, or by not using my hands in shooting practise.' This habit of not using his hands is remembered with awe by an impressed Pat Nevin too, but Southall is perhaps understating his acts of retribution. Kevin Sheedy says that if you ever dared to try it 'you'd better look out!' while Mark Ward is less vague about the threat posed by an irate Nev on the warpath. Ward found out all about it the day he dared to send the ball up and over Nev's head. Demanding satisfaction, Southall chased him 'like a raging bull' and when he caught up with him, Ward says, 'He grabbed me with his massive hands and pummelled me from head to toe. He picked me up, then threw me back on to the turf and his parting shot was to jump on me with his studs scraping the skin off my back.'[142] It makes me think that once the cameras stopped rolling on that infamous 'Well done, he's 13' video, he furiously chased Michael Owen all over that pitch.

---

142 Southall's parents, by the way, are named Fred and Rose. I don't know where that gets us, I just thought you might like to know.

FINAL THIRD

It will surprise absolutely nobody to learn that Peter Schmeichel also has a zero-tolerance policy on being chipped. Unfortunately for him, at Manchester United training sessions he had to contend with the supernaturally talented footballer and all-round cheeky scamp, Paul Scholes – so he got chipped a lot. Alex Ferguson remembers him threatening to kill Scholes and chasing him for having the temerity to do a Philippe Albert on him. But, of course, he did it anyway. Scholes is bemused by the goalkeepers' union policy on being chipped in training, saying, not unreasonably, 'Chipping is part of the game, so why wouldn't we want to practise it?' He has found that many of them are the same though: 'It was always against the law with Ben Foster, and when I was with England, Dave Seaman hated it too.' Far be it from me to tell David Seaman his business, but perhaps if he had had asked people to practise getting the ball over his head while he tried to stop them a bit more, we wouldn't have witnessed him glancing skywards as the likes of Nayim of Real Zaragoza, Ronaldinho of Brazil, Gareth Farrelly of Bolton, Artim Sakiri of Macedonia and Serge of Kasabian all sent the ball sailing over his various ill-advised hairdos.

For the record, old fusspot Schmeichel was also very touchy about having any balls in his goal during training. At Man City, Darren Huckerby therefore naturally took great delight in filling the net with balls when Peter wasn't looking. No points for guessing what happened next: 'He'd chase me, but he was so old and big that he had no chance of catching me.' It seems that Schmeichel spent more time chasing people than 'The Beast' and 'The Governess' put together, because Ben Thornley also has a story which has him fleeing the scene with the keeper in hot pursuit. Thornley was a Manchester United sub at Southampton one day and as such it was his job to warm Schmeichel up, by firing half-volleys at him in the goalmouth. All well and good until Schmeichel got distracted by some jibes from fans behind the goal and turned back just in time to see one of Thornley's cultured kicks fly 'straight into his bugle'. Fearing the worst, the youngster took off as Schmeichel 'went berserk' and chased him the length of The Dell pitch, down into the dressing room and into the toilets, where he hid until Alex 'The Schmeichel Whisperer' Ferguson calmed his goalie down.

If all this paints a picture of your average goalkeeper as being a bit grumpy then I don't think that's unfair, based on the evidence at hand. John Burridge, again, is a case in point as he tells the tale of leaving Aston Villa and being asked to return his club Alfa Romeo so that somebody else could have it. Put yourself in his shoes for a moment. Perhaps you're disappointed to be leaving, but you can't expect to retain the club car if you're no longer at the club, right? Perhaps your next club will provide you with one. With that in mind do you:

a) Get the car professionally valeted in preparation for the next owner. After all, you should leave things as you found them.

b) Hand it over in its present condition. After all, it's not your problem anymore.

c) Take your car to a farm on your way to dropping it off, ask the farmer to lend you ten chickens to throw inside and let them shit everywhere. After all, you might be John Burridge.

If you chose C you might just have what it takes to make it as a goalkeeper. Budgie says that his 'little surprise' was awful to look at and smell. What he leaves out of his version of the story is how he then got the car from the farm to the ground and what they said when he got there. Presumably he had to climb back in and take it there himself, so maybe it's not quite the win he sees it as, even if he wound all the windows down and put some newspaper on the seat.

Despite his petty poultry party piece and constantly nagging people to chuck healthy snacks at him, Budgie is by no means the least popular goalkeeper according to our sources. That title should probably go to Harald 'Toni' Schumacher, who famously put Patrick Battiston in a coma and knocked his teeth out with the worst challenge most of us have ever seen, at the 1982 World Cup for West Germany against France. He compounded his villainy by responding to a question about it on TV by pulling a wad of cash out of his pocket and saying, 'Well. I'll buy him a new set of teeth.'

Tony Woodcock and Jens Lehmann are both full of tales of Schumacher's arrogance and general unpleasantness, but purely in terms of word count, he does not appear to be the keeper to have rubbed the most people up the wrong way. It is no exaggeration to say that across over 300 books read in research, there is one goalkeeper that stands head and shoulders above all others in terms of upsetting his fellow pros, in print at least. Which is ironic, because the defining image of this goalkeeper is of Diego Maradona being head and shoulders above him. It is, of course, Peter Shilton.

None of us, outside Scotland at least, can be without sympathy for Shilts about that infamous Maradona goal – it was cheating, after all. However, neither is it unreasonable to hope that, nearly 40 years on and with Diego dead and buried, the unfortunate keeper might have got over it, at least a little bit. Newsflash – he hasn't. Let's not pretend, however, that the Maradona incident is the only thing about him that people question. The autobiographies covered here are littered with disputes with Shilts over any number of things (some of which we've covered in previous volumes) – even though they were all written before he became one of those Twitter controversialists you get these days.

Gordon Banks claims that Peter the protege gave the Leicester board an ultimatum that he should play in the first team, or he would leave, which set Banks on his way out of the door to Stoke. Shilton then followed him to Stoke as well where Alan Hudson says he was so unpopular that team-mates would sneakily put weights in his bag while he was in the shower. Alan Curtis played alongside Shilton at Southampton, a few years after he had been badly injured in a collision with the keeper while playing for Swansea. Curtis is clearly a little put out that Shilton 'never actually mentioned the incident once during the time we played together at The Dell'.

With the usual caveats about the unquestionable ability of Shilton, Curtis goes further, saying that Saints players were upset that, due to reputation and status, 'his training schedule was sometimes a little more flexible than the majority of the rest of the squad'. This is interesting, because at Southampton around that time, Lawrie McMenemy was juggling a lot of big stars. If he had afforded the luxury of an easier training regime to all these big guns (the likes of Ball, Channon and Mills) he would have barely had enough players left for a game of headers and volleys, so it's interesting that Shilton got the VIP treatment. David Armstrong goes further still, saying of Shilts, 'Nobody at Southampton was close to him,' and that he would talk to team-mates 'as if they were somehow inferior and everyone except him was at fault if a goal went in'.

I imagine that Shilton wouldn't be alone in apportioning blame elsewhere when the net bulges behind him, but it clearly rankles enough with Armstrong that he picks Jim Platt over him in his all-time XI, which is controversial. He says it's not a personal grudge, but it certainly feels like one. Maybe it was triggered because Shilton swore at him in a restaurant once, which clearly rocked him to his core. 'I won't say what he called me ... but I was quite shocked at what he said and where he said it.' This is all I can think about now. Why is he so shocked at a swear word? Did he call him a bastard at the bar, a tosser in the toilets or something else in the carvery queue? If Armstrong won't tell, I guess we'll never know, but he does say Shilton later apologised, so he's not a monster.

The keeper's winning way with people continued into his brief management stint at Plymouth. Things went sour quickly at Argyle, and Andy Morrison was there to witness it. Morrison writes in *The Good, The Mad and the Ugly* that Shilton introduced John McGovern as his assistant by telling his players, 'Remember, he's lifted the European Cup, something that none of you will ever do so don't forget that,' which may have turned out to be true but doesn't seem to be quite the boost the players were looking for.

Unimpressed by Shilts the gaffer, he describes him curiously as 'so fucking wooden that I wondered if he had ever been mistaken for a door'. Given Morrison's pre-match routine, Shilton is lucky he didn't get the nut stuck on him before each game.

Roy McDonough is a similarly abrasive character to Morrison and takes against Shilton despite never even having played with him. Much of his disgust seems to stem from Shilton not putting Maradona in hospital and going 'straight through the Argie' at that Hand of God moment. Apparently had Roy been in goal himself, 'I'd have made sure Maradona left the field on a stretcher.' Clearly a bit of a selection oversight by Bobby Robson there, ignoring lower league striker McDonough in favour of one of the world's greatest, albeit bitterest, keepers. Although in fairness to Roy, it's a sentiment shared by Peter Reid in his snapshot of the time, *Everton Winter Mexican Summer*. He says, 'I just had the feeling that Shilts might have taken everything – the ball was there so he had the chance to take Maradona as well,' and he was on the pitch that day. McDonough just won't let it lie. Elsewhere in the relentlessly entertaining *Red Card Roy*, he says that he barely counts the penalty he scored past Shilton once for Southend against Derby because of the keeper's poor efforts at saving the German penalties at Italia '90. Roy rants that the England keeper 'never took a gamble and just waited to see which way the ball went', and you can hear his blood boiling from here. He may have a point though. It certainly seems to have come up in the post-match dressing room on that night in Turin.

Paul Parker says that Shilton was 'the only one not apparently overwhelmed' in the aftermath and he 'was telling himself and those around him how unlucky he had been because he had guessed the right way every time and had dived accordingly'. Then, Parker says, Stuart Pearce piped up to shout, 'You should have bloody gambled,' which is bold considering he had just missed his kick, so it must have been something he felt strongly about. Tantalisingly,

Parker doesn't say how Shilton reacted or what happened next and now that dressing room is the only place I'd want to go in a time machine. He does say, 'In my view there was no point in blaming Shilton any more than we should have blamed Pearce or Waddle,' which is good of him to say, but is perhaps motivated by the fact that some people have pointed the finger at him over the years, for his part in the Andy Brehme goal. Shilton doesn't, which comes as a relief, saying he did his job in closing the ball down, but nor does the keeper see anything wrong with his own part in what remains a pretty farcical goal to concede. Please look it up if you're not old enough to wake up screaming about it most nights. Shilton is right to say that the deflection off Parker meant that 'my momentum suddenly had to change', but a few of us may dispute his assertion that 'I felt I'd made a good job of readjusting quickly' and that 'if I had remained rooted to the spot and looked on helplessly as the ball sailed over my head, I'm sure not a word would have been said'. I think it might have come up in conversation, Peter.

Pearce recalls having to defend his buddy, Des Walker, from an undeserved Shilton rant on one occasion and says that the keeper 'used to go through black moods and was often at loggerheads with several of the players'. It's a view backed up by Bryan Robson, a man who was skipper for a good chunk of Shilton's England caps. Robbo is keen to stress how highly he rated him as a keeper and says that 'Shilts was a good mate' but concedes that after defeats 'he had an irritating habit of blaming somebody else and telling them they weren't good enough' to the point where Robbo would have to have a word with him. Not only was 'bad feeling in the camp a concern' but on one occasion 'Terry Butcher was going to kill him on a flight from Los Angeles until I stepped in'. It sounds like it was a good job that Robson was there, keeping a lid on things with his diplomatic captaincy skills.

His role as peacemaker worked just fine until Shilton turned his critical gaze on Robson himself after England were dumped out of the 1988 European Championship. Robson says that 'one or two of us were having a drink at the hotel bar and Peter started having a go at me', calling him a bottler and 'taunting me about the "Captain Marvel" stuff and saying he was number one'. Technically he was number one and Robbo was number seven and perhaps this was all a silly misunderstanding. It's also possible that the few drinks were playing their part, but Shilton had apparently pressed one too many buttons and after keeping his temper for a good while Robson exploded, telling the keeper, 'Get up and I'll show you who's a bottler.'

'He wouldn't get up, but I was so angry I punched him.' Obviously, captains punching their team-mates isn't on and Robbo did the right thing and apologised over the Rice Krispies the following morning.

Maybe it's no wonder Shilton gets grumpy if even the people who like and respect him put a bit of side on their compliments. Kevin Keegan says of him, 'I am not being unkind in saying that nature intended Peter Shilton to be a thickset lad with a weight problem.' I mean, it seems unkind, Kev. What he means, of course, is that 'his fitness and agility are an inspiring example', but it feels like he could say the good thing without saying the bad thing, and maybe then the list of people Shilton has fallen out with wouldn't be longer than his arms after a long session hanging off the banister.

Maybe what makes Shilts and his goalkeeping brethren so irascible is what they have to put up with, and I'm thinking specifically about the things that get thrown at them from behind the goal. I can remember playing in a school match where there were kids behind the goal whacking golf balls at our keeper, and let me tell you, that lad would be in good company. Goalkeepers have people constantly talking behind their back while they're at work, which is enough to make you paranoid. If they're lucky it will just be about their ability or lack of it, but sometimes it gets personal. Amid the taunts and spit that some of them sadly remember raining down from the stands, there are also a surprising variety of objects, and here's the roll call:

Bruce Grobbelaar
Second-hand toilet paper
Fresh fruit
Rockets and flares
A magnesium stick (Don't really know what one is or where you would get one)

Pat Jennings
Bottles
Coins
Stones
Doorknobs (Please note the plural, suggesting this happened more than once)
A billiard ball
Steel staples (Fired by elastic bands)
Sharpened coins
Snowballs (A bit Christmassy, at least)

Shay Given
Oranges
Food (Disconcertingly vague)
Bits of the stadium
Concrete
Firebombs

Shay Given's list here all comes from the World Cup Play-Off Ireland played against Iran, which sounds a bit lively. He remembers that at one point a firebomb 'landed about a metre away, dug into the pitch and exploded, sending dirt and soil right into my face'. Bloody hell.

Interacting with the fans as a goalkeeper isn't all bad. Alan Curtis remembers Swansea keeper Tony Millington getting a pasty sent down to him through the crowd from the snack bar at the back of the stand and leaning against a post eating it during a game. Even if the filling was really hot it doesn't count as an incendiary device. Unfortunately, manager Harry Gregg, a legendary keeper himself, didn't see the funny side of it and 'went crazy, screaming obscenities at Millie', when he saw what was going on. In the dressing room 'Millie was lifted off his feet by his neck and told, in no uncertain terms, what a disgrace he was to his profession'. With a name like Gregg, you would think that Harry might be sympathetic to any transgressions to do with bakery goods, but no. Besides which, I thought that goalkeepers were supposed to stick together.

Commentators and pundits regularly talk about 'The Goalkeepers' Union'. As far as I can see from a cursory online check, such a union isn't listed as a TUC affiliate, but it seems to have a lot of members regardless. Given says that when he had surgery for a terrible stomach injury sustained away at West Ham, he received messages of support from other players and that 'Petr Cech and Edwin van der Sar both texted, telling me to stay positive', which is nice as it isn't easy with gloves on.

Dave Beasant recalls that in the moment of his greatest triumph his thoughts turned to his opposite number. Having saved a penalty and lifted the trophy in Wimbledon's 1988 FA Cup win over Liverpool, pleasant Beasant sought out Bruce Grobbelaar to offer his commiserations. The pair swapped shirts and, having done a newspaper article in which he had asked '"Wimbledon, they play tennis don't they?", presented me with a case containing a pair of racket-shaped [sic] glasses.' It's not clear if he means crystal tumblers here or spectacles like Elton John might wear on Centre Court, but it's a lovely, contrite gesture and it speaks of a mutual respect between two men with a difficult job. However, you have to wonder exactly why Grob was carrying the glasses with him that day. Call me a cynic, but it must surely have been with the intention of making fun of their conquered London foes, mustn't it? Or maybe I just don't understand the ties between this Band of Brothers between the sticks.

However, solidarity from one end of the field to the other is one thing, but at the same team where two goalkeepers are competing for one spot? That's quite different. As Jens Lehmann says, 'The fight for the goalposts, in contrast, is like *Highlander*: there can only be one.' He's right, although fewer heads get chopped off in the world of goalkeeping. Some managers will try to placate two talented goalkeepers and let them take turns like children on a slide, but it doesn't always work. Genial Ron Greenwood juggled Ray Clemence and Peter Shilton to good effect when he was England manager, but they had nowhere else to go and no choice but to suck it up.[143] When Tommy Docherty tried the same thing at Chelsea with Peter Bonetti and Alex Stepney, he just upset both of them, with Stepney labelling it 'bordering on the absurd' on his way out of the door to Manchester United.

Nick Tanner remembers that when David James first arrived at Liverpool as competition to Bruce Grobbelaar, the two were like rutting stags, trying to establish dominance like you see in those Attenborough shows on the telly. The pair even had a diving competition 'while a couple of beers in' on the summer club holiday before they got down to business.[144] A diving competition between two goalkeepers should have been fairly spectacular. I wonder if it's easier to teach an Olympic diver to be a goalkeeper, or a goalkeeper to be an Olympic diver? It's like *Armageddon* where they trained some deep-core drillers to be astronauts, rather than teach some astronauts to do a bit of drilling. I've gone off topic again, haven't I? You really should say something when that happens.

Competing keepers, was it?

---

143 Clem even stayed friends with Shilton long enough to record a single together – a version of 'Side by Side', which I urge you to seek out.

144 Jamo made quite the early impression on his Liverpool team-mates after sharing a room with Torben Piechnik (it was a golden age) and trying to beat him up while sleepwalking. Tell me you want a room of your own without telling me you want a room of your own, as the kids say.

Jens Lehmann spends a good amount of his book on his rivalry with Oliver Kahn for a place in the Germany team, which was about as cordial as you might expect at times, while Bryan Gunn remembers joining Norwich from Aberdeen to find a frosty welcome from fellow keeper, Peter Benstead, who told him, 'If you think you're going to waltz in here and take my place, you've got another thing coming.' Reader, he took his place.

A 16-year-old Andy Goram was thrown into the first team at Oldham, upsetting resident goalie Peter McDonnell in the process. Faced with the challenge of the younger man, the incumbent keeper did his best to hang on to his role by hiding the youngster's boots. As Goram says, 'He was an experienced pro, and yet he did that.' Goram got around the fiendishly clever plan by simply buying another pair of boots and playing anyway. McDonnell is hardly The Hooded Claw, is he?

The dream pairing of club-mate keepers appears to be Shay Given and Steve Harper at Newcastle. Given was usually number one, Harper played his share of games and everyone got along famously. So much so in fact that Given talks less about their rivalry on the pitch and more about the various scrapes he got into, and that Harper got him out of. There was one occasion when a night out in Liverpool after the races went sideways, with Given essentially being abducted by some local lads he got talking to and being taken to 'the roughest house party I've ever been to'. At 6am Given finally made it back to his Formby Hall hotel, to find that his bed had been taken by someone else in their group. He then says, 'There was nothing else for it. Two hours later, Harps woke up in the luxurious surroundings of Formby Hall to find me next to him in bed, still pissed, snoring. And stark bollock naked.' I mean, he says there was nothing else for it, and it's great that he's got a friend he can turn to in his hour of need, but this doesn't explain the nudity. Break into his room, by all means; kip in an armchair or bunk down on the floor, by all means; take all your clothes off and spoon him – that feels like a step too far – but thankfully Harper doesn't seem to have cared. Given also tells of a time in St Andrews when he did a drunk wee down an alleyway on a night out, only for Harper to talk a policeman out of arresting him for it. What a save!

* * *

Goalkeepers then – what have we learned? Hopefully we can leave this chapter behind with a bit more tolerance for their moods, awareness of their flaws and respect for their craft. Matt Busby calls them 'a race apart' and perhaps he's right, after a fashion. Pepe Reina nails the goalkeeper's lot when he says, 'It is easier to recall the mistakes than the great saves,' and that's something they just live with, particularly in an age of endless TV replays and internet memes – just ask Loris Karius. However, US legend Hope Solo takes a more positive view of her chosen trade. She lives by the words, 'A goalkeeper cannot win a game. A goalkeeper saves it.' So moved was she when this revelation was first pointed out to her that 'I made those words my computer screen-saver'. There can be no higher compliment. From that moment on she was motivated by them as she watched them bounce slowly around her monitor at all the different angles.

Some of us might labour under the impression that we can throw just anyone in the nets – the biggest player, or the one that hasn't brought the right shoes with them, or even just take turns depending on who gets puffed out, but there's clearly more to it than that. You can't just put anyone in – if Gary Plumley taught us anything, he taught us that. Plumley played for Watford when they were without first-choice keeper Tony Coton for the 1987 FA Cup semi-final against Tottenham. Presumably they were also without their second, third, fourth or fifth choices as well, because although he had previously been a professional for Newport County, at the point he stepped in for the Hornets, he was the manager of a wine bar in Wales. Crucially, however, he was the son of the club's chief

FINAL THIRD

executive. A fairytale nepotism ending was not to be, however, as Spurs thumped them 4-0, and Gary went back to Newport with just his expenses paid for his trip out. Hindsight is a wonderful thing, but I think a good many people could have told them before kick-off that they might have stood a better chance with an actual professional goalkeeper in nets rather than a wine bar manager. Still, Gary bought a new fridge with his expenses, so it wasn't all bad news.

14.

Always Finish with a Song – Or a List

'The Selection Pistol'

AND SO, as we collapse, exhausted, under the weight of all the football anecdotes, we can take our rest and ponder exactly how best to end a book such as this. Having been told by the otherwise incredibly tolerant publishers that it apparently 'just wasn't possible' to have a firework burst out upon turning the final page, instead I thought that if more conventional methods were the order of the day, we might finish with a list.

Football fans love a list, don't we? Barely a day goes by where we aren't poring over league tables, or successful dribble stats lists (if you're one of those people) or coming up with our own 'All-Time Foreign Players that Played for Our Club Whose Names Begin with Vowels XI'.[145] Well the good news is that those inside the game love them just as much. Faced with finishing their own books, many turn to a list to crystalise their thoughts. Often, the go-to is a Best Of ..., a celebration of the great and good that the author has played with, against, managed or whatever they like really. Ron Atkinson may talk about being 'forced into a corner with the selection pistol pointed at the temple', but we're pretty sure it's just

---

145 I give it half an hour before you're having a go.

FINAL THIRD

a bit of fun. What on earth is a selection pistol anyway? I've heard of starting pistol, but this seems to be a different thing entirely, like it's a pistol that only comes out of the drawer and takes aim while someone struggles to choose their 'All-Time Wales XI with Moustaches'.[146] Silly Ron – although that's not making a top ten list of the worst things he's said.

Sometimes, these Best XIs work well and bring home the high-calibre company these players have kept. Paul Merson's best XI looks like it would take some beating; solid at the back and with Vieira and Gascoigne in midfield, though Paul Parker's best boys would give them a game. Others throw up surprising results. As well as snubbing Shilton, David Armstrong doesn't find room for Mick Channon either, while Graeme Souness picks a best Liverpool XI and leaves out John Barnes on the grounds that 'he didn't do it for me when I went back as manager' (ooh, get him). Elderly relatives might be outraged that Eddie Hapgood left Stanley Matthews out of his black-and-white dream team, but surely the most heartbreaking omission of them all occurs in Sam Allardyce's list of the best players he has managed. He's certainly coached some greats and predictably Okocha, Djorkaeff and Anelka all make the cut, but here comes the bomb … there's no room for Kevin Nolan.

Just to clarify, Kevin Nolan must be the most Sam Allardyce player there's ever been. He might just as well have been created in a Sam Allardyce lab by Sammy Lee and the other Minions. He's a player that dutifully followed him from Bolton to Newcastle to West Ham and I cannot imagine how crestfallen Kev would have been to receive the news. It would really take the spring out of that chicken dance.

One man who takes these lists to heart is the hyper-sensitive Rodney Marsh. Marsh is fuming about a link a friend sent him, you

---

146 Big Nev and Rushy are absolute shoo-ins, aren't they?

know, 'on the internet' in which he was only number eight on a list of Man City's greatest players. Rod was so outraged he said he was tempted to 'write in and say, "What the fuck do you think you're doing?"'. Personally insulted, it sends Marsh off into a furious spiral about his standing at City generally. He not only believes that 'my name should be up with the City greats around the stadium' and claims that he isn't 'because it's no longer a people's club'. Ah, yes, that'll be it. A dozen or so trophy-laden years on at the Etihad since he wrote this and we can only imagine where Rodney would appear on such a list now, with the likes of Agüero, Touré, Sterling and David Silva to compete with. He must be fuming every time he plugs the internet in. Don't worry, Rodney, just write your own and put yourself top.

One list of his own that he comes up with is his own top ten 'Loose Cannons', players, after his own irrepressible heart. It's a fairly arbitrary list in which he finds room for both Diego Maradona and Vinnie Jones, and his entry for Gazza is quite something: 'Whether he was pushing a pie into someone's face, eating worms and spitting them out on camera or belching into the mike, he was never fully under control. He even wore a pair of false tits once!' Yes. Yes, he did, didn't he? Get him in a top ten.

Some like lists so much they lean on them throughout. In fact, in the case of Harry Redknapp and Robbie Savage, they have now written so many between them that their later efforts are almost just a list of lists.

In A Man Walks Onto a Pitch Redknapp devotes chapter after chapter to his teams of every decade since the fifties. His time spent on the seventies is particularly interesting as he spends pages and pages extolling the virtues of the mercurial talents of maverick geniuses Rodney Marsh (who would, no doubt, be delighted), Alan Hudson, Frank Worthington and Stan Bowles, subscribing to the commonly held opinion that it's criminal how few international caps they got between them. So how many of these geniuses does he include when he selects his team of the decade? You guessed it. Not a single one.

Previous volume, *Booked!* dealt with king of the lists, John Aldridge, who gives us a series of 'Top 8s' throughout his book including his favourite celebrations ('8. Hands in the air (simple)') and best of all 'Most Difficult Grounds to Get To', which surely depends on where you're starting from, Aldo? But he's not alone in mixing things up. Johann Cruyff goes high end with his Perfect XI and 'The Fourteen Rules of Johann Cruyff' (14. 'Bring beauty to the sport'). while Peter Reid keeps things grounded by alluding to 'a league table of drinkers'. He does stop just short of writing it out in a table but tells us that Bryan Robson and Terry McDermott would be firmly established in the Champions League spots 'although if brandy was involved Sam Allardyce would take some beating'. Or pints of wine, presumably.

Matt Le Tissier and Muzzy Izzet each give off negative energy by creating a worst XI for Southampton and Leicester, respectively, which seems a bit unnecessary, but we'll let Muzzy off because he goes even further and lists his most hated player, which is priceless gossip. Tim Sherwood, since you ask, 'for general obnoxious mouthiness'. Who'd have thought?

The reasoning is often part of the fun. Some of these team lists, best or worst, are clearly born out of having a few axes to grind. For example, Emlyn Hughes picks a greatest Liverpool XI and leaves out his famous dressing-room rival Tommy Smith, saying, 'It's a shame that Tommy Smith must go into the reserve slot', with barely contained glee.

He does, of course, find room for himself and Phil Thompson, with whom he clearly got along better, adding, 'I like to think that we brought a new dimension to defensive techniques.' Even if you do say so yourself, Emlyn.

Mickey Thomas picks football enigma Steve Coppell in his best XI to conclude his book but the entry for him raises more questions than it answers. Mentioning Coppell's degree, he says, 'Some cruel jibes now say it must have been a degree in depression. I got mine in shagging.' I can't find either of these in any prospectus I've looked in, and it seems a bit off-topic, unless you read Mickey's book and find his lustful boasts fighting for room with the football on practically every page. On Coppell he continues, 'He was a great bloke. I went to his house once after a game and it was bloody cold. He didn't have any heating on. So he gave me this lovely England top to keep me warm.'

Why didn't Steve Coppell have any heating on? It's never explained. But keeping yourself and visitors warm with accumulated England shirts is surely not practical. Does he keep his head warm indoors with his international caps too? Finally, Mickey says of his chilly chum, 'I admired Steve in more ways than one. Everyone said I had two lungs. He had three legs by the way – make your own assessment of that one.' Firstly, most people have got two lungs – this is not much of a compliment if people do indeed say it. Secondly, well I think he's either saying that Steve could run really fast, or that he's got a big winkle, and given Mickey's constantly below-the-waist, one-track mind, it's more likely to be the latter that gets him into his best XI.

Let's finish with an absolute favourite of all the lists, from Chelsea legend Didier Drogba, who presents his 'top five Chelsea 'players'. Now let's stress once again that this is Didier's book. Nobody is holding Big Ron's 'selection pistol' to his head and he can write what he wants. This could be the top five things that make Chelsea great, or a full list of top ten Chelsea players. Instead, his 'players' list is as follows:

1. 'Roman Abramovich, as without him, we would never have achieved what we did'.

Strong start. Roman put in so much tainted money that it earns him top spot despite not even being a player.

FINAL THIRD

2. 'Jose'.

Right. The reasons for Drogba praising Mourinho are long and obvious, but he's not a Chelsea player, is he? Stepping on the pitch once and kicking Olly Murs at Soccer Aid, while admirable, doesn't make you a player. But we're only on number two. There's still time if we're quick.

3. 'JT, Frank Lampard and Petr Cech'.

I mean, that's three players. A decision he justifies by claiming that 'they should be considered as one'. Okay then, we're back on track. Two more slots to complete his top five players. Here we go.

4. 'Claude Makelele'.

Why does he get his own slot then? Would the other three not have him in their gang?

So which Chelsea player gets the coveted final slot in Didier's definitive list of Stamford Bridge's best players?

5. 'The fans – they are, quite simply, essential'.

Ah. Well, those aren't players either are they Double-D? What on earth is going on? You've called a list top five Chelsea players, then picked an owner, a manager, tied three players at third, put one of his own at fourth, then said 40,000-odd people are fifth. You didn't need to make this fit, mate. Oh well, as long as he's happy, I suppose.

As a bluff old traditionalist, I'm going to finish with my own lists. As a nod to John Aldridge, here's a Top 8 books that I would happily recommend from the additional reading done for Final Third! Some of these were so good, it makes you wonder why I didn't read them sooner.

In no particular order:

Mick 'Baz' Rathbone – *The Smell of Football*

What a legend. A man who successfully bounced back from Sir Alf Ramsey breaking character to tell him, 'Who's going to sign you? You are fucking crap!', to become a cult figure on and off the pitch at Preston, Halifax and Everton.

Peter Taylor – *With Clough by Taylor*

The inside line on the best double act in football.

Howard Gayle – *61 Minutes in Munich*

Particularly good around his early Liverpool years, giving a good snapshot of the time. Inevitably, given when he played, there's racism and how he faced it.

Jimmy Hill – *The Jimmy Hill Story*

You might not want to enjoy it, but you will. It's a wild ride full of surprises. That man has done pretty much everything.

Matt Piper - *Out of the Darkness*

A promising career ruined by injury. An excellent, honest book, both funny and tragic in places.

Peter Swan - *Swanny: Confessions of a Lower-League Legend*

Full of loads of funny stories and not all of them are even about showbiz chum Robbie Williams.

Steve Hunt – *I'm with the Cosmos*

Played with any number of superstars while at New York Cosmos. Tells it very well.

Arsène Wenger – *My Life in Red and White*

Something highbrow for the deep thinkers out there.

FINAL THIRD

And finally, because I couldn't resist, it's an XI. From well over 300 books read for this odyssey, from gritty well-written life stories to pure fun anecdote gold, here is my Autobiography XI.

Every one of these is worthy of your time, whoever you support. Enjoy, and thanks for reading.

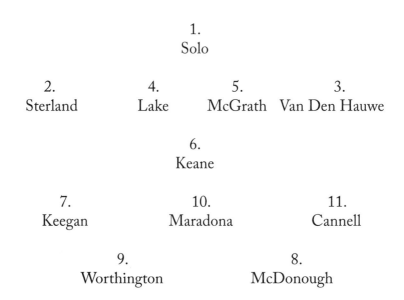

1.
Solo

2.   4.   5.   3.
Sterland   Lake   McGrath   Van Den Hauwe

6.
Keane

7.   10.   11.
Keegan   Maradona   Cannell

9.   8.
Worthington   McDonough

Sub: Whiteside

Manager: **Malcolm Allison**
Assistant Manager: **Peter Taylor**
Physio: **Mick Rathbone**
Chairman: **Elton John**

BIBLIOGRAPHY

Adams, Tony with Ian Ridley, *Sober: Football. My Story. My Life* (Simon & Schuster UK, 2017).

Akinfenwa, Adebayo, *The Beast: My Story* (Headline, 2017).

Aldridge, John with John Hynes, *Alright Aldo: Sound as a Pound. On the Road with Everybody's Favourite Irish Scouser* (Trinity Mirror Sport Media, 2010).

Allardyce, Sam, *Big Sam: My Autobiography* (Headline, 2015).

Allen, Clive with James Olley, *Up Front: My Autobiography* (deCourbetin Books, 2019).

Allison, Malcolm with James Lawton, *Colours of My Life* (Everest Books Ltd, 1975).

Anderson, Viv, *First Among Unequals: The Autobiography* (Fullback Media, 2010).

Ardiles, Ossie, *Ossie's Dream: My Autobiography* (Transworld Digital, 2010).

Armstrong, David and Pat Symes, *The Bald Facts: The David Armstrong Biography* (Pitch Publishing, 2013).

Atkinson, Ron, *Big Ron: A Different Ball Game* (Andre Deutsch Ltd, 1999).

Atkinson, Ron, *The Manager* (deCoubertin Books, 2016).

Ball, Alan, *Playing Extra Time* (Pan; New edition edition, 2005).

Banks, Gordon, *Banksy: The Autobiography* (Penguin, 2019).

Barnes, John, *The Autobiography* (Headline Book Publishing, 1999).

Barton, Joey, *No Nonsense* (Simon & Schuster UK, 2017).

Bassett, Dave, *Settling the Score* (John Blake, 2002).

Bassett, Dave and Downes, Wally, *The Crazy Gang* (Bantam, 2016).

Batty, David, *The Autobiography* (Headline, 2002).

Beasant, Dave with Dave Smith, *Tales of the Unexpected* (Mainstream Publishing Company, 1989).

Beattie, Kevin, *The Beat* (Skript Design & Publishing, 1998).

Bellamy, Craig with Oliver Holt, *Goodfella* (Trinity Sport Media, 2013).

Bergkamp, Dennis, *Stillness & Speed: My Story* (Simon & Schuster UK, 2014).

Best, Clyde, *The Acid Test* (deCoubertin Books, 2016).

Blanchflower, Danny, *The Double and Before …* (Nicholas Kaye Ltd, 1961).

Bonds, Billy, *Bonzo* (Arthur Barker, 1988).

Botham, Ian, *Head On: The Autobiography* (Ebury Press, 2007).

Bowles, Stan, *The Autobiography* (Orion, 2005).

Brady, Karren, *Brady Plays the Blues: My Diary of the Season* (Pavilion Books, 1995).

Brady, Karren, *Strong Woman: The Truth About Getting to the Top* (HarperCollins, 2013).

Brazil, Alan with Mike Parry, *There's an Awful Lot of Bubbly in Brazil: The Life and Times of a Bon Viveur* (Highdown, 2007).

Bright, Mark with Kevin Brennan, *My Story – From Foster Care to Footballer* (Constable, 2019).

Brooking, Trevor, *My Life in Football* (Simon & Schuster Ltd, 2014).

Bruce, Steve, *Heading for Victory: An Autobiography* (Bloomsbury, 1994).

Bullard, Jimmy, *Bend it Like Bullard* (Headline, 2014).

Burridge, John, *Budgie: The Autobiography of Goalkeeping Legend John Burridge* (John Blake, 2011).

Busby, Matt, *Soccer at the Top – My Life in Football* (Wiedenfeld & Nicolson, 1973).

Butcher, Terry, *Both Sides of the Border: An Autobiography* (George Weidenfeld & Nicolson Ltd, 1989).

Cahill, Tim, *Legacy* (HarperSport, 2015).

Cannell, Paul, *Fuckin' Hell It's Paul Cannell* (Createspace Independent Publishing Platform, 2012).

Canoville, Paul, *Black and Blue* (Headline, 2008).

Cantona, Eric, *Cantona on Cantona* (Andre Deutsch, 1996).

Carragher, Jamie, *Carra: My Autobiography* (Corgi, 2009).

Case, Jimmy, *Hard Case: The Autobiography of Jimmy Case*, (John Blake Publishing Ltd, 2014).

BIBLIOGRAPHY

Channon, Mick, *Man on the Run: An Autobiography* (Littlehampton Book Services Ltd, 1986).

Chapman, Lee, *More than a Match – A Player's Story* (Stanley Paul, 1992).

Charles, John with Bob Harris, *King John – The Autobiography* (Headline, 2003).

Charlton, Bobby, *1966: My World Cup Story* (Yellow Jersey, 2017).

Charlton, Jack, *The Autobiography* (Partridge Press, 1966).

Charnley, Chic with Alex Gordon, *Seeing Red: The Chic Charnley Story* (Black and White Publishing 2009).

Chisnell, David, *Gunny – A Year in the Life of Bryan Gunn* (Parrot Publishing, 1994).

Clark, Lee with Will Scott, *Black or White No Grey Areas* (Mojo Risin' Publishing, 2016).

Clough, Brian, *Cloughie – Walking on Water – My Life* (Headline, 2002).

Cole, Andy with Peter Fenton, *The Autobiography* (Manchester United Books, 1999).

Cole, Ashley, *My Defence: Winning, Losing, Scandals and the Drama of Germany 2006* (Headline Publishing Group, 2006).

Collina, Pierluigi, *The Rules of the Game* (Macmillan, 2003).

Collymore, Stan, *Tackling My Demons* (Willow, 2013).

Conroy, Terry, *You Don't Remember Me, Do You? The Autobiography of Terry Conroy* (Pitch Publishing, 2015).

Cottee, Tony with Tony McDonald, *Claret & Blues* (Independent UK Sports Publications, 1995).

Cottee, Tony, *West Ham: The Inside Story* (Philip Evans Media Ltd, 2012).

Crouch, Peter, *How to Be a Footballer* (Ebury, 2019).

Cruyff, Johan, *My Turn: The Autobiography* (Macmillan, 2017).

Curbishley, Alan, *Valley of Dreams* (HarperCollins, 2018).

Curbishley, Alan, *Game Changers – Inside English Football* (Harper Collins, 2016).

Curran, Terry with John Brindley, *Regrets of a Football Maverick: The Terry Curran Autobiography* (Vertical Editions, 2013).

Curtis, Alan with Tim Johnson and Stuart Sprake, *Curt – The Alan Curtis Story* (Mainstream Publishing, 2009).

Dalglish, Kenny with Henry Winter, *My Autobiography* (Hodder & Stoughton, 1996).

Dalglish, Kenny, *My Life* (Trinity Mirror Sport Media, 2013).

Di Canio, Paolo with Gabriele Marcotti, *The Autobiography* (Willow, 2001).

Dixon, Kerry with Harry Harris, *Up Front: My Autobiography* (John Blake Publishing, 2016).

Docherty, Tommy, *Call the Doc* (Littlehampton Book Services Ltd, 1981).

Dougan, Derek, *The Sash He Never Wore* (Allison & B., 1972).

Dougan, Derek, *How to Run Football* (All Seasons, 1981).

Dougan, Derek, *Doog* (All Seasons, 1980).

Dougan, Derek and Percy M. Young, *On the Spot: Football as a Profession* (Stanley Paul, 1974).

Drinkell, Kevin, *Drinks All Round: The Autobiography* (Black and White Publishing, 2010).

Drogba, Didier, *Commitment: My Autobiography* (Hodder & Stoughton, 2016).

Dunphy, Eamon, *Only a Game?* (Penguin, 1987).

Duxbury, Mick with Wayne Barton, *It's Mick Not Mike: The Autobiography of Mick Duxbury* (Pitch Publishing, 2015).

Dyer, Kieron with Oliver Holt, *Old Too Soon, Smart Too Late: My Story* (Headline, 2018).

Dyson, Terry with Mike Donovan, *Spurs Unsung Hero of the Glory Years: My Autobiography* (Pitch Publishing, 2015).

Edghill, Richard with Dante Friend, *Once a Blue Always a Blue: The Autobiography of Richard Edghill* (Pitch Publishing, 2014).

Edwards, Maurice, *Brian and Peter: A Right Pair – 21 Years With Clough and Taylor* (DB Publishing, 2010).

Elleray, David, *Referee! A Year in the Life of David Elleray* (Bloomsbury Publishing, 1998).

Eriksson, Sven-Göran, *Sven: My Story* (Headline, 2014).

Fenwick, Terry with Brian Woolnough, *Earning My Spurs* (Mainstream Publishing, 1989).

Ferdinand, Les, *Sir Les: The Autobiography of Les Ferdinand* (Headline Book Publishing, 1997).

Ferdinand, Rio, *#2sides: My Autobiography* (Blink Publishing, 2014).

Ferguson, Alex, *My Autobiography* (Hodder & Stoughton, 2013).

Ford, Trevor, *I Lead the Attack!* (Stanley Paul, 1957).

Fowler, Robbie, *Fowler: My Autobiography* (Pan, 2009).

BIBLIOGRAPHY

Francis, Trevor with David Miller, *The World to Play For: A Great Footballer's Own Story* (Granada Publishing Limited, 1983).

Fry, Barry, *Big Fry: Barry Fry: The Autobiography* (Willow, 2011).

Gayle, Howard, *61 Minutes in Munich – The Story of Liverpool FC's First Black Footballer* (deCoubertin Books, 2016).

Gemmill, Archie, *Both Sides of the Border: My Autobiography* (Hodder & Stoughton, 2005).

Gerrard, Steven, *My Story* (Penguin, 2015).

Giggs, Ryan with Joe Lovejoy, *Giggs: The Autobiography* (Michael Joseph, Penguin, 2005).

Giles, John, *A Football Man: The Autobiography* (Hodder & Stoughton, 2010).

Gillespie, Keith with Daniel McDonnell, *How Not to Be a Football Millionaire – Keith Gillespie My Autobiography* (Trinity Mirror Sport Media, 2013).

Given, Shay with Chris Brereton, *Any Given Saturday – The Autobiography* (SportMedia, 2017).

Goater, Shaun with David Clayton, *Feed the Goat* (The History Press, 2006).

Gold, David, *Pure Gold: My Autobiography* (Highdown, 2006).

Goram, Andy with Iain King, *The Goalie: My Story* (Mainstream Publishing, 2010).

Gorman, John with Kevin Brennan, *Gory Tales: The Autobiography* (Green Umbrella, 2008).

Goss, Jeremy with Edward Couzens-Lake, *Gossy: The Autobiography* (Amberley Publishing, 2014).

Gould, Bobby and David Instone, *24 Carat Gould* (Thomas Publications, 2010).

Gray, Andy, *Gray Matters – Andy Gray: The Autobiography* (Pan Books, 2005).

Greaves, Jimmy, *This One's On Me* (Hodder & Stoughton, 1980).

Greaves, Jimmy, *The Heart of the Game* (Sphere, 2009).

Greaves, Jimmy, *Greavsie: The Autobiography* (Time Warner, 2003).

Grobbelaar, Bruce, *More than Somewhat* (HarperCollins, 1986).

Groves, Perry, *We All Live in a Perry Groves World* (John Blake Publishing, 2007).

Gullit, Ruud, *How to Watch Football* (Penguin, 2017).

Gunn, Bryan with Kevin Piper, *In Where it Hurts – My Autobiography* (Vision Sports Publishing, 2006).

Halsey, Mark with Ian Ridley, *Added Time: Surviving Cancer, Death Threats and the Premier League* (Floodlit Dreams Ltd, 2013).

Hamann, Dietmar, *The Didi Man: My Love Affair with Liverpool* (Headline, 2012).

Alan Hansen, *Tall, Dark and Hansen – Ten Years at Anfield* (Mainstream Publishing, 1988).

Hansen, Alan, *A Matter of Opinion* (TransWorld Digital, 2011).

Hapgood, Eddie, *Football Ambassador* (Sporting Handbooks Limited, 1945).

Hasselbaink, Jimmy Floyd, *Jimmy: The Autobiography of Jimmy Floyd Hasselbaink* (HarperSport, 2011).

Heskey, Emile with Dean Eldridge, *Even Heskey Scored: My Story* (Pitch Publishing, 2019).

Hilaire, Vince, *Vince: The Autobiography of Vince Hilaire* (Biteback Publishing, 2018).

Hill, Gordon with Wayne Barton, *Merlin: The Autobiography of Gordon Hill* (Vertical Editions, 2014).

Hill, Jimmy, *The Jimmy Hill Story – My Autobiography* (Hodder & Stoughton, 1998).

Hill, Ricky with Adrian Durham, *Love of the Game* (Pitch Publishing, 2021).

Hoddle, Glenn with David Davies, *Glenn Hoddle: My World Cup Story* (Andre Deutsch, 1998).

Hoddle, Glenn with Harry Harris, *Spurred to Success: The Autobiography of Glenn Hoddle* (Queen Anne Press, 1987).

Hodge, Steve, *The Man with Maradona's Shirt* (Orion, 2011).

Holland, Matt, *From Wembley to Moscow: A Diary of a Tractor Boy* (Greenwater Publishing, 2001).

Holloway, Ian with David Clayton, *Ollie: The Autobiography of Ian Holloway* (Green Umbrella Publishing, 2009).

Horton, Brian with Tim Rich, *Two Thousand Games – A Life in Football* (Pitch Publishing, 2020).

Howey, Lee, *Massively Violent and Decidedly Average* (Biteback Publishing, 2018).

Huckerby, Darren, *Hucks: Through Adversity to Great Heights, My Autobiography* (Wensum Publishing, 2011).

BIBLIOGRAPHY

Hudson, Alan, *The Working Man's Ballet* (London Books, 2017).

Hughes, Emlyn, *Crazy Horse* (Arthur Baker, 1980).

Hughes, Mark with Peter Fitton, *Sparky – Barcelona, Bayern & Back* (Cockerel Books, 1989).

Hunt, Steve with Ian McCauley, *I'm with the Cosmos – The Story of Steve Hunt* (Pitch Publishing, 2021).

Hunter, Norman, *Biting Talk: My Autobiography* (Hodder & Stoughton, 2004).

Hurst, Geoff with Michael Hart, *1966 and All That: My Autobiography* (Headline, 2001).

Ibrahimović, Zlatan, *I Am Zlatan Ibrahimović* (Penguin, 2013).

Izzet, Muzzy with Lee Marlow, *Muzzy: My Story* (Trinity Mirror Sport Media, 2015).

Jennings, Pat, *An Autobiography* (Panther Books, 1984).

Jones, Vinnie, *It's Been Emotional: My Story* (Simon & Schuster, 2013).

Jordan, Joe, *Behind the Dream: The Story of a Scottish Footballer* (Hodder & Stoughton, 2004).

Jordan, Simon, *Be Careful What You Wish For* (Yellow Jersey, 2013).

Kamara, Chris, *Mr Unbelievable* (HarperSport, 2010).

Keane, Roy with Roddy Doyle, *The Second Half* (W&N, 2015).

Keegan, Kevin, *Kevin Keegan* (Readers Union, 1978).

Keegan, Kevin, *My Autobiography* (Warner Books, 1998).

Keegan, Kevin with Mike Langley, *Kevin Keegan Against the World* (Sidgwick and Jackson Limited, 1979).

Kendall, Howard with Ian Ross, *Only the Best is Good Enough: The Howard Kendall Story* (Mainstream Publishing, 1991).

Kimmage, Paul, *Full Time: The Secret Life of Tony Cascarino* (Simon & Schuster Ltd, 2000).

King, Ledley, *King: My Autobiography* (Quercus, 2014).

Lake, Paul: *I'm Not Really Here: A Life of Two Halves* (Arrow, 2012).

Lampard, Frank, *Totally Frank: My Autobiography* (HarperSport, 2010).

Laws, Brian with Alan Biggs, *Laws of the Jungle: Surviving Football's Monkey Business* (Vertical Editions, 2012).

Lee, Rob, *Come In Number 37* (CollinsWillow, 2000).

Lehmann, Jens, *The Madness is on the Pitch* (De Coubertin, 2017).

Leighton, Jim with Ken Robertson, *In the Firing Line: The Jim Leighton Story* (Mainstream Publishing, 2000).

Le Saux, Graeme, *Left Field: A Footballer Apart* (HarperSport, 2010).

Le Tissier, Matt, *Taking Le Tiss: My Autobiography* (HarperSport, 2009).

Lyall, John, *Just Like My Dreams: My Life with West Ham* (Penguin, 1990).

Macari, Lou, *Football, My Life* (Bantam Press, 2008).

MacDonald, Malcolm, *An Autobiography* (Arthur Baker Ltd, 1983).

MacDonald, Malcolm with Jack Hobbs and Roger Millington, *Football Makes Me Laugh* (M&J Hobbs, 1979).

MacDougall, Ted with Neil Vacher, *MacDou-GOAL! The Ted MacDougall Story* (Pitch Publishing, 2016).

Mackay, Dave with Martin Knight, *The Real Mackay: The Dave Mackay Story* (Mainstream Publishing, 2004).

Maradona, Diego Armando, *El Diego: The Autobiography of the World's Greatest Footballer* (Yellow Jersey, 2005).

Marsh, Rodney, *Shooting to the Top* (Sportsmans Book Club, 1969).

Marsh, Rodney with Brian Woolnough, *I Was Born a Loose Cannon* (Optimum Publishing Solutions, 2010).

Mason, Rob, *Zero to Hero: The Gareth Southgate Story* (SJH Group, 2018).

Matthews, Stanley, *The Way it Was: My Autobiography* (Headline, 2001).

Matthews, Stanley & Mila with a helping hand from Don Taylor, *Back in Touch* (Arthur Barker Limited, 1980).

McAteer, Jason, *Blood, Sweat & McAteer: A Footballer's Story* (Hachette Books Ireland, 2016).

McAvennie, Frank, *Scoring: An Expert's Guide* (Cannongate Books, 2003).

McCarthy, Mick, *Captain Fantastic: My Football Career and World Cup Experience* (O'Brien Press Ltd, 1990).

McCarthy, Mick with Cathal Dervlin, *Ireland's World Cup 2002* (Pocket Books/TownHouse, 2002).

McClair, Brian, *Odd Man Out: A Player's Diary* (Andre Deutsch, 1997).

McCulloch, Lee, *Simp-Lee the Best: My Autobiography* (Black & White Publishing, 2013).

McDonough, Roy with Bernie Friend, *Sex, Booze and Early Baths: The Life of Britain's Wildest Ever Footballer* (Vision Sports Publishing, 2015).

McGovern, John, *From Bo'ness to the Bernabeu: My Story* (Vision Sports Publishing, 2015).

BIBLIOGRAPHY

McIndoe, Michael, *Wildling: My Autobiography* (Michael McIndoe, 2017)

McKenzie, Duncan with David Saffer, *The Last Fancy Dan: The Duncan McKenzie Story* (Vertical Editions, 2009).

McMahon, Steve with Harry Harris, *Macca Can! The Steve McMahon Story* (Penguin Books 1990).

McMenemy, Lawrie, *A Lifetime's Obsession: My Autobiography* (Trinity Mirror Sports Media, 2017).

McMenemy, Lawrie, *The Diary of a Season* (Arthur Barker, 1979).

Merson, Paul, *How Not to Be a Professional Footballer* (Harper Sport, 2012).

Merson, Paul with Ian Ridley, *Hero and Villain: A Year in the Life of Paul Merson* (Willow, 1999).

Miller, Charlie with Scott McDermott, *The Proper Charlie: The Autobiography* (Black & White Publishing, 2014).

Milne, Ralph with Gary Robertson, *What's It All About, Ralphie? My Story* (Black & White Publishing, 2010).

Mølby, Jan with Grahame Boyd, *Jan the Man: From Anfield to Vetch Field* (Orion, 1999).

Moore, Brian with Norman Giller, *The Final Score – An Autobiography* (Coronet Books 1999).

Morrison, Andy, *The Good, the Mad and the Ugly: The Andy Morrison Story* (Fort Publishing, 2011).

Mullery, Alan, *The Autobiography* (Headline, 2007).

Neal, Phil, *Attack from the Back* (Littlehampton Book Services, 1981).

Negri, Marco with Jeff Holmes, *Moody Blue: The Story of Mysterious Marco* (Pitch Publishing, 2018).

Nelson, Garry, *Left Foot Forward: A Year in the Life of a Journeyman Footballer* (Headline, 1996).

Neville, Gary, *Red: My Autobiography* (Transworld Digital, 2011).

Neville, Gary & Phil with Sam Pilger & Justyn Barnes, *For Club and Country – The Hunt for European and World Cup Glory* (Manchester United Books, 1998).

Nevin, Pat, *The Accidental Footballer* (Monoray, 2021).

Newley, Patrick, *You Lucky People! The Tommy Trinder Story* (Third Age Press, 2008).

Nicholas, Charlie with Ken Gallacher, *Charlie: An Autobiography* (Stanley Paul & Co., 1986).

Nicol, Stevie, *My Autobiography: Five League Titles and a Packet of Crisps* (Trinity Mirror Sport Media, 2016).

O'Leary, David, *Leeds United on Trial* (Little, Brown, 2002).

Owen, Michael, *Reboot: My Life, My Time* (Reach Sport, 2019).

Palmer, Carlton with Steve Jacobi, *It is What it Is: The Carlton Palmer Story* (Vertical Editions, 2017).

Parker, Paul with Pat Symes, *Tackles Like a Ferret* (Know the Score Books, 2006).

Parlour, Ray, *The Romford Pelé: It's Only Ray Parlour's Autobiography* (Cornerstone Digital, 2016).

Partridge, Pat and John Gibson, *Oh Ref!* (Souvenir Press 1979).

Pearce, Stuart, *Psycho: The Autobiography* (Headline, 2014).

Pelé, *Pelé: The Autobiography* (Simon & Schuster 2007).

Pennant, Jermaine with John Cross, *Mental: Bad Behaviour, Ugly Truths and the Beautiful Game* (John Blake, 2018).

Piper, Matt with Joe Brewin, *Out of the Darkness – My Story in Football* (Pitch Publishing 2020).

Pirlo, Andrea with Alessandro Alciato, *I Think Therefore I Play* (Backpage Press 2014).

Platt, David, *Achieving the Goal: An Autobiography* (Richard Cohen Books Ltd, 1995).

Poll, Graham, *Seeing Red* (HarperSport, 2018).

Powell, Hope, *Hope: My Life in Football* (Bloomsbury, 2016).

Rathbone, Mick 'Baz', *The Smell of Football* (Vision Sports Publishing, 2011).

Quinn, Mick with Oliver Harvey, *Who Ate All the Pies? The Life and Times of Mick Quinn* (Virgin Digital, 2011).

Redfearn, Neil, *There's Only One Neil Redfearn: The Ups and Downs of My Footballing Life* (Headline, 2006).

Redknapp, Harry, *A Man Walks on to a Pitch: Stories from a Life in Football* (Ebury Press, 2014).

Redknapp, Harry, *My Autobiography* (CollinsWillow, 1998).

Redknapp, Harry with Martin Samuel, *Always Managing: My Autobiography* (Ebury Press, 2013).

Regis, Cyrille with Chris Green, *Cyrille Regis: My Story* (Andre Deutsch, 2010).

Reid, Peter, *Everton Winter, Mexican Summer* (The Book Service Ltd, 1987).

BIBLIOGRAPHY

Reid, Peter, *Cheer Up Peter Reid* (Trinity Mirror Sport Media, 2018).

Reina, Pepe, *Pepe – My Autobiography* (Sport Media, 2011).

Reynolds, George, *My Wicked Life* (Blake Publishing, 2003).

Ridsdale, Peter, *United We Fall: Boardroom Truths About the Beautiful Game* (Pan Books, 2008).

Roberts, Graham with Colin Duncan, *Hard as Nails: The Graham Roberts Story* (Black and White Publishing, 2008).

Robertson, Alistair with Bill Howell, *Thou Shalt Not Pass: The Alistair Robertson Story* (Pitch Publishing, 2017).

Robertson, David with Alistair Aird, *The Quiet Man Roars – The David Robertson Story* (Pitch Publishing 2021).

Robertson, John with John Lawson, *Super Tramp: My Autobiography* (Mainstream Publishing, 2011).

Robson, Bobby with Bob Harris, *Against the Odds: An Autobiography* (Hutchinson, 1990).

Robson, Bryan, *Robbo: My Autobiography* (Hodder & Stoughton, 2012).

Rosenior, Leroy with Leo Moynihan, *'It's Only Banter': The Autobiography of Leroy Rosenior* (Pitch Publishing, 2017).

Rosler, Uwe, *My Autobiography – Knocking Down Walls* (Trinity Mirror Sport Media, 2013).

Ruddock, Neil, *Hell Razor: The Autobiography of Neil Ruddock* (Willow, 1999).

Ruddock, Neil with James Hogg, *The World According to Razor – My Closest Shaves* (Constable, 2020).

Rush, Ian, *Rush – The Autobiography* (Ebury Press 2008).

Ryan, John, *Dare to Dream* (Scratching Shed Publishing, 2010).

Sansom, Kenny, *To Cap it All: My Story* (John Blake, 2010).

Savage, Robbie with Janine Self, *Savage!: The Robbie Savage Autobiography* (Mainstream Publishing, 2010).

Schmeichel, Peter with Egon Balsby, *Schmeichel. The Autobiography* (Virgin Publishing, 2000).

Scholes, Paul, *My Story* (Simon & Schuster, 2011).

Seaman, David, *Safe Hands: My Autobiography* (Orion Media, 2000).

Sharpe, Lee with David Conn, *My Idea of Fun: The Autobiography* (Orion Books Ltd, 2006).

Shearer, Alan, *Alan Shearer's Diary of a Season* (Virgin Books, 1995).

Sheedy, Kevin, *So Good I Did it Twice: My Life from Left Field* (Trinity Mirror Sports Media, 2014).

Sheringham, Teddy with Mel Webb, *Teddy: My Autobiography* (Little, Brown and Company, 1998).

Shilton, Peter, *The Autobiography* (Orion, 2004).

Sitton, John, *A Little Knowledge is a Dangerous Thing: A Life in Football* (John Sitton, 2016).

Smith, Alan *Heads Up – My Life Story* (Constable, 2018).

Smith, Kelly, *Footballer: My Story* (Corgi, 2013).

Snodin, Ian with Alan Jewell, *Snod This for a Laugh* (Trinity Mirror Digital Media, 2013).

Solo, Hope, *Solo: A Memoir of Hope* (HarperPaperBacks, 2013).

Souness, Graeme, *Football: My Life, My Passion* (Headline, 2017).

Souness, Graeme with Ken Gallacher, *Graeme Souness: A Manager's Diary* (Mainstream Publishing, 1989).

Southall, Neville, *The Binman Chronicles* (deCoubertin Books, 2012).

Southgate, Gareth and Andy Woodman, *Woody & Nord: A Football Friendship* (Penguin, 2003).

St John, Ian with James Lawton, *The Saint – My Autobiography* (Hodder & Stoughton, 2005).

Stam, Jaap, *Head to Head* (Collins Willow, 2003).

Stepney, Alex, *Alex Stepney* (Littlehampton Book Services Ltd, 1978).

Sterland, Mel with Nick Johnson, *Boozing, Betting and Brawling: The Autobiography of Mel Sterland* (Green Umbrella Publishing, 2008).

Stewart, Ray, *Spot On with 'Tonka'* (West Ham Football Club, 1991).

Stiles, Nobby, *After the Ball: My Autobiography* (Hodder & Stoughton, 2003).

Storey, Peter, *True Storey: My Life and Crimes as a Football Hatchet Man* (Mainstream Digital, 2011).

Sturrock, Paul with Charlie Dudby and Peter Rondo, *Forward Thinking: The Paul Sturrock Story* (Mainstream, 1989).

Sturrock, Paul with Richard Cowdery, *Paul Sturrock's Championship Diary* (Plymouth Argyle Football Club, 2002).

Sturrock, Paul with Bill Richards, *Luggy: The Autobiography of Paul Sturrock* (Pitch Publishing, 2015).

Suárez, Luis, *Crossing the Line: My Story* (Headline, 2014).

Sugar, Alan, *What You See is What You Get: My Autobiography* (Pan, 2011).

Sutton, Chris with Mark Guidi, *Paradise and Beyond: My Autobiography* (Black & White Publishing, 2011).

BIBLIOGRAPHY

Swan, Peter, *Swanny: Confessions of a Lower-League Legend* (John Blake Publishing, 2008).

Tanner, Nick with Steve Cotton, *From a Field to Anfield* (Pitch Publishing, 2017).

Taylor, Peter with Mike Langley, *With Clough By Taylor* (Sidgwick and Jackson / New English Library, 1981).

Ternent, Stan with Tony Livesey, *Stan the Man – A Hard Life in Football* (Blake Publishing, 2003).

Thomas, Clive, *By the Book* (HarperCollins, 1984).

Thomas, Mickey, *Kickups, Hiccups, Lockups: The Autobiography* (Century, 2008).

Thompson, Phil, *Stand Up Pinocchio: Thommo from the Kop to the Top – My Life Inside Anfield* (Trinity Mirror Sport Media, 2013).

Thornley, Ben with Dan Poole, *Tackled* (Pitch Publishing, 2018).

Tomlinson, Barrie, *Real Roy of the Rovers Stuff* (Pitch Publishing, 2016).

Toshack, John, *Tosh: An Autobiography* (Arthur Baker, 1982).

Trundle, Lee with Chris Wathan, *More than Just Tricks* (Mainstream Publishing, 2010).

Tueart, Dennis, *My Football Journey* (Vision Sports Publishing, 2011).

Tutt, Graham with Matt Eastley, *Never Give Up – The Graham 'Buster' Tutt Story* (Pitch Publishing, 2021).

Van Den Hauwe, Pat, *The Autobiography of the Everton Legend* (John Blake Publishing Ltd, 2015).

Vardy, Jamie, *From Nowhere: My Story* (Ebury Press, 2017).

Venables, Terry, *Born to Manage: The Autobiography* (Simon & Schuster UK, 2015).

Vieira, Patrick, *Vieira: My Autobiography* (Orion, 2006).

Vine, Phillip, *Visionary: Manchester United, Michael Knighton and the Football Revolutions 1989-2019* (Pitch Publishing, 2019).

Walcott, Theo, *Theo: Growing Up Fast* (Corgi, 2012).

Walsh, Paul, Walshie, *My Autobiography: Wouldn't it Be Good* (Trinity Mirror Sport Media, 2015).

Walters, Mark with Jeff Holmes, *Wingin' It: The Mark Walters Story* (Pitch Publishing, 2018).

Ward, Mark, *From Right-Wing to B-Wing ... Premier League to Prison* (Football World, 2009).

Wark, John, *Wark On: The Autobiography of John Wark* (Know the Score Books, 2009).

Warnock, Neil, *Made in Sheffield: My Story* (Hodder & Stoughton, 2008)

Warnock, Neil, *The Gaffer: The Trials and Tribulations of a Football Manager* (Headline, 2013).

Webb, Howard, *The Man in the Middle: The Autobiography of the World Cup Final Referee* (Simon & Schuster UK, 2017).

Weller, Paul with Dave Thomas, *Not Such a Bad Life: Burnley, Gazza, Wrighty, Waddle and Me* (Pitch Publishing, 2021).

Wenger, Arsène, *My Life in Red and White* (Weidenfeld & Nicolson, 2020).

Whelan, Ronnie, *My Autobiography. Walk On: My Life in Red* (Simon & Schuster UK, 2011).

Whiteside, Norman, *Determined: The Autobiography* (Headline, 2007).

Wilson, Bob, *Behind the Network – My Autobiography* (Hodder and Stoughton, 2003).

Wilson, Davie and Alistair Aird, *Wilson on the Wing – The Davie Wilson Story* (Pitch Publishing, 2020).

Windass, Dean, *Deano: From Gipsyville to the Premiership* (Great Northern Books, 2011).

Winter, Jeff, *Who's the B*****d in the Black? Confessions of a Premiership Referee* (Ebury Press, 2006).

Woodcock, Tony with Peter Ball, *Inside Soccer* (The Book Service Ltd, 1985).

Worthington, Frank with Steve Wells, Nick Cooper and Ian Worthington, *One Hump or Two? The Frank Worthington Story* (ACL & Polar Publishing, 1994).

Wright, Ian, *A Life in Football: My Autobiography* (Constable, 2016).

Wylde, Rodger, *Wylde Man of Football: Dressing Room Banter* (2013).

Yorath, Terry, *Hard Man, Hard Knocks* (Celluloid, 2004).

Yorke, Dwight, *Born to Score: The Autobiography* (MacMillan, 2009).